The Preamble

The daring publisher, Universal Law Publishing Company, among the foremost in the law publishing field and progressive in venturing to bring out rare legal literature of avant garde *character has rightly enriched the* corpus juris *of India*

Justice V R Krishna Iyer
Random Reflections, page 14

The Preamble

Deepa Kansra
LL.M., LL.B.
Assistant Professor of Law
Indian Law Institute, New Delhi

Universal
Law Publishing Co. Pvt. Ltd.
NEW DELHI - INDIA

2013 Edition

ISBN: 978-93-5035-373-8

Published by

Universal
Law Publishing Co. Pvt. Ltd.
NEW DELHI - INDIA

A-58, G.T. Karnal Road Industrial Area,
(Near Azadpur Metro Station), Delhi-110033
Tel. : 011-47082254, 27458529, 27215334 Fax : 011-27458529
e-mail: unilaw@vsnl.com

- Showroom : C-27, Connaught Place, New Delhi-110001
  e-mail: sales@unilawbooks.com
- Editorial : edit@unilawbooks.com
- Website : **www.unilawbooks.com**

Join us on Facebook
www.facebook.com/unilawbooks

Recommended citation: Deepa Kansra, *The Preamble* (New Delhi: Universal Law Publishing Co. Pvt. Ltd., 2013).

Computer Typeset at Aesthetic and *Printed* at Mudrak, Delhi

Preface

The ever rising complexities faced by the populace in India have over the years created misgivings about the politico-legal system that has been in place. The lack of stability in interpretation, and the lack of vision in politics, has made people look askance about the limitations and dimensions of their constitutional existence. It is no longer sufficient and viable to look into the formal source of constitutional values, but rather the dilemmas and contestations of their meaning and relevance to the community.

This book makes an attempt at portraying the cultural, political and global realities of a constitutional polity like India. The contributors reflect upon the progress and dynamics of foundational values embodied in the Preamble; sovereignty, socialism, secularism, fraternity, justice, and so on. The aim is to highlight the day to day relevance of the broader principles in the Preamble, the ideological inspiration that they generate, and their commonly attached meanings.

Introduction

Is fraternity a forgotten ideal? Is socialism outdated? What advantage does republicanism offer? Is secularism politically motivated? Are there any global ethics?

Questions of this genre are multiple and willing to multiply. Very few legal systems are exploring the foundation of their constitutions to educate the young minds about the principles/ideals that affect them day to day. Nevertheless, constitutions over the world are propelling significant reforms and innovations for their respective societies and political systems. What ushers such dynamism is a fundamental question for our generation.

Taking the case of India, the Constitution – "the supreme deed of independent India"[1] is a strong edifice for a functional system of rules, structures and principles. The constitutional philosophy over the years has permitted expansion in the value based thought, rights, opportunities, institutions, and structures. The underlying philosophy to such dynamism is located in the text of the Preamble of the Constitution. It can very safely be gathered that the dynamism is a resultant of the evolving character of the basic tenets like justice, democracy, socialism and secularism.

More recently, a consensus at the global platform has emerged on the role of preambles in constitutional interpretation and adjudication. The Preambles have been found to have "integrative power", a more "binding force" as a "substantive source of rights" or as a "guide for constitutional

1. Justice V.R. Krishna Iyer, "The Indian Constitution in 2050", Halsbury's Law Monthly (October 2008).

interpretation"[2] Each preamble expresses a unique quality in terms of the ideals incorporated therein and the history that has given birth to it.

This book is inspired by the very strength of the Constitutional philosophy, placed in the Preamble to the Constitution of India. The layout of the book is designed to provide the theoretical dimensions/complexities of the ideals in the Preamble. The authors have contributed immensely to put forth a more contemporary and a larger picture of the basic ideals that govern several constitutions like that in India. It is more rightly a *Political and Contemporary Reading of the Preamble.*

Chapter I on the *Preamble of the Constitution of India* gives a brief outline of the basic tenets of the Preamble. It lays special emphasis on the qualitative characteristics/values under the Preamble, which enable the Constitution to deliver and progress with dignity.

The ideals highlighted under this chapter have been discussed in detail by the other authors.

Chapter II on *We the People* is an exciting narrative of the power of the people – 'the colonized' in the colonial context, and the 'the suppressed' in the post-colonial context. The *power* has been personified under the right to self determination; the building block of the post-colonial world. The chapter describes the journey of the *peoples* in their struggle for self-governance amidst the recurring politics behind the said right.

An attempt is made to capture the larger and restricted interpretation of the right in context of the third world countries (India) and the United Nations.

Chapter III on *Sovereignty* highlights the changing and complex conception of sovereignty. The chapter determines the nature of sovereignty in general in context of transnational law, and in specific in the context of the Indian Constitution.

---

2. Liav Orgad, "The Preamble in Constitutional Interpretation", Vol. 8 Issue 4 International Journal of Constitutional Law (October 2010).
   Also see *Keshavananda Bharati* v. *State of Kerala*, (1973) 4 SCC 225.

Special emphasis in this regard is placed on how global integration and interdependence have resulted in the diminishing authority of the states in the matters of both local and global relevance.

Chapter IV on *Socialism* highlights the relevance and impact of socialism in India. In this regard, specific reference is made to the Constitution of India, which reflects a commitment to socialism under the Preamble, and under Part IV and Part III.

An attempt is made to explore the status of India's commitment to the socialist ideology post 1991 in the context of liberalization and globalization.

Chapter V on *Secularism* tests the efficiency and effectiveness of the constitutional promise of secularism. The chapter dwells upon the judicial discourse on the "essential practices test" that carves out the practices that must be constitutionally protected.

The author with several judicial and political incidents to his support raises the need to seriously consider the theoretical ramifications of "religion", "secular" in post-modern multicultural societies.

Chapter VI on *Democracy* aims at carving out an acceptable definition of democracy encompassing both of its functional and political virtues.

On the relevance of democracy, the chapter incorporates the vision of the United Nations General Assembly, experts like Robert Dahl and Brian Tamanaha.

In the context of India, the meaning and working features of democracy have been highlighted by referring to (a) the authoritative apex court's rulings (b) the legislative reforms and initiatives (c) civic participation (also labelled as the deliberative feature of democracy) (d) the expanding notions of social justice through Public Interest Litigation etc.

Since democracy has been defined as the basic structure of the Constitution of India, both the Indian and global vision of democracy have been discussed.

Chapter VII on *Republicanism* conceptually establishes an understanding of republicanism, in the narrow and wider sense. It incorporates the contemporary nuances of republicanism; anti-monarchism, non-domination, civic virtue/participation and institutional accountability. In the context of India, reference is made to the constitutional debates in favor and against the inclusion of the term "republic" in the text of the Preamble.

Reference is also made to writings of Dr. Subhash Kashyap, D.D. Basu etc. to carve out a meaning of republicanism in India. On a larger frame, the chapter is highly informative on the practices adopted globally (United States, Ireland, Germany, China) to describe the forms of republic governments that exist, similar or in comparison to India.

Chapter VIII on *Justice, Liberty, and Equality* highlights the value-based and contextual grounding of constitutional ideals such as justice, equality and liberty.

Justice in specific has been explained in the general and particular sense, taking shape in the name of distributive justice, corrective justice, commutative justice, retributive justice, and so on. In this regard, the relevant provisions of the Indian constitution have been discussed vis-à-vis political, economic and social justice.

Equality, in specific has been referred to as an aspect of justice; equality as an end to justice, equality as the means of doing justice. In the Indian context, Article 14 has been discussed as encompassing both the dimensions.

Liberty, in specific has been recognized and referred to be a product of social and economic justice, without which all freedoms are rendered meaningless.

Chapter IX on *Fraternity* draws attention to the forgotten ideal in contemporary constitutional discourse.

Specific reference is made to the academic enthusiasm in several other states aiming to bring fraternity back to the mainstream of political and historic discussions. In the context of India, emphasis is placed on the need to explore fraternity as a constitutional ideal amidst mass conflict and social disintegration in its various forms.

June 2013 **Deepa Kansra**

CONTENTS

CHAPTER III

Sovereignty

CHAPTER IV

Socialism

CHAPTER V

Secularism

CHAPTER VI

Democracy

CHAPTER VII

Republic

CHAPTER VIII

Justice, Equality, Liberty

CHAPTER IX

Fraternity

TABLE OF CASES

O

P

R

S

ABOUT THE CONTRIBUTORS

Amit Bindal

Amit Bindal is currently Assistant Professor and Assistant Director, Centre for Penology, Criminal Justice and Police Studies at Jindal Global Law School. Amit Bindal obtained his Master of Laws (LL.M.) from the Indian Law Institute (Batch of 2009). He has published on the topic of Retributive Theory of Punishment in the Journal of Indian Law Institute; a comment on Law of suicide in India in Bangalore Law Review [2010]. He has contributed various short articles and comments in magazines such as 'Combat Law' (Human Rights Law Network), and 'AWAZ Times'.

Bhrigu Vishwakarma

Bhrigu Vishwakarma is a practicing advocate at the Durgapur Court in West Bengal and Guest Lecturer of the Law College Durgapur, The University of Burdwan. He did his LL.M. from the University of Burdwan. He is a prolific writer and has contributed numerous papers, rejoinders and case comments to Law Journals and Law Reviews such as Indian Bar Review, Indian Human Rights Law Review, All India Reporter, Criminal Law Journal, besides contributing book Chapters in Edited books. He has co-edited a book: *Re-Thinking The Law: Perspective and Challenges*, AUTHORSPRESS, New Delhi (2013).

Deepa Kansra

Deepa Kansra is Assistant Professor at the Indian Law Institute, New Delhi. Her areas of interest include Human Rights Law, Public International Law, and Jurisprudence. She has previously worked at the University of Delhi (Campus Law Centre 2010-2012) and is currently pursuing Ph.D. in Law from the Faculty of Law, Jamia Millia Islamia.

She is the author of the book *India and the Dynamics of Socialism in the Global Order* (Authors Press 2012). She has also published in reputed journals like the International Journal of Law and Policy Review (2013), Indian Human Rights Law Review (2012), Indian Law Review (2011), Social

Action Journal (2011), and the Journal of the Indian Law Institute (2009). In 2008, she worked as a Legal Researcher at the Indian Law Institute for a project assigned by the Rajya Sabha Secretariat on *A Compendium of Judicial Pronouncements Relating to Parliamentary Privileges since Independence.*

Latika Vashist

Latika Vashist is currently Assistant Professor and Assistant Director (Clinical Program) at Jindal Global Law School. She obtained Master of Laws (LL.M.) from Indian Law Institute (I.L.I.), New Delhi where she was awarded the Scholarship of Merit. She has published in Bangalore Law Journal, Combat Law, Awaz Times and Perspectives. She was also the co-editor of I.L.I. Law Review (Jan, 2010). She has worked on a project on the condition of women in the unorganized sector under National Commission for Women. Her areas of research include feminist legal theory, multiculturalism, poverty and policy of criminalization and constitutional law.

Mallika Ramachandran

Mallika Ramachandran is a Ph. D Scholar at the Indian Law Institute, New Delhi, where she obtained her LL.M. Her interest areas are Competition Law and Human Rights. She has worked as a Researcher on several projects including a 'Regional Study for Harmonization of Anti-Trafficking Legal Framework in India, Bangladesh and Nepal' with the South Asian Law Schools Forum, 'Reasons for Delay in Disposal of Murder Cases and to Suggest Management of Case Flow of Such Cases' (2011) with the Indian Law Institute (Delhi), and more recently on the 'Preparation of Module and Handbook on Human Trafficking for the Training of the Judiciary' (2012) with Save the Children, India.

P. Puneeth

Dr. P. Puneeth is Assistant Professor at the Indian Law Institute, New Delhi. He has done his LL.B and LL.M. and Ph.D. from Bangalore University, Karnataka. His subject of specialization is Constitutional Law and Legal Order. His areas of interest are Constitutional Law and Administrative Law. He has participated in many national and international seminars and conferences and presented papers in couple of national/international seminars. Before joining the Institute, he was practicing as an Advocate at High Court of Karnataka, Bangalore and also worked as Lecturer at Dr. RML College of Law, Bangalore.

Rabindra Kumar Pathak

Rabindra Kr. Pathak is currently an Assistant Professor at National University of Study and Research in Law, Ranchi. He did his LL.M. (2009) from Indian Law Institute with a Gold Medal in Jurisprudence. He is currently pursuing his doctoral research on "Constitutional Adjudication".

He has authored a book, and has several publications in national and international journals such as the Bond Law Review, Asian Journal of International Law, Journal of the Indian Law Institute, Indian Bar Review, Indian Human Rights Law Review, Madras Law Journal, to name a few. He has also worked as a Legal Researcher for a project assigned by the Rajya Sabha (2008), and for a project on Centre-State Relations for the Indian Law Institute (2009).

CHAPTER I

The Preamble of the Constitution of India

Bhrigu Vishwakarma

The Constitution of India begins with a Preamble. It embodies the basic purpose of the Constitution. It contains the spirit of the Constitution. It embodies inalienable ideals and aspirations in a solemn form with the stamp of deep deliberation.[1]

Accordingly, to quote the observation of the Supreme Court in *re Berubari* case,[2] the Preamble to the Constitution is a key to open the mind of the makers and shows the general purpose for which they made the several provisions of the Constitution. M. Hidayatullah, CJ, said, "Preamble resembles the Declaration of Independence of the United States of America, is more than a Declaration. It is the soul of our Constitution which lays down the pattern of our political society which it states is Sovereign Democratic Republic. It contains a solemn resolve which nothing but a revolution can alter."[3]

So, the Preamble of the Indian Constitution contains the visions of the Founding Fathers. It discloses the quality of the

1. M.C. Jain Kagzi, The Constitution of India, Vol. 1, 322 (2004).
2. *In re Berubari*, AIR 1960 SC 845: 1960 SCJ 933: (1960) 3 SCR 250. Also *see*, *L.C. Golak Nath* v. *State of Punjab*, AIR 1967 SC 1643: 1967 (2) SCJ 486: (1967) 2 SCR 762.
3. V.D. Mahajan, Constitutional Law of India, 37 (1991).

Constitution. It is a dignified part of the Constitution, which indicates the goals that the Constitution intends to achieve by the written provisions.

The Preamble can be divided into three parts on the basis of its qualitative characteristics. The first is *'declarative'*, the second is *'resolutionary'* and the third is *'promissory'*.[4] In other words the Preamble broadly reflects three things:

(i) the source of the Constitution;

(ii) objects or goals including rights and freedoms for the Indian citizens living under the Constitution; and

(iii) the date of the adoption of the Constitution.

In this connection, Prof. M.P. Jain in his book on *Indian Constitutional Law* says, "the purpose of the Preamble is to clarify who has made the Constitution, what is its source, what is the ultimate sanction behind it; what is the nature of the polity which is sought to be established by the Constitution and what are its goals and objectives?"[5] In short, the Preamble embodies solemnly all the ideals and aspirations for which India had struggled during the British regime.[6]

1. Framing of the Preamble

The Government of India Act, 1935 had no Preamble of its own. It kept the Preamble of the Government of India Act, 1919.[7] The Preamble had been crafted with the chosen words

4. In the declarative part, the people of India adopted, enacted and gave to themselves the Constitution of India. In the resolutionary part, the people of India resolve to constitute India into a SOVEREIGN SOCIALIST SECULAR DEMOCRATIC REPUBLIC. Finally, in promissory part, the people of India committed to secure to all its citizens Justice, Liberty, Equality, Fraternity, unity of the nation and assurance of dignity of the individual. *See* Justice R.C. Lahoti, Preamble: The Spirit and backbone of the Constitution of India 3 (2004).

5. Prof. M.P. Jain, Indian Constitutional Law 11 (2004).

6. See *Kesavananda Bharati* v. *State of Kerala*, AIR 1973 SC 1461: (1973) 4 SCC 225.

7. The omission to have a Preamble in the Government of India Act, 1935 was criticized. Sammuel Hoare, the Secretary of State for India made plea that there was no necessity to enshrine in an Act words and phrases which have added nothing new to declaration of the Preamble. Later the mistake was realized and the Preamble of the Act of 1919 was adopted. For more *see* Kanahailal Sharma, Reconstitution of the Constitution of India 26 (2002).

by the Framers of the Constitution. Each and every chosen word of the Preamble has a meaning and philosophy of its own. Even the arrangement of words in the Preamble has also importance and is suggestive. The total chosen words, collectively called Preamble, reflect the struggle of Indians during the British yoke. Therefore, the vision of the framers of Constitution "was of an independent and united nation, a democratic polity and a just social and economic order, free from exploitation."[8] In this relation, K.M. Munshi stated that the Preamble reflected the changes that had come over the country as a result of the partition and integration of the Indian States.[9]

In November 1946, the Constituent Assembly came into being. During the election of Constituent Assembly, an Expert Committee, headed by Pandit Jawaharlal Nehru, was formed to prepare Aims and Objectives of the Constitution in the form of declaration on July 8, 1946. The Committee had formed the following objectives:

> This Constituent Assembly declares its firm and solemn resolve to proclaim India as an Independent Sovereign Republic, and to draw up for her future governance a Constitution wherein the territories that now form the Indian States and such other territories

---

8. Dr. Subhash C. Kashyap, Constitutional Law of India, Vol. 1 284 (2008). In 1931, Mahatma Gandhi while replying to a spokesman in London on the question: what Constitution he would bring back if he could help it? Gandhiji replied, "I shall strive for a Constitution which will release India from all thraldom and patronage, and give her, if need be, the right to sin. I shall work for an India, in which the poorest shall feel that it is their country in whose making they have an effective voice; an India in which there shall be no high class and low class of people; an India in which all communities shall live in perfect harmony. There can be no room in such an India for the curse of untouchability or the curse of intoxicating drinks and drugs. Women shall enjoy the same rights as men. Since we shall be at peace with all the rest of the world, neither exploiting nor being exploited, we should have the smallest army imaginable. All interests not in conflict with the interest of the dumb millions will be scrupulously respected, whether foreign or indigenous. Personally, I hate distinction between foreign and indigenous. That is the India of my dreams." See, M.V. Pylee, India's Constitution 46 (1999).
9. K.M. Munshi, Pilgrimage to Freedom at 191 in Indian Constitutional Documents (Vol. I).

and parts of India as are outside British Independent Sovereign India, shall be a Union of them all; and the said territories, either with their present boundaries or with such others as may be determined by the Constituent Assembly, and thereafter according to the law of the Constitution, shall possess and retain the status of autonomous units, together with residuary powers, and exercise all functions and powers of the government and administration, save and except those that are assigned to and vested in the Union, and save and except such powers and functions as are inherent in the Union by virtue of the sovereignty of the Union;

And wherein all power and authority of the Sovereign Independent India, its constituent parts, and organs of government are derived from the people; and wherein shall be guaranteed to all the people of India by law and secured to them by declared social objectives and purposes, economic organization and administrative machinery

(a) Justice, social economic and political,

(b) Equality of status, of opportunity, and before the law,

(c) Freedom of thought, belief, vocation, association and action subject of law and public morality;

and wherein adequate safeguards shall be provided for minorities, backward areas and classes; and whereby shall be maintained the integrity of the territory of the Republic and its sovereign rights on land, sea and air according to justice and law of the civilized nations; and this ancient land attain its rightful and honoured place in the world and make its full and willing contribution to the promotion of world peace and the welfare of mankind.[10]

The recommended Resolution with the text recommended by the Expert Committee on aims and objectives of the

10. For more *see*, B. Shiva Rao, et al, (ed), The Framing of India's Constitution, Select Documents, Vol. 1, IIPA 329-330 (1966-1968).

Constitution was moved by Pt. Jawaharlal Nehru on December 13, 1946. With certain alteration and debate the resolution was adopted by the Constituent Assembly on 22nd day of January, 1947.[11] On 18th day of July, 1947 the Union Constitution Committee said that the Preamble was largely covered by the objective resolution and would be included in the final Constitution with modifications necessitated by the partition of the country under 3 June plan. Under the scare of partition of India the Drafting Committee took the initiative to consider the text of the Preamble afresh according to the changed circumstances.

"Firstly, the Preamble was drafted by B.N. Rao in his memorandum of May 30, 1947 and later on it was reproduced in the draft of October 7, 1947. The Drafting Committee considered it formally and decided that it should be restricted in defining the special features and the basic Socio-economic objectives of the Republic."[12] In order to provide strong centre, the Framers thought to establish Union with strong Centre. So, the Drafting Committee confined the text of the Preamble essentially to a statement of basic objectives of the Constitution.[13] Finally, the Preamble was presented before the Constituent Assembly for the adoption on October 17, 1949. Explaining the late adoption of the Preamble, Dr. Rajendra Prasad said, "the Constitution as a whole has to be passed in its second reading and the Preamble forms part of the Constitution."[14] Thereafter, the Preamble was put before the Assembly for debate and after the mature consideration the Preamble was adopted and added to the Constitution. Thus, the Preamble came into being.[15]

2. Deciphering the Preamble

The words used in the preamble have an inherent meaning. They conceal more than they convey. These are

---

11. *See*, CAD Vol. 1, 65-153, 269-324.
12. *Supra* note 1 at 322.
13. *See Supra* note 10 at 287.
14. CAD Vol. X, at 432, 429.
15. *See*, CAD Vol. IV at 710. *See* also, Dr. Subhash C. Kashyap, Constitutional Law of India, Vol. 1, 284-288 (2008).

the words of great constitutional importance. Each of the ideals embodied under the Preamble needs to be analyzed separately.

Sovereign

The preamble declares India as a Sovereign. The Constitution has been framed by the people of India themselves so the ultimate sovereignty vests in the people of India. Justice R.M. Sahai said in *N. Nagendra Rao & Co.* v. *State of Andhra Pradesh.*[16] that "sovereign as used in the Constitution is different from the old and archaic concept of sovereignty which has ceased to survive. Sovereignty now vests in the people of India and the United States and both recognized that people are the basis of all sovereignty. The legislature, the executive and the judiciary have been created and constituted to serve the people."

Socialist

The term *socialist* made an explicit appearance in the Preamble by the 42nd Amendment in 1976. In order to implement new socio-economic reform effectively, the Swarn Singh suggested the alteration of the Constitution.[17] The term 'Socialist' has different meanings and connotation in different countries depending on their socio-economic condition.[18] However, certain basic concepts can be found to be common.[19] Sometimes, it refers to a system of social organization in which private property and the distribution of the income are subject to social control and the political system helping that system in practice.[20] The Supreme Court

16. AIR 1994 SC 2663: (1994) 6 SCC 205: 1994 AIR SCW 3753.
17. The Statement, dated 30-05-1976. Shri Swarn Singh explained in A.I.C.C. (1976):"the Prime Minister's new economic programme was a major move for socio-economic reform. We must, therefore, alter the Constitution suitably so that these and other socio-economic reforms can be effectively implemented."
18. See *Minerva Mills Ltd.* v. *Union of India,* AIR 1980 SC 1789: (1980) 3 SCC 625: 1980 Ker LT 573.
19. See *Excel Wear* v. *Union of India,* AIR 1979 SC 25: 1978 Lab IC 1537: (1978) 4 SCC 224.
20. Britanica Ready Referencer Encyclopedia, Vol. 9, at 87.

in *D.S. Nakara* v. *Union of India*,[21] observed that the basic framework of socialism is to provide a decent standard of life to the working people, particularly security from cradle to grave; the object is to achieve economic equality and distribution of income. This is a blend of Marxism and Gandhism leaning towards Gandhian Socialism."

Democratic Republic

Democracy is a form of government in which the sovereign power is vested in the people, which they enjoy on the principle of equal political rights. The Constitution has established representative democracy by ensuring universal adult suffrage and free and fair periodic elections.[22] Every citizen of India who has attained the age of 18 years has the right to cast vote and choose representatives of their own choice in a democratic manner. The citizens of India have no direct share in the political power but they can enjoy it indirectly, through their chosen representatives.

A Republic is a government for the protection of the citizen against the exercise of all unjust power. It is a government administered by a few, as the representatives of the people and for their benefit.[23] India is a Republic. The head of the State is not a monarch, but an elected person for a definite period. In this relation, D.D. Basu points out that "it may be said that the Preamble to our Constitution uses the term in both senses. For, not only shall we have an elected President instead of a hereditary King as the head of our State, but the State will also be characterized by the absence of any ruling or privileged class, and all offices – from the humblest to the highest (including that of the President) – will be open to all citizens without any distinction of caste, creed, religion or sex. Thus Indian citizens will be subjects and free citizens at the same time."[24]

21. AIR 1983 SC 130: (1983) 1 SCC 305: 1983 (1) SCJ 188. *See* also *Randhir* v. *Union of India*, AIR 1982 SC 879: (1982) 1 SCC 618: 1982 (1) SCJ 283; *S.R. Bommai* v. *Union of India*, AIR 1994 SC 1918: 1994 AIR SCW 2946: (1994) 3 SCC 1.
22. J.C. Johari, Indian Government and Politics, Vol. 1, 389 (1998).
23. P. Ramanatha Aiyer, The Law Lexicon 1663 (2004).
24. See *Supra* note 24 at 390.

The Supreme Court in *Kesavananda Bharati* case,[25] held while explaining Democratic Republic of India that "the concept of Democracy as visualized by the Constitution presupposes the representation of people in the Parliament and State Legislatures by the method of election…it is obvious that a power must be lodged somewhere to judge the validity of the election, for, otherwise, there would be no certainty as to who were legitimately chosen as members, and any intruder or usurper might claim a seat and thus trample upon the privileges and liberties of the people. Indeed elections would become under such circumstances a mockery."

Secular

In order to emphasize the Secular nature of the Constitution, the term 'secular' was inserted by the 42nd amendment in 1976. The term 'secular' means "non-spiritual, having no concern with religious, or spiritual matters, anything which is distinct oppose to, or not connected with religion or ecclesiastical things, temporal as oppose to spiritual or ecclesiastical."[26] In this relation, V.P. Luthera states that secular is materialistic in tone and holds that human improvement can be sought through material means alone.[27] Sardar Swaran Singh stated that "when we talk of secularism we have our concept of equal respect for all religions."[28]

In the Preamble, the term 'secular' has been used with the term 'republic'. Therefore, the State according to the Constitution is a Secular State. There are many provisions[29]

25. See *Supra* note 7.
26. Encyclopedia Britannica, Vol. XX, 264 (1967).
27. V.P. Luthera, The Concept of Secular State and India 19 (1964).
28. *The Times of India* (Delhi) dated 29-08-1976.
29. Preamble (Sovereign… Secular… Republic… liberty of… belief, faith and worship); Part II (Only one citizenship, no citizenship on the basis of religion); Article 14 (Equal treatment to all before the law without giving any preference on the basis of religion); Article 15 (No discrimination on the basis of religion); Article 16 (In public employment, no discrimination on the basis of religion); Article 17 (Abolition of untouchability); Articles 25-28 (Freedom to propagate, practice or follow any religion); Article 44 (Uniform civil code for whole India); Article 51A(e) (Duty of every citizen to promote harmony and the spirit of common brotherhood amongst the people of India); Article 325 (No person to be in-eligible for inclusion on in or to claim to be included in special electoral roll on ground of religion); and article 326 (Adult suffrage to all without the basis of any religion).

under the Constitution which reflect the secular nature of the Constitution. The Supreme Court in *Commissioner, Hindu Religious Endowments, Madras* v. *Lakshmindra Swamiar*,[30] stated that 'Secular' means religion as a matter of faith with individual or communities which is not necessarily 'theistic'.

Again in *St. Xavier's College Society* v. *State of Gujarat*,[31] the Supreme Court held that there is no mysticism in the Secular character of the India. It is neither anti-God nor pro-God. It treats alike the devout, the agnostic and the atheist. It eliminates God from the matter of the State and ensures that no one shall be discriminated against on the ground of religion. Above all, the Supreme Court in *S.R. Bommai* v. *Union of India*,[32] recognized Secularism, whatever may be the meaning, as a basic feature of the Constitution of India.

Justice, Liberty, Equality and Fraternity

The term 'justice' has been used in the Preamble in three distinct forms: social, economic and political. The social, economic and political justice is the Constitutional goal as well as legitimate expectation of the people of India. The Supreme Court in *Valsamma Paul* v. *Cochin University*,[33] observed that "social democracy means 'a way of life which recognizes liberty, equality and fraternity as principles of life.' They are not separated items in a trinity but they form union of trinity. To diverse one from the other is to defeat the very purpose of democracy. Without equality, liberty would produce the supremacy of the few over the many. Equality without liberty would kill individual initiative. Without fraternity, liberty and equality could not become a natural course of things. Articles 15(4) and 16(4), therefore, intend to remove social and economic inequality to make equal opportunities available in reality. Social and economic justice is a right enshrined for the protection of society."

Being a dynamic concept, the concept of social justice aims at mitigating the suffering of poor, tribes, Dalits and

30. AIR 1954 SC 282: 1954 SCJ 335: 1954 SCR 1005.
31. AIR 1974 SC 1389: (1974) 1 SCC 717: (1975) 1 SCR 173.
32. AIR 1994 SC 1918: 1994 AIR SCW 2946: (1994) 3 SCC 1.
33. AIR 1996 SC 1011: 1996 AIR SCW 492: (1996) 1 SCR 128.

deprived section of people. The main object of social justice is to bring the status of these weaker sections of society to level of equality to live a life full of dignity. Social justice is not a simple concept of the society but it is an essential part of complex change to relieve poor. So, Social Justice and equality are complementary to each other so that both should maintain their vitality. Rule of law is a potent instrument of social justice to bring equality in result.[34] The Court in India has given effect to social justice after passing orders in various social matters such as abolition of bonded labour,[35] protective discrimination in favour of backward classes,[36] child welfare,[37] woman welfare,[38] right to livelihood,[39] and so on.

Economic Justice is undefined under the Constitution. The concept of economic justice demands a socialistic pattern of society for the establishment of welfare State. It demands that there should be no discrimination between man and man on the basis of economic values.[40] The concept of economic justice is envisioned in various Articles of the Constitution, in particular articles 14, 19(g), 19 (6)(ii), 39 (b) & (c), 31A, 41 and 43. Therefore, economic justice, on individual level means the legitimate proceeds of his labour. To work according to needs, seems, yet to be a distant goal. Work, whether mental or manual, being condition for the subsistence of an individual being, the meaning to be basically assigned to economic justice, is to ensure that one who puts in any labour must take the deserts of his labour.[41]

34. For more see *Air India Statutory Corporation* v. *United Labour Union*, AIR 1997 SC 645: 1997 AIR SCW 430: (1997) 9 SCC 377.
35. See *Bandhua Mukti Morcha* v. *Union of India*, AIR 1984 SC 802: (1984) 3 SCC 161: 1984 Lab IC 560.
36. See *State of Kerala* v. *Jacob Mathew*, AIR 1964 SC 316: 1964 Ker LJ 498: ILR (1964) 2 Ker 53.
37. *See* article 39(f) of the Constitution of India
38. See *Vishaka* v. *State of Rajasthan*, AIR 1997 SC 3011: (1997) 6 SCC 241: 1997 AIR SCW 3043.
39. See *Olga Tellis* v. *Bombay Municipal Corporation*, AIR 1986 SC 180: (1985) 3 SCC 545: 1986 Cr LR (SC) 23.
40. See *Supra* note 3 at 43.
41. *See* Dr. R.G. Chaturvedi, Justice: Social, Economic and Political, 707 (1997); *see* also CAD. Vol. II, at 302 (*see* Pandit Jawaharlal Nehru's view on economic justice).

For the smooth working of a democracy, political justice is *sine qua non*. Political justice is to ensure the people's participation in the political life of a country. Indian Constitution ensures this through the article 325 and 326. These Articles ensure the general electoral roll for every constituency and universal adult suffrage. Therefore, the main theme of political justice is those aspects of life which are the subject matter of politics or touched by politics, the political justice must be there. The other aspects of "Political Justice" are adequate representation of women and minorities and curbs on money powers.[42]

Liberty covers the area of thought, expression, belief and worship. Liberty of thought enables liberty of expression. Belief occupies a place higher than thought and expression. Belief of people rests on liberty of thought. In a triangle, the belief occupies the upper angle and thought and expression would be at the two corner angles on the base line. See the illustration below:[43]

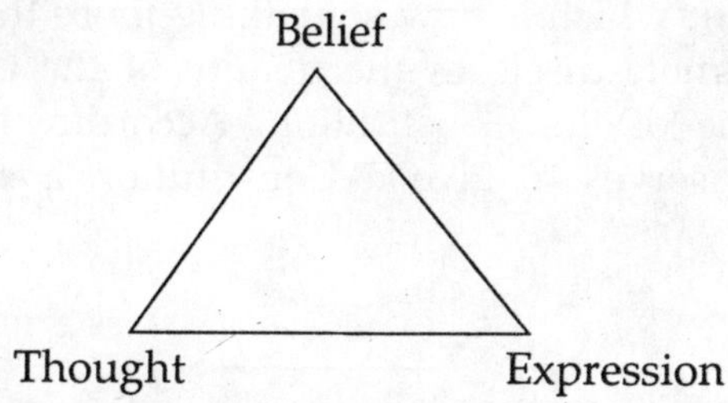

Further, one who has neither thought nor expression nor belief, is lacking in faith. Respect for thought, expression, belief and faith of one by the other would give a meaning to worship and it is such worship which would pose no risk and no danger to liberty of one at all.[44]

Equality of status and opportunity is ensured by the Preamble. The Constitution provides equality of status by prohibiting discrimination on artificial grounds and equality

---

42. *See* B. Sivaramayya, Inequalities and The Law 117-129 (1984).
43. Justice R.C. Lahoti, Preamble: The Spirit and Backbone of the Constitution of India 11 (2004).
44. *Ibid.*

of opportunity has been assured by the Constitution by the guarantee of rule of law. Justice R.C. Lahoti states that[45] "if Justice, Liberty and Equality have been secured, "fraternity" is assured. Fraternity cannot be inculcated; it can be promoted *i.e.* held forward and furthered. Dignity of the individual is the prime constituent of fraternity, while fraternity assures the dignity of the individual. Both are interdependent and intertwined. Unity and integrity of nation cannot survive unless the dignity of every individual citizen is guaranteed."

Prof. Ernest Barker in his book *Principles of Social and Political Theory* observed that "I ought to explain, as I end, why the Preamble to the Constitution of India is printed after the table of contents. It seems to me, when I read it, to state in brief and pithy form the argument of much of the book; and it may accordingly serve as a key note. I am the more moved to quote it because I am proud that the people of India should begin their independent life by subscribing to the principles of political tradition which we, in the West call Western, but which is now something more than Western".[46] Thus, Preamble discloses the quality of the Constitution. It is backbone of the Constitution. According to Kelsen the "preamble serves to give a Constitution a greater dignity and efficacy."[47]

---

45. *Ibid.*
46. K.C. Markandan, Spirit of The Constitution 243 (1986).
47. Kelson, Theory of Law and State 261 (1946).

CHAPTER II

We the People

Latika Vashist

The enactment and commencement of the Constitution of India was the moment of giving a meaning to the right to "swaraj" that the people had been fighting for against centuries of colonial oppression. To realize *swaraj i.e.,*"rule by self"/"rule over self", the Constitution proclaims that political sovereignty rests in "We, the People of India". It is the sovereignty of people that renders meaning to the sovereignty of Indian nation state. And in this metonymic claim of the modern Indian state rests the *peoples'* right to self-determination.[1]

In the discourse of human rights, right to self-determination is one right that transcends the on-going East-West debate of *Are Human Rights Western*?[2] The authorship of this right, asserts Baxi, "rests with communities in struggle against illegitimate power formation and the politics of cruelty".[3]

1. Here the term peoples' is remarkable. Though the state is also a reference to a collectivity of people, self-determination is not a right of the Governments but a right of 'peoples'. This may not be this clear in case of other peoples' rights, for instance the rights to international peace and security. See for details, James Crawford, The Right of Peoples: 'Peoples' or 'Governments'? in Rights of Peoples 55-68 (James Crawford ed., 1988).
2. A detailed excellent account provided in Arvind Sharma, are Human Rights Western? (2006).
3. Upendra Baxi, the Future of Human Rights 158 (2008). Baxi believes that destruction of 'narrative monopolies' is of utmost importance to recognize that the authorship of human rights rests with the suffering communities.

Decades before the international human rights discourse recognized self-determination, Lokmanya Tilak had given the freedom call to India: *Swaraj is my birthright and I shall have it!* Being a firm answer to the colonial hegemony – territorial, economic and cultural – self-determination was the building block of the post-colonial world scholarship.

The 20th Century is witness to the great prowess, power and potential of this right. While on the one hand, it awakened the masses from an *opiumated* slumber, on the other hand, it had grave implications for the sovereignty, integrity and unity of states. Consequentially, with the integration of right to self-determination in the modern human rights discourse, limits were set on it and now the only place it acquires is one of 'soft law', being an offspring to the third generation human rights. The journey of self-determination from the local to global spaces of *politics of human rights* corroded its contours to the extent that for the contemporary human rights discourse it is a 'riddle wrapped in an enigma shrouded in mystery'. There are unfathomable ambiguities about who constitutes 'self', what it means to have a right to self-determination and if self-determination is also an inalienable human right of the peoples.

There has been a great increase in the secessionist movements in the past.[4] The Indian sub-continent itself has been the contested site for movements of self-determination which has often resulted in brutal violations of humans as well as their human rights. The struggles for independence and self-governance from Kashmir[5] to

4. At present there are about 26 ongoing armed self-determination conflicts. In addition to these armed conflicts, it is estimated that there are another 55 or so campaigns for self-determination which may turn violent if left unaddressed, with another 15 conflicts considered provisionally settled but at risk of re-ignition. Quinn, "Self-determination movements and their Outcomes" cited in Marc Weller, Settling Self-Determination Conflicts: Recent Developments, 20 EUR. J. INT'L L 111 (2009).

5. The most controversial aspect of the Kashmir issue is the question of plebiscite. There is no unanimity of opinion on this aspect. While some authors completely rule out the possibility of plebiscite, some hold that a UN monitored plebiscite can be the only panacea. See, for arguments in favour of holding plebiscite, Umozurike OJI Umozurike, Self-Determination in International Law 236-244 (1972).

Nagalim[6] and from Tibet[7] to Tamil Eelam[8] - have been viewed with scorn and suspicion that is attached to the seditious schema of a few unpatriotic people. The rhetoric of territorial sovereignty clothed in the suave language of international law has attempted to silence all claims – even the legitimate ones – of self-determination and peoples' freedom movements.

This chapter attempts to locate the limits of self-determination beyond the shadow lines of nation by freeing it from the rhetoric of unmindful secessionism and nationalistic jingoism. The first part of the chapter unravels the world politics behind the evolution of self-determination from a political principle to a right. The chapter in the second part questions the confinement of self-determination to the colonial context, especially in the context of India's reservation to article 1 of ICCPR. The third and the fourth part deals with the scope of self-determination, with the focus on carving space for a right to secede in some contexts. The concluding part of the chapter delves into the realm of *post national* politics from whose spectacle secession (no matter how radical in itself) would appear to be an extremely conservative response to the state authority. This chapter is not an exhaustive account of the scope of the right to self-determination. Though the complex

6. The Hydari Agreement (especially article 9) that was signed in 1948 between the Naga Leaders and Sir Akbar Hydari, Governor of Assam on behalf of India created much resentment in Nagas, along with the unfulfilled promises made to them by Gandhi and the then Governor General. But it is believed that a political solution within the Constitution can effectuate their right to self-determination. *Id.* at 245-251.
7. With the invasion of Tibet in 1950 and the subsequent Seventeen Point Agreement, the People's Republic of China asserted control over Tibet. While the Chinese sources generally claim progress towards a prosperous and free society in Tibet, with its pillars being economic development, legal advancement, and peasant emancipation, Tibet Government-in-Exile and some indigenous Tibetans refute these claims, alleging gross violation of most human rights by the Chinese Government.
8. The history of the dispute can be traced back to the Sinhala only Act which was enacted in 1956 and the state sponsored violence unleashed on Tamils in 1958 which pushed the Tamils in the Tamil provinces of North and East. What started as a non-violent struggle took the form of the most violent struggle of independence. Though the Government seemed to have silenced the guns of LTTE, the situation for Sri Lankan Tamils is grim as they continue to live as refugees in their own country.

questions like who is the 'self', determination with respect to which part of the state's territory, self-determination as the minorities right for cultural preservation *et al.* are only given a passing reference, but the silence on these issues should not be taken to mean that these issues are less important or secondary; they merely fall outside the scope of the present chapter.

1. Dark Dualities of Evolution of Self-Determination

Pre World War II

What is today proclaimed as the 'first'[9] human right of people began its life as a political principle, rather than a legal right. Even as a political principle it was not absolute. There were two conflicting models of human rights – socialist model of human rights advocated by socialist Russia and progressive liberal notions of human rights advanced by US – which worked in opposition to each other, premised primarily on the 'doctrine of vested interests'! There was bound to be grave inconsistency and contradiction in the application of principle of self-determination, when the theoretical foundations of the principle were in doldrums. The only policy that governed the right to self determination was of double standards. While Stalin supported the secessionism of anti-colonial movements in India, Egypt, Morocco and elsewhere, he rejected similar demands for succession within the regions bordering Russia and defended this duality in the 'interests of the revolution'.[10] On exactly similar lines the European powers favoured the independence of the nationalities in the Balkans but ignored the appeals for self-determination of their colonies.

There were huge differences in the understanding of the national question amongst leading socialists themselves. For instance, Bauer in his *Question of Nationalities and Social Democracy* (1907), rather than acknowledging a right to secede, which could prove economically and politically disruptive

9. Here, 'first' doesn't mean that it has a heightened status. It merely refers to its special place in the international documents-being the first and sole article in the first part of both the human rights covenants.
10. Micheline R. Ishay, The History of Human Rights 187 (2004).

to neighbouring nationalities, proposed the establishment of cultural autonomy within a greater federal state. Questioning the *national unity imposed from above* wherein local regions kept clinging to fragmented parochial loyalties, he proposed 'the implementation of the nationality principle' a rule by which an external federal power would serve local communities.[11] While federal state would be concerned with foreign policy and domestic economic policy between different nationalities, the representative national entities would be responsible for matters related to their cultural and national life. Thus, he called for resolution of ethnic conflicts by proposing multicultural existence within states, relying perhaps on Marx's and Engel's early view of the national question- 'proletarians have no country'.[12]

Rosa Luxemberg, another leading socialist, while dealing with nationalist calls of Polish movement expressed apprehension about a right to self–determination in Poland. Warning of the costs of secession for economically weak nationalities, she argued that ''national movements' and struggles for 'national interests' are usually class movements of the ruling strata of the bourgeoisie, which can in any given case represent the interest of the other strata of the population only insofar as under the form of 'national interests' it defends progressive forms of historical development, and insofar as the working class has yet distinguished itself from the mass of the 'nation' (led by the bourgeoisie) into an independent, enlightened political class'.[13] Her circumspection about right to self-determination and the nationalist sentiment was again inspired by the spirit of Marx and Engels who approached the nationality question from an economic materialist standpoint rather than 'from the 'eternal' sentimental formulae of liberalism'. Keeping economic materialism as the

---

11. Bauer, The Question of Nationalities and Social Democracy cited in *supra* note 12 at 184.
12. Karl Marx and Frederick Engels, "Manifesto of the Communist Party" in Karl Marx and Frederick Engels, Selected Works 108 (1977).
13. Rosa Luxemberg, The National Question And Autonomy in *supra* note 12 at 185.

vintage point, she concluded that for industrially backward countries like Poland, secession (here from Russia) would only undermine the interests of the proletariat, by not only perpetuating their economic dependence on the parent country but also diminishing their potential to co-ordinate struggle with workers of the parent country against the state's authoritarianism. This, however, implied that when people attained self-sufficiency, their hitherto abstract right to self-determination could be concretized and secession could be taken as a workable proposition.

Lenin, on the other hand, did not share Luxemberg's anti-secessionist position. According to him the repression suffered by colonized nationalities warranted a 'tactical alliance' with the bourgeois class in the struggle for self-determination.[14] Contending that, economic materialism could not be the only factor justifying nationalist claims, Lenin supported the liberation movements of the oppressed nations. While extending support for the cause of nationalists, he drew a distinction between nationalism from 'above' and nationalism from 'below', former signifying the oppressive nationalism of an authoritarian state and the latter referring to the justifiable nationalism of an oppressed nation.[15]

Lenin's position *vis-a-vis* self determination was echoed after World War I in Woodrow Wilson's 'Fourteen Points Address' (1918). It called for the independence of nationalities in the Balkan states, proclamation of a Polish homeland, sovereignty for Turkish portion of the Ottoman Empire and invoked the right to self-determination which would secure 'justice to all peoples and nationalities, and their right to live on equal terms of liberty and safety'[16] . It concluded with the hope that these rights 'could be realized by a League of Nations, which would *establish borders for homogenous ethnic groups, thereby presumably removing a major cause of war.*'[17] But

14. *Supra* note 12 at 186.
15. *Id.*
16. Woodrow Wilson, The Fourteen Points Address (1918). *Available at* http://wwi.lib.byu.edu/index.php/President_Wilson%27s_Fourteen_Points.
17. *Supra* note 12 at 188.

the hope cast upon League of Nations to redeem the future of oppressed nations and peoples was soon shattered. Right to self-determination was not laid down in the League of Nations. The League gave in to the pressure of major colonial powers and devised a system of mandates to legitimately allocate Asian and African colonies to the victors as the 'prize of war'.[18]

Hitherto developed principle of self-determination– grounded partially in Wilson's 'borders for homogenous ethnic groups' thesis and partially in realities of colonialism – acquired destructive form with the rise of aggressive nationalism in Europe. Wilson's notions of national unity and territorial sovereignty for homogenous ethnic groups were invoked by the Nazi regime to justify its occupation of Sudetenland (there being three million Germans within Czechoslovakia's borders). Self-determination was robbed off its inherent value of justice and dignity of all human beings as the grotesque face of national consolidation unveiled under the hegemony of fascist forces. While Hitler prophesied a Third Reich,[19] Mussolini strove to receive the lost grandeur of ancient Rome, both exercising self-determination. Thus, the

---

18. The Covenant of the League of Nations (1919), article 22. To pacify the critics of mandate system the Covenant included clauses urging colonial powers to bring the mandate territories towards self-government and guarantee under the mandatory system, the political advancement of indigenous people, freedom of conscience and religion, just law and the prohibition of abuses (such as trafficking in slaves, arms or alcohol). In the *Aaland Islands* case (a dispute between Sweden and Finland as to whether the islanders who were under Finnish jurisdiction could opt to join Sweden in the exercise of their right to self-determination, especially in view of the fact that Finland itself obtained independence from Russia in exercise of that right) it was held that in the case of nations within established states, there was no legal right of self-determination or secession, the composition of a state being a matter within its exclusive domestic jurisdiction.
19. The Nazis sought to legitimize their power historiographically by portraying their rule as a continuation of a Germanic past. They coined the term Das Dritte Reich ("The Third Empire" or "The Third Reich"), counting the Holy Roman Empire of middle ages as the first and the 1871-1918 monarchy as the second. Third Reich is the common English name for Germany between 1933 and 1945, while it was led by Adolf Hitler and the National Socialist German Worker's Party (NSDAP).

right of the oppressed turned into the merciless sword of tyrants themselves!

Post World War II Developments: First Phase of Right to Self-Determination

We have seen in the preceding section how the fledgling right to self-determination was abused by the fascist parties with their ideological whip and military might. At the twilight of World War II when the victorious Allied powers proposed to the world a new Charter of hope and security, the occasion necessitated a comprehensive and well-defined (though justifiably 'confined' after the Nazi experience) right to self-determination for the peoples, but what came along was only a cautious promise and a hazy principle.

The United Nations Charter has an express mention of self-determination right of peoples. Article 1(2) provides that one of the purposes of the United Nations (UN) is 'to develop friendly relations among nations based on respect for the principle of equal rights and self-determination of peoples.' Concurrently, article 55, on Economic and Social Co-operation, instructed the UN to promote higher standards of living, solutions to health and cultural problems and universal respect for human rights – all in order to create conditions necessary for peaceful and friendly relations among nations 'based on equal rights and self-determination'. But in both article 1(2) and article 55, the context seems to be the rights of the peoples of one state to be protected from interference by other states. In other words, the right to self-determination was merely a right against interference of one state by other state.

The use of expression 'equal rights' with 'self-determination' is particularly noteworthy as it was equal rights of states that were being provided for, not of individuals[20] (particularly bearing in mind that international law at that time was a law between sovereign nations). Moreover, both these articles are not couched in the language of a specific obligation- article 1 being aspirational (self-determination

20. The travaux preparatoires of the Charter confirms this understanding of the phrase. See, VI UNCIO 300.

being the 'basis' of the 'purpose' of developing 'friendly relations among nations') and article 55 being promotional ('the United Nations shall promote'). Thus, the provision of self-determination in the Charter neither referred to a right of dependent peoples to be independent nor secured them a right to vote for it 'spoke cautiously of an obligation to develop, rather than immediately to grant, self-government'[21] and prolonged the full realization of self-determination of the trust territories.

The aforesaid observation might be a striking and unpleasant revelation, but any other interpretation of the Charter which brings it in conformity with the correct understanding (howsoever confusing that might be) of the term, would amount to 'a retrospective rewriting of history'.[22] The fact gets crystallized by the stark absence of the term 'self-determination' in Chapter XI and XII of the Charter which deal with non-self-governing territories and trusteeship system respectively.[23] But despite the cautious articulation

---

21. R.J. Vincert, Human Rights and International Relations 79 (1986).
22. Rosalyn Higgins, Problems and Process: International Law and how we use it 111 (2003).

    Higgins points out that when the Charter of the UN was drawn up, there were fifty one original members, all independent, with the exception of India (which shortly became independent), Ukraine and Byelorussia (which were treated as independent UN members while still republics of Soviet Union). In 1946, the focus was on the rights and obligations of Sovereign member states and not of the dependent territories. Though it was recognized that colonial powers had certain duties towards the peoples they governed, it did not include any duty to grant independence.
23. There was a division of category of colonial territories into two groups purely for historical reasons. Those territories that had been mandates were brought under the trusteeship system, while the remaining colonial territories were covered under Chapter XI as Non-Self Governing Territories. A categorical right of self-determination was not given to either of the two. Though article 73(b) refers to the duty of the governing state 'to develop self-government, to take due account of the political aspiration of the peoples, and to assist them in the progressive development of their free political institution, according to the particular circumstances of each territory and its people and their ranging stages of advancement', it falls quite short of what today is generally thought of as self-determination. Even article 76 while delineating the basic objective of Trusteeship in its

Contd. on next page

of self-determination in the Charter, there was a significant development of the principle in the post war years.

It is rather surprising to note that the Universal Declaration of Human Rights assumed silence on this question[24] and did not give much assertion to the rights of nations and peoples.[25] The *politics of human rights* (especially during Cold War) surfaces some disturbing realities about the inconsistencies in the invocation and protection of this right. For example, it becomes extremely difficult to reconcile United States' call for the liberation of Eastern Europe from communism, demand Soviet respect for the Yugoslavia's anti-Soviet communist state on one hand and fund the French colonial War to deny the self-determination to Indo-China, on the other hand. Similarly, Soviet Union's support for 'national liberation movements abroad, but gross denial of self-determination for those actually living under socialism'[26] was quite appalling.

Second Phase of Self-Determination

Initial resistance of the colonial powers against the idea of self-determination as a legal right (according to them it was merely a political aspiration) was gradually muted and 'self-determination was historically bound up with decolonization – with the growing agreement that it was obligatory to bring forward dependent peoples to independence if they so chose, even though article 73 had spoken only of self-government.'[27] With this recognition as a legal right in the

---

Contd. from previous page

clause (b) – 'to promote... their progressive development towards self Government or independence as may be appropriate to the particular circumstances of each territory and its people and the freely expressed wishes of the peoples concerned' – does not assume independence as the only proper outcome of the colonized territories.

24. There was no reference to self-determination even in the American Convention or the European Covenant on Human Rights.
25. Though it is suggested that article 21 does deal with internal self-determination by stipulating the right of everyone to participate in the government of his country, directly or through democratically elected representatives, it is only a soft version of self-determination.
26. The history of Hungary and Czechoslovakia is testimony to the Soviet double standards.
27. *Supra* note 24.

context of decolonization, it took various forms – choice of independence[28] or a choice by the peoples of a territory to join with another state[29] or choice to remain in a constitutional relationship with the former colonial power.[30]

Self-determination as a legal obligation in the process of decolonization was strengthened by the two resolutions of the General Assembly in 1960: General Assembly Resolution 1514 (XV) and General Assembly Resolution 1541 (XV). In Resolution 1514 – the Declaration on the Granting Independence to Colonial Countries and Peoples – right of all peoples to self-determination is recognized by virtue of which all peoples subject to colonial rule have the right to 'freely determine their political status and freely pursue their economic, social and cultural development.'[31] Resolution 1541 (XV) clarified that this exercise in self-determination could result in various outcomes[32] and stipulated that processes required to ensure that informed, free and voluntary choices were being made. However, the scope of the applicability of self-determination was considerably regulated by defining non-self governing territory as 'a territory which is geographically separate and is distinct ethnically and/or culturally from the country administering it'[33] .

28. It was executed through a referendum or plebiscite very often under the aegis of UN. *See e.g.,* GA Res. 944 (X), 15 Dec. 1955 and the ensuing plebiscite in British Togolands in May 1956; GA Res. 1580 (IV) and the ensuing referendum in Rwanda of Sept. 1961, and many others.

29. *E.g.,* the integration of Northern Cameroons into Nigeria and the Southern Cameroons into Cameroon.

30. *E.g.,* Gibralter *vis-a-vis* the UK and Puerto Rico *vis-a-vis* the USA.

31. The fact that this Declaration strictly applied to colonial context and does not give right of secession to peoples is substantiated by its sixth principle- 'Any attempt aimed at the partial or total disruption of the national unity and the territorial integrity of a country is incompatible with the purposes and principles of the Charter of the United Nations'.

32. Principle VI: A Non-Self-Governing Territory can be said to have reached a full measure of self-government by:

(a) Emergence as a sovereign independent State;

(b) Free association with an independent State; or

(c) Integration with an independent State.

33. Principle IV. This is known as the 'salt water barrier' or 'salt water' theory of decolonization which requires that colonies be physically separated

Contd. on next page

Once the right to self-determination was accepted as a right of the peoples under colonial rule against colonization to be recognized and respected by the colonial powers[34], the next question that arose was whether self-determination has any application outside the colonial context.

2. Self-Determination: Beyond the 'Logic' of Colonization...Illegality of India's Reservation

The blatant omission of right to self-determination from UDHR was a historical *faux pas* which unravelled the impious intentions of colonial powers. Though the General Assembly made quite a few references to this principle as a human right,[35] its recognition as a fundamental human right was still dubious.

It took almost two decades for the international human rights order to recognize explicitly the right to self-determination. The common article 1 of the two Covenants on Civil and Political Rights and Social, Economic and Cultural Rights provides:

1. All peoples have the right of self-determination. By virtue of that right they freely determine their political status and freely pursue their economic, social and cultural development.

Contd. from previous page

from the colonial power with 30 miles of open water. According to the resolution, the nations dominated by nation to which they are contiguous or within which they are encapsulated are not colonies *per se*, but they are 'minorities' domestic to the dominating power. This interpretation of decolonization was challenged by Belgium through its 'Belgian Thesis' which 'contended that decolonization should extend to all colonized peoples, even if they are bound in enclaves entirely surrounded by the colonizing states'. The thesis especially drew attention to the conditions of the indigenous people and called for application of right to self-determination to them as well, but the international order remained pre-dominated by the 'salt-water thesis'.

34. *See*, Namibia Advisory Opinion, ICJ REPORTS (1971) 16 at para 52. Also *see*, Western Sahara Advisory Opinion, ICJ REPORTS (1975) 12 at para 162.

35. *See*, General Assembly Resolutions 421 D, S.U.N.G.A.O.R. SUPP. (NO. 2042), UN DEC. A/2119, (1952) GA RES. 637, (VIII) OF DEC 16, 1952, GA RES. 1314 (XVII) of Nov. 1955.

2. All peoples may, for their own ends, freely dispose of their natural wealth and resources without prejudice to any obligations arising out of international economic co-operation, based upon the principle of mutual benefit, and international law. In no case may a people be deprived of its own means of subsistence.
3. The States Parties to the present Covenant, including those having responsibility for the administration of Non-Self-Governing and Trust Territories, shall promote the realization of the right of self-determination, and shall respect that right, in conformity with the provisions of the Charter of the United Nations.

An ordinary interpretation of this article indicates that article 1 cannot be limited to the colonial cases only.[36] Article 1, paragraph 1 does not say *some people* (limited to the colonial context) rather it is *all peoples* who have the right to self-determination and then paragraph 3 deals expressly, and non-exclusively, with colonial territories.[37] When a text first says 'all peoples' have a right and then in another paragraph of the same article, it says that the term 'peoples' includes the people of colonial territories, it can be conveniently inferred that the term is being used in a broad, general sense. This interpretation receives further corroboration from paragraph 2. The right of peoples over their natural wealth and resources has never been suggested to be limited to the colonial territories only as the principle of permanent sovereignty over natural resources applies to all the nations and states of the world equally.[38] The point here being very simple, that

36. James Crawford, "The Right of Self-Determination in International Law: Its Development and Future" in Peoples' Rights 27 (Philip Alston ed., 2005).

37. *Id.*

38. There are differences in dealing with the notion of permanent sovereignty as a right of peoples rather than states. If it is a right of peoples then can the people hold their Government internationally accountable for the stewardship of its resources? And if it is right of the state pre-existing in the doctrine of state sovereignty which was inalienable then what need did its re-affirmation serve except as reiteration against neo-colonialism and economic imperialism? These issues though pertinent in themselves are outside the scope of our present discussion.

it is not legally possible to argue (without crossing the limits set by reason and logic in the fervor of nationalistic jingoism) that the use of words 'peoples' means different things in the two paragraphs of the same article.[39] The term 'peoples' in paragraph 1 cannot be argued to have a narrower meaning than it evidently has in paragraph 2; since in paragraph 2 it applies to people inside as well as outside the colonial context, even in paragraph 1 it must apply to peoples inside as well as outside the colonial context.

Notwithstanding the clear disposition of article 1, some governments have insisted that self-determination extends only to the situation of 'classic' colonization and hence though it was the decisive factor between them and their former colonial masters, it is not available to their own peoples under the new found sovereignty. The third world countries which fought so valiantly to end colonialism and imperialism themselves stifle the growth of post-colonial self-determination owing to their threat (which is not always unreasonable) of fragmentation of new nation states and secession demands by ethnic groups or national minorities. The contention is that right to self-determination is available *only once* to the peoples, which once exercised to acquire a sovereign status, gets exhausted for all times to come. This rationale '(presumes) that the 'logic' of colonialism which made all sorts of different peoples, cultures and territories vessels of imperial unity should continue in the post-colony.'[40] Unveiling the crude realities of the theory and practice of self-determination one finds that the 'decolonizing world was in the process, yet again of recolonization'.

'The post-colonial state was *somehow* to create – out of many nations – a single 'nation-state''[41] – this gigantic task of nation building mutilated the hitherto cherished

39. Though it has been so argued by many. For instance *see*, M.H. Mendelson, Self-Determination In Jammu and Kashmir, 36 INDIAN J. INT'L L., 13 (1996); While broadly arguing against the right of self-determination to Jammu and Kashmir, Mendelson, *interalias*, asserts that though article 1(2) cannot be confined to colonial peoples, paragraphs 1 and 3 are confined to colonial and trust territories.
40. *Supra* note 5, at 51.
41. *Id.*

ideal of self-determination. The contradictions of the third world logic amounted to deep fragmentation of right to self-determination. The ultimate defeat was of the mute subjects of human rights. Baxi aptly summarizes the fate of the strife ridden, politicized self-determination:[42]

> '... we see the emergence of contradiction between human rights norm creation at the global level (political *for* human rights) with a claim, in the name of 'nation-building', to violate these with impurity at home (politics *of* human rights)'.

In this context, consider the Indian reservation to article 1 of ICCPR and ICESCR:[43]

> '...the Government of the Republic of India declares that the words `the right of self-determination' appearing in [this article] apply only to the peoples under foreign domination and that these words do not apply to sovereign independent States or to a section of a people or nation—which is the essence of national integrity.'

The reservation invited strong objections by the Netherlands, France[44] and the Federal Republic of Germany[45] and even Pakistan.[46] The erroneousness of the

---

42. *Id.*

43. Also note the declaration made by Bangladesh *vis-à-vis* art. 1:

'It is the understanding of the Government of the People's Republic of Bangladesh that the words "the right of self-determination of Peoples" appearing in this article apply in the historical context of colonial rule, administration, foreign domination, occupation and similar situations.'

44. The French objection to Indian reservation is because '(it) attaches conditions not provided for by the Charter of the United Nations to the exercise of the right of self-determination. The present declaration will not be deemed to be an obstacle to the entry into force of the Covenant between the French Republic and the Republic of India'.

45. The German objection reads as follows:

"The Government of the Federal Republic of Germany strongly objects, ... to the declaration made by the Republic of India in respect of article 1 of the International Covenant on Economic, Social and Cultural Rights and of article 1 of the International Covenant on Civil and Political Rights.

"The right of self-determination as enshrined in the Charter of the United Nations and as embodied in the Covenants applies to all peoples and

Contd. on next page

Indian reservation gets corroborated by the reference to self-determination in various other international instruments that clearly articulate self-determination in non-colonial contexts. Following three instruments are particularly significant:

- In the UN Declaration on Friendly Relations of 1970[47] it was postulated that right of self-determination is also available to peoples subject to 'alien subjugation, domination and exploitation'. This expression is not elaborated upon anywhere in the declaration 'but the reference to 'a government representing the whole people belonging to the territory without distinction as to race, creed or colour', in the penultimate paragraph, would be unnecessary and even irrelevant if the

Contd. from previous page

not only to those under foreign domination. All peoples, therefore, have the inalienable right freely to determine their political status and freely to pursue their economic, social and cultural development. The Federal Government cannot consider as valid any interpretation of the right of self-determination which is contrary to the clear language of the provisions in question. It moreover considers that any limitation of their applicability to all nations is incompatible with the object and purpose of the Covenants."

46. The objection raised by Pakistan is interesting for its incompleteness (perhaps deliberate due to political reasons). It states that right of self-determination applies to all peoples under foreign occupation and alien domination but does not proceed to say that it even applies to people outside the colonial context:

'The Government of Islamic Republic of Pakistan objects to the declaration made by the Republic of India in respect of article 1 of the International Covenant on Economic, Social and Cultural Rights and article 1 of the International Covenant on Civil and Political Rights.

The right of Self-determination as enshrined in the Charter of the United Nations and as embodied in the Covenants applies to all peoples under foreign occupation and alien domination.

The Government of the Islamic Republic of Pakistan cannot consider as valid any interpretation of the right of self-determination which is contrary to the clear language of the provisions in question. Moreover, the said reservation is incompatible with the object and purpose of the Covenants. This objection shall not preclude the entry into force of the Covenant between the Islamic Republic of Pakistan and India without India benefiting from its reservations.'

47. GA RES. 2625 (XXV) 1970.

principle of self-determination applied only to colonial territories.'[48]

- The African Charter of Human and Peoples' Rights which was adopted by the OAU in 1981 elaborates upon self-determination in articles 19[49] and 20.[50] The contrast in the language of article 20(1) and 20(2)-former using the term *all peoples* and latter using *colonized or oppressed peoples*-divulges the fact that the principle of self-determination as applicable to peoples is intended to be general in scope.
- Similar positioning is evident from the provisions of the Helsinki Final Act.[51] Though the Final Act was only concerned with Europe which had no Chapter XI territories (perhaps except Gibraltar),[52] yet the principle

48. *Supra* note 38, at 31. Despite this reference the wording of UN Declaration on Friendly Relations is many a times interpreted to support the view that self-determination is limited to a specific moment of decolonization as it provides, *inter alia,* that a colonial or non-self governing territory continues its separate existence 'until the people of the colony or Non-Self Governing Territory have exercised their right of self-determination in accordance with the Charter'.
49. Article 19 reads 'All peoples shall be equal; they shall enjoy the same respect and shall have the same rights. Nothing shall justify the domination of a people by another'.
50. Article 20 provides:
    1. *All peoples* shall have the right to existence. They shall have the unquestionable and inalienable right to self-determination. They shall freely determine their political status and shall pursue their economic and social development according to the policy they have freely chosen.
    2. *Colonized or oppressed peoples* shall have the right to free themselves from the bonds of domination by resorting to any means recognized by the international community.
    3. All peoples shall have the right to the assistance of the States parties to the present Charter in their liberation struggle against foreign domination, be it political, economic or cultural.
51. Helsinki Final Act, Helsinki Accords or Helsinki Declaration, was the final act of the Conference on Security and Co-operation in Europe held in Helsinki, Finland during July and August of 1975. It was an attempt to improve the relations between the Communist bloc and the West. Though it is merely a declaration of non-binding nature, it is important for understanding the international understanding of self-determination.
52. The sovereignty of Gibraltar has been a major point of contention in Anglo-Spanish relations. Gibraltar was ceded by Spain to the Crown of Great Britain in perpetuity, under the 1713 Treaty of Utrecht, though Spain

Contd. on next page

of self-determination finds a categorical mention in Principle VIII of the Act:

> '...By virtue of the principle of equal rights and self-determination of peoples, all peoples always have the right, in full freedom, to determine, *when and as they wish,* their *internal and external political status,* without external interference, and to pursue as they wish their political, economic, social and cultural development...'

The expression *internal and external political status* is remarkable as it clearly implies that even within a sovereign and independent state, self-determination continues to have striking significance. Even the once-and-for-all argument gets ruptured with the unequivocal phraseology of *when and as they wish.*

Thus, the international understanding of the principle is in contradistinction with the stand taken by the Indian government. Self-determination is a right against suffering and as history testifies, suffering has not only been inflicted by the colonial masters but even by sovereign states on its own countrymen.[53] Limiting self-determination only to the moment of de-colonization would thus mean blatant denial of any right to peoples against the state induced violence and legitimizing 'third world colonialism'.

There is an urgent need for the Indian state to re-consider the reservation to article 1, especially on account of the contemporary understanding of self-determination.

Contd. from previous page

asserts a claim to the territory and seeks its return. The overwhelming majority of Gibraltarians strongly oppose this, along with any proposal of shared sovereignty.

53. Amin's atrocities in Uganda and Pol Pot's in Cambodia are the most glaring examples of violence being perpetuated by a sovereign state on its own people. Recognizing this fact, General Assembly's Third Committee in 1985 by the United Kingdom affirmed that 'self-determination is a right of peoples and not of Governments...it is not only peoples suffering occupation by the foreign power which are deprived of their right of self-determination...(and thus) self-determination is not a single event, but a continuous process'. *See,* General Assembly's Third Committee in 1985 cited in *supra* note 38, at 29.

Self-determination right operates on a continuum. There are various degrees of self-determination secession being only one, though most extreme, manifestation of it. The Indian reservation to article 1, by linking right to self-determination only to peoples under foreign rule, views the doctrine as an all-or-nothing proposition. This position is erroneous for two reasons; it narrows down both the subject and content of this right. In international law, all 'peoples' have the right to self-determination who constitute 'peoples', needs to be construed for every case, thus subject of the right is not fixed.

The reservation by restricting self-determination only to 'peoples' under colonial rule, illegitimately curtails the subject of the right. With respect to the content of the right there is even an assumption implicit in the reservation that self-determination merely refers to complete independence or full autonomy. This assumption discards the multi-facetedness of self-determination; claim of self-determination may be to external self-determination (the establishment of a sovereign and independent state, the free association or integration with an independent state, or the emergence into any other political status freely determined by a people) and/or internal self-determination (the pursuit of a people's political, economic and social development within the framework of an existing state which can acquire the form of federalism, devolution and autonomy). With such an anachronistic approach towards self-determination, India fails to offer innovative solutions to the concerns of ethnic minorities, tribals, displaced peoples and even the peoples of strife ridden areas. Moreover, the reservation seems to be ridden with the fear of fragmentation and hence completely illegalizes all claims of secession for the sake of 'national integrity'. Being absolutely blind to all secession assertions, the state refrains from investigating into the claims, thereby leaving even the legitimate demands unaddressed.

3. Self-Determination in the Post-Colonial Context

Self-determination has gradually evolved 'from its modest beginnings in the UN Charter to a legal entitlement of decolonization and to a free-standing human right' in the post-colonial context. Notwithstanding this impressive journey, self-determination continues to be highly controversial and volatile because of its political character. The issues of territorial unity and integrity cast a dark shadow on the human rights oriented interpretation of self-determination – and some very basic questions of object, subject and scope still continue to plague the efforts of concretization. Following sections delve into some of these aspects to surface the underlying problems and identify the horizons of self-determination.

Range of Self-Determination

In the post-colonial context, self-determination has acquired varied dimensions. It is not just the traditional right to independence (as it was understood in the colonial context) but has a range of options within it- right to secession, right of divided states to be united,[54] right of limited autonomy, short of secession for groups defined territorially or by common ethnic, religious and linguistic bonds,[55] right of minorities within a larger political entity[56] and right to choose one's form of government or even more sharply the right to a democratic form of government.[57] Broadly the aforesaid options can be classified into external self-determination and internal self-determination. Those political arrangements that endeavour to locate self-determination within the existing boundaries of the state and within the overriding political system of the state manifest the internal right to self-determination, while those arrangements (secession, dissolution, unification) that rupture the borders of the parent state are manifestations of external right to self-determination.[58]

---

54. As in unification of East Germany and West Germany.
55. As in autonomous areas within confederations.
56. As recognized in article 27 of ICCPR and in the General Assembly's 1992 Declaration on the Rights of Persons Belonging to National, Ethnic, Religious and Linguistic Minorities.
57. As was exercised in Haiti and more recently in Nepal.
58. Some writers erroneously hold that when people fight for independence against colonial domination and alien occupation, it is called external self-determination, and when in an independent country, any one or other minority groups struggle for secession or self-government, it is called internal self-determination. Anupam Jha, Self-Determination and Terrorism, XXVI DELHI L. REV. 116 (2004).

Since right of self-determination outside colonial context is still a fluid concept, different movements for self-determination cannot be equated with each other without running the risk of injustice owing to uniformity of treatment. Each case needs to be individualized and evaluated independently on the touchstone of the key variables of the right. Evaluation mandates addressing the *by whom* and *how* questions. International law posits the degrees of self-determination-"dismemberment is at the end of a scale of claims, ranging from modest to extremely destabilizing".[59] The correct determination of 'authentic' and legitimate claims necessitates an evaluation closely tied to the degree of representative government existing *de facto* in the state. Frederic Kirgis reduces the complexity of the problem to a 'manageable form' by establishing this relationship between degrees of claim and degrees of representative government:[60]

> 'The relationship is inverse between the degree of representative government on the one hand, and the extent of destabilization that the international community will tolerate in a self-determination claim, on the other.'

In this emerging perspective, a separatist group's claim of right to secede from a representative democracy may not be considered as a legitimate exercise of right to self-determination, but the same demand may be acceptable in a dictatorial or unrepresentative regime. It need not be said that the inquiry must necessarily be into the *de facto* situation and not be based on the *de jure* claims of the state.[61] Hence, even a state with constitutionally established democratic institutions may not be completely immune from rightful claim to secede if it fails to materialize democracy for all people, in all regions. Democracy might be failing in some areas where regional

---

59. Frederic Kirgis Jr., The Degrees of Self-Determination in the United Nations Era, 88 AMJ INT'L L 306 (1994).
60. *Id.*
61. Notwithstanding the fact that self-determination is now a legal precept, claims are bound to be entangled with the power politics of the state because of the insistence on *de facto* enquiry into the state of affairs. This means that it is not completely freed from the political considerations both at national and international level.

aspirations are thwarted under a powerful centre-militarily or financially. It might be failing when the ethnic groups are engulfed under a universalizing rhetoric of one-nation, one-language or when the state excludes the people from development and robs them off their customary rights.

Internal Self-Determination and its Relation to Secession

The internal rights of self-determination can be easily bargained as they are less threatening to the territorial sovereignty of the state being exercised within the state but the threat of potential secession casts the shadow on them. Minority cultural rights (article 27 of ICCPR) present one option under internal self-determination. Though minority cultural rights loosely include the right of peoples to wear their distinctive cultural dress, to practice their cultural or religious rituals as well as the state support for teaching and preserving their language and culture, when being argued under the right to self-determination they acquire the form of political rights. These then include not only right of self-administration but genuine rights of self-government, including rights to regulate the use of land and development of natural resources, which requires regulations of property rights and rights to raise and disburse tax revenues. Federal and quasi-federal forms of territorial autonomy are the most familiar instance of internal right of self-determination[62] that enable self-government for the peoples.

The option of federalism as an alternative to secession, when debated for the expression of self-determination rights of national minorities and indigenous peoples, itself becomes ridden with suspicious and consequent problems. Federalism is viewed 'as a way-station on the road to secession'.[63] The

62. In the Indian context, article 370 of Constitution of India defines the relationship between India and Jammu & Kashmir is a special form of federalism that secured people of Kashmir their internal right to self-determination. How a re-structured article 370 can form the basis of future centre-state relationship based on equality and mutuality in contemporary globalized economy is well explained by Professor S.P. Sathe. *See*, S.P. Sathe, Article 370 and Jammu and Kashmir: For a Future Federalisation of Polity Mainstream 13 (July 25, 1992) and S.P. Sathe, Article 370 and Jammu and Kashmir: For a Future Federalisation of Polity-II Mainstream 19 (August 1, 1992).
63. Allen Buchanan, Federalism, Secession and the Morality of Inclusion, 37 ARIZ L REV 56 (1995).

past of liberal democracies of West[64] and the present of Eastern Europe, Africa and Asia testifies that federal and quasi-federal forms of territorial autonomy are not easily acceptable to the states. Fears of disloyalty, secession and state security disrupt all discussions between the contesting groups and even internal self-determination is hard to achieve for the fears cast upon by transformation of the political agenda into external right of self-determination. It is sometimes also feared that self-governing national minorities will embark on illegal forms of nation-building, restricting the rights of their own members or of other groups.[65]

Though in most Western democracies, territorial autonomy is now an accepted principle and the 'old self-image of states as unified nation-states is being replaced with the new self-image of states as multination federations and/ or as partnerships between two or more peoples'[66], many countries in Eastern Europe and the Third World still prefer to 'cling to the old model of unitary nation-states, in which minorities ideally are politically weak, deprived of intellectual leadership and subject to long term assimilation'.[67] Latter's ambivalence and suspicion towards the model of multination emanates from the fact that these states view secession as unthinkable and secessionist mobilization as intolerable.

But these reasons need to be dismantled for the preservation of values of democracy, peace and individual rights. The fear of secession has to be challenged for the promotion of federal structures of territorial autonomy. The states need to accept and permit secessionist political mobilization which means granting self-governing minorities the right to freely debate their future including the right to elect secessionist parties to

64. At various points in 18th and 19th C Liberal Democracies have tried to suppress their sort of minority nationalism for instance, France banned the use of the Basque and Breton languages in schools and publications and banned any political associations which aimed to promote minority nationalisms.

65. Will Kymlicka, rightly, rejects, this assumption as having little basis.

66. Will Kymlicka, Federalism and Secession: At Home and Abroad, 13 CAN. J.L. & JURIS. 218 (2000).

67. *Id.*

power. Further, the states must be willing to live with the risk of secession; rather than concentrating on eliminating secession from the political agenda and labeling any act challenging the 'sacredness of its borders' as seditions, the 'first goal of the state should be to promote democracy, human rights, justice and well being of citizens'.[68] If territorial integrity can only be sustained at the cost of justice and human rights, former must make way for latter.

Moreover, the multination model of federation would reduce the actual likelihood of secession by reducing the states of secession. A well protected autonomous and self-governing national minority a multi-nation state would have little to gain by seceding from a multi-nation federation to an independent state. While advocating for multi-nation federations, though this writer has argued for a 'willingness to live with the risk of secession', it may not be presumed that national minorities have a categorical right to secede which they can exercise after securing self-government rights. Unlike, Kymlicka who while drawing this intriguing relationship between federalism and secession seems to be accepting an unfettered unilateral right to secede within the right to self-determination-'...if Quebec, Scotland, Puerto Rico and Catalonia votes one day for secession, there is little that the state, or the international community, can do to present it'[69] -, I would argue for a 'remedial right only' to secede.

Forgotten Rights of Indigenous Peoples

One category that has recently been conferred with the express right to internal self-determination is indigenous peoples.[70] The UN Declaration on the Rights of Indigenous

68. *Id.*

69. *Id.*

70. Indigenous peoples are defined as follows:

'Indigenous communities, peoples and nations are those which having a historical continuity with pre-invasion and pre-colonial societies that developed on their territories, consider themselves distinct from others sectors of the societies now prevailing in those territories or parts of them. They form at present non-dominant sectors of society and are determined to preserve, further develop and transmit to future generations their ancestral territories and their ethnic identity, as the basis of their

Contd. on next page

Peoples[71] gives a new salience to the notion of internal autonomy. Article 3 of the Declaration recognizes the indigenous peoples' right to self-determination 'to freely determine their political status and freely pursue their economic, social and cultural development'[72]. In exercising their right to self-determination, they 'have the right to *autonomy or self-government* in matters relating to their internal and local affairs, as well as ways and means for financing their autonomous functions'.[73] They also have 'the right to maintain and strengthen their distinct political, legal, economic, social and cultural institutions, while retaining their right to participate fully, if they so choose, in the political, economic, social and cultural life of the State.'[74]

Despite this international commitment towards the indigenous peoples whose very existence is under threat, the idea of internal self-determination appeals little to the development-obsessed states. When Indian authorities gave Vedanta Aluminium Limited and the State-owned Orissa Mining Corporation permission to mine bauxite for the next 25 years in the Niyamgiri Hills, in the eastern state of Orissa, they not only breached the constitutional protection granted to the tribals,[75] but even disregarded the internationally recognized right to internal self-determination. The mine falls within the traditional lands of the Dongria Kondh community, an indigenous community with special protection under Indian law.

Contd. from previous page

continued existence as peoples, in accordance with their own cultural patterns, social institutions and legal systems.' This is most common is the "working definition" formulated by Special Rapporteur for the Sub-Commission, José Martinez Cobo in Problem of Discrimination against Indigenous Populations (1986).

71. Adopted by General Assembly Resolution 61/295 on 13 September, 2007.
72. UN Declaration on the Rights of Indigenous Peoples (art. 3).
73. *Id.* (art. 4).
74. *Id.* (art. 5).
75. Indian Constitution, Schedule V.

Though the Kondhs 'fear the mine will destroy their sacred sites, decimate their forests, pollute their water source and cause an influx of traffic and people that would threaten their traditional way of life',[76] quite in violation to international human rights standards, the Indian authorities approved the project without obtaining the 'free and informed consent'[77] of the Dongria Kondh; thus completely disregarding their right against forced assimilation[78] , the right to own, use, develop and control the lands, territories and resources[79] and the right to determine and develop priorities and strategies for the development or use of their lands or territories and other resources.[80]

4. Right to Secession as a Form of Self-Determination

Secession in the classic sense refers to the creation of a new state by the territorial division of an existing state. It is the most extreme exercise of the right to self-determination as at stake, is the much cherished sovereignty and territorial integrity of state. As it tends to be the most controversial aspect of self-determination, international law is still ambivalent in recognizing a *right* to secede and has been largely unsuccessful in clearly demarcating its legitimate bounds. At least one thing is clear that international law does not recognize (and rightly so) an unconditional and absolute right to secession, except some Constitutions like the Constitution of Ethiopia.[81] Recognizing such a right would

---

76. *See* for details Dongria Kondh Livelihoods And Cultural Identity Threatened By Vedanta Mine In Niyamgiri Hills available at

http://indigenouspeoplesissues.com/index.php?option=com_content&view=article&id=1128%3Adongria-kondh-livelihoods-and-cultural-identity-threatened-by-vedanta-mine-in-niyamgiri-hills&catid=63%3Acentral-asia-indigenous-peoples&Itemid=85&lang=en.

Also *see* a scathing critique of the Governmental apathy to the peoples' wishes, Arundhati Roy, *Mr. Chidambram's War* in OUTLOOK 30-46 (9th November, 2009).

77. *Supra* note 74 (art. 32)

78. *Id.* (art. 8).

79. *Id.* (art. 26).

80. *Id.* (art. 32).

81. ETHIOPIA CONST, article 39.

amount to repudiation of the idea of redistributive state[82] as it would be perfectly legitimate for the 'haves' to secede from the 'have-nots' and divest themselves of the obligations to the latter.[83]

This necessitates concrete theorization about secession so that 'legitimate' demands of secession are accepted and 'illegitimate' demands dealt with by lesser forms of self-determination. What falls within the sphere of legitimacy and what outside it can only be determined by analyzing the reasons behind every secessionist movement, meaning thereby that secession *per se* can't be denied or accepted. The states torn by secessionist claims are required to indulge in a constructive dialogue with the secessionists to understand the nature and reasons of their demands. International order is required to be vigilant and sensitive to such claims and if the claims appear to be legitimate, then 'interfere' giving up its restraint *vis-a-vis* domestic sovereignty. This merely means that the states' complete refusal to secession as a part of self-determination is unreasonable and inconsistent and must be questioned within the human rights discourse. The landmark *Quebec case* seems to be reaching similar conclusions.

Quebec's Claim to Secede

The Supreme Court of Canada's pronouncement on Quebec's claim to secede[84] responded to questions related to the unilateral secession of Quebec from Canada. A brief reference to the issues is given as follows:

- ***The constitutional capacity of the national assembly, legislature or government of Quebec to effect the unilateral secession of Quebec from Canada***

In responding to this question, the Court stated that 'a clear majority vote in Quebec on clear question in favour of

---

82. A redistributive state is one whose fundamental functions is the redistribution of wealth from the better off to the worse off citizens or the achievement of distributive justice.
83. Attempted secession of the 'haves' from the 'have nots' can be seen in cases of Biafra's secession from Nigeria, Katanga's from Congo and Slovenia's from Yugoslavia.
84. *Reference Re Secession of Quebec*, (1998) 2 SCR 217.

secession would confer democratic legitimacy on the secession initiative which all the other participants in Confederation would have to recognize'.[85] But it could not be construed to mean, despite a clear referendum result, that Quebec could 'purport to invoke a right of self-determination to dictate the terms of a proposed secession to the other parties to the federation.'[86] Explaining the position, the Court observed:[87]

'The democratic vote, by however strong a majority, would have no legal effect on its own and could not push aside the principles of federalism and the rule of law, the rights of individuals and minorities or the operation of democracy in the other provinces or in Canada as a whole... The other provinces and the federal government would have no basis to deny the right of the government of Quebec to pursue secession should a clear majority of the people of Quebec choose that goal, so long as in doing so, Quebec respects the rights of others...Negotiations would need to address the interests of the other provinces, the federal government, Quebec and indeed the rights of all Canadians both within and outside Quebec, and specifically the rights of minorities.'

Thus, it was held that no absolute legal entitlement to secede can be assumed; under a negotiation, however, the possibility of secession can be contemplated, which can be granted by an amendment of the Canadian Constitution.

• ***Whether a right to unilateral secession exists under international law?***

While addressing this question the Court observed that under international law, right to secession only arises in a colonial context *or* where peoples are subject to alien subjugation, domination or exploitation or where peoples are 'denied any meaningful exercise of its right to self-determination within the state of which it forms a part'.[88] The Court further clarified that right to secede cannot be

85. *Id.* (para 150).
86. *Id.* (para 151).
87. *Id.*
88. *Id.* (para 154).

granted to peoples who constitute part of '(the) state whose government represents the whole of the people or peoples resident within its territory, on the basis of equality and without discrimination, and respects the principles of self-determination in its internal arrangements' and such a just state is 'entitled to maintain its territorial integrity under international law and to have that territorial integrity recognized by other states'.[89]

Thus, it was held that the National Assembly, the legislature or the government of Quebec does not enjoy a right in international law to effect the secession of Quebec from Canada unilaterally. But at the same time the Court pronounced the 'Effectivity' principle, *i.e., de facto* secession may result regardless of the legality of the steps leading to the creation of the reality. Thus, an unconstitutional declaration of secession may lead to *de facto* secession if the international community backs it with recognition. But even if it is granted, it 'would not, however, provide any retroactive justification for the act of secession, either under the Constitution of Canada or at international law'.[90]

It is clear that the *Quebec case* does not rule out the possibility of secession in international law. Though it lays down certain situations when right to secede arises, it is important to discover the jurisprudential basis of such a right. Understanding secession and locating its legitimacy within self-determination mandates a discussion of the normative theories of secession. This paper is only concerned with the moral right to secede unilaterally, as opposed to consensual secession.[91] Further, the paper delves into the issue of

89. *Id.*
90. *Id.* (para 155).
91. Consensual secession results either through constitutional processes (it is achieved either by the exercise of an explicit constitutional right to secede, which a few constitutions contain– 1993 Ethiopian Constitution or by constitutional amendment, something akin to what Supreme Court of Canada envisioned for secession of Quebec) or from a negotiated agreement between the state and secessionists (as occurred when Norway seceded from Sweden in 1905) or by enforcing the secession clause (implicit or explicit) of the agreement by which the state was initially created out of previously independent political units (as it is sometimes argued by the American Southerners as being true of the states of the Union).

unilateral secession in the sense of the group having a moral *right* to secede (in the sense of having a claim-right) and not merely a moral 'justification' to secede (which implies a mere moral permission of liberty-right).[92]

There are two main types of theories of right to secede (understood as a unilateral claim-right) – Remedial Right Only Theories and Primary Right Theories. The two are discussed in detail as follows.

Remedial Right only Theories/Just Cause Theories

According to this type of theory, 'a group has a general right to secede if and only if it has suffered certain injustices, for which secession is the appropriate remedy of last resort.'[93] The (*general*)[94] right to secede is similar to the right to revolution as typified by John Locke's theory of social contract. According to Locke, people have the right to overthrow the government if and only if their fundamental rights are isolated.[95] The main difference however, is that object of right to secede is only to sever the government's control over a portion of state's territory, while object of right to revolution is to overthrow the government. The former right accrues when injustice is perpetuated not against the citizenry at large, but against a particular group concentrated in a region of the state.

Right to secede is seen as the right of persons who are subject to a political authority to defend themselves from

92. The distinction between the two is crucial while talking about 'the right to secede'. Having the liberty-right implies that a group might morally justified in seceding but it does not caste a duty on others (including the parent-state) to refrain from interfering with the group's attempt to secede. Claim-right, on the other hand, would impose a corresponding duty on other (including the parent-state) not to interfere with the attempted secession. See for the different connotations of the term 'right', W.H. Hohfeld, "Some Fundamental Legal Conception as Applied in Judicial Reasoning" in Rights and Duties 16 (Carl Wellman ed., 2002).

93. Allen Buchanan, Theories of Secession, 26(1) Philo. & Pub. Affairs 31-61 (1997).

94. It is important to bear in mind that Remedial Right Only Theories do not deny that there can be *special* rights to secede in the absence of injustice but only deny that there is a general right to secede that is not a remedial right.

95. *Supra* note 95, at 31.

serious injustices, as a remedy of last resort.[96] Injustice suffered by the group can take different forms. Different Remedial Right Only theories identify different injustices as warranting the remedy of secession. To argue for a right to secession one of these grounds should be present.[97]

- when the physical survival of its members is threatened by actions of the state (as with the policy of the Iraqi government towards Kurds in Iraq) or
- when the group suffers violations of basic human rights (as with the East Pakistan which seceded in 1970) or
- when the group's previous sovereign territory was unjustly taken by the state (as with the succession of Baltic Republic from the Soviet Union in 1991 and also the Indonesian occupation East Timor[98]) or
- state's major violation of intrastate unilateral agreements[99] (as with Milosovic's destruction of Kosovo's autonomy in 1989).
- discriminatory redistribution[100] practiced by the state (but it is the most contested form of remedial right, least accepted within the self-determination discourse.)

---

96. What constitutes justice and injustice, no doubt depends on the subjectivities/whims of the international lawyers/state/the dominant majority, and this makes one wonder whether self-determination is the right of 'peoples' or the state.
97. Allen Buchanan, *Self-Determination, Secession and the Rule of International Law* in the Morality of Nationalism 310 (Robert Mckim and Jeffrey McMahan eds.,1997).
98. For details on the right to self-determination exercised as a remedial right in East Timor and Kosovo see, Ved P. Nanda, Self-Determination and Secession under International Law, 29 DENV. J. INT'L L. & POL'Y 305 (2001).
99 A reference to the State of Jammu and Kashmir's accession would be quite relevant at this juncture. Kashmir's accession to India was conditional on the article 370 of the Constitution and the Jammu Kashmir Order. The relationship between India and Jammu & Kashmir is based upon mutuality and thus India cannot unilaterally abrogate article 370, as is demanded by the right wing parties in India. Any such step would amount to violation of the basic condition of accession and would invoke a remedial right to secession for the people of Kashmir.
100. It is sometimes referred to as 'internal colonialism' or 'regional exploitation'. Discriminatory discrimination occurs whenever the state indulges in unequal economic treatment, implements taxation schemes, property rights systems, regulatory policies or economic development programmes that are prejudicial to the interests of some groups and benefit others exclusively.

This basically means that to successfully argue for a right of secession, there should be consistent denial of internal right to self determination as well as right to economic self-determination by the state.[101] For the recognition of the right to secede, some other conditions also ought to be satisfied- for instance the terms of secession require that the new state must respect the human rights of all its citizens, including minority rights, there must be a fair division of national debt, a negotiated determination of new boundaries *et al.*

Primary Right Theory/Choice Theories

These theories recognize that 'certain groups can have a (general) right to secede in the absence of any injustice.'[102] According to these theories, there exists a right to unilateral secession over and above the remedial right. Different Primary Right Theories elaborate different conditions that groups need to satisfy to have the unilateral right to secede in the absence of injustice. Primary Right Theories do not deny that there can be a remedial right to secede; they only deny that right to secede is only a remedial right. Primary Right Theories are of two types – Ascriptive Group Theories and Associative Group Theories.[103]

According to Ascriptive Group versions of Primary Right Theories certain groups whose memberships are defined by ascriptive characteristics have the right to secede unilaterally (even in the absence of injustices). Ascriptive characteristics are certain non-political characteristics of groups which are ascribed to individuals independently of their choice and include being of the same nation or being a 'distinct people'. The most common Ascriptive theory is based on the

---

101. The decision of the African Commission on Human and Peoples' Rights on Katangese peoples' liberation from Zaire is premised on the remedial right only theory. Denying the claim the Commission noted that since there was no violation of peoples' human rights at the hands of the state it could not be called a genuine case of secession. *Supra* note 100 at 311.
102. *Supra* note 95, at 31.
103. *Id.*

Nationalist Principle according to which nations[104] have a right of self-determination that includes right to secede in order to have their own state. Nationalist Principle is adhered to by Margalit and Raz when they ascribe the right to secede to "encompassing cultures".[105] By encompassing cultures, they mean large scale, anonymous group having a common culture and character that encompasses many important aspects of life of its members and where membership in the group is 'a matter of belonging, not of achievement.'

Associative Group Theories, on the other hand, do not require the group to have any ascriptive characteristics to acquire a right to secede. Instead they 'focus on the voluntary political choice of members of a group (or the majority of them), their decision to form their own independent political unit.'[106] The group may be completely heterogeneous but still can claim the right to secede which is an instance of right of political association. Plebiscitary theory is the simplest version of Associative Group Primary Right Theory. Different variants of this theory are provided by Harry Beran[107] and Christopher Wellman.[108]

104. Being a nation or people is an ascriptive characteristic. What makes a group a nation or people is the fact that it has a common culture, history, language, a shared sense of its own distinctiveness and perhaps a shared aspiration for constituting its own political unit.

105. Avishai Margalit and Joseph Raz, National Self-Determination cited in supra note 88, at 33. It is submitted that this view is quite ignorant of the politics of 'fourth world' that seems more meaningful in the multicultural world of today.

106. *Supra* note 95, at 34.

107. Beran grounds his theory of right to secede in 'consent theory of political obligation' wherein he argues that *actual* consent (and not "ideal contractarian") of the governed is a necessary condition for political obligation, and consent cannot be assumed unless those who wish to secede are allowed to secede. According to Beran a group is entitled to secede if it constitute a substantial majority in its portion of state and express its wish to secede and secondly, it will be able to secure all necessary resources for its independent existence and thirdly, if secession does not harm the parent states essential military, economic and cultural interests. See for discussion, Harry Beran, The Consent Theory of Political Obligation 42 (1987).

108. Wellman also argues for – primary right of political association or 'political self-determination', which is the right of any group that reside

Contd. on next page

The chief distinction between Remedial Rights Only Theories and Primary Right Theorites as stated earlier is that in the former type, a group must have suffered injustices at the hands of the parent state to claim its right to secede, while in the latter the group can even claim on general right to secede from a perfectly just state, which is flawlessly performing all its legitimating functions and zealously guards human rights of all its members. The next section argues against the basis of Primary Right Theories of Secession and to this extent seeks to curtail the scope of right to self-determination and in favour of the claims of secessionists who seek their remedial right to secede, which must fall well within the bounds of right to self-determination.[109]

Remedial Rights Only* v. *Primary Right Theories

It is the principle of territorial integrity of existing states that becomes a valid touchstone to accept remedial right to secede and discard primary right to secede, not because it is in the self-interest of existing state (which it definitely is) but because 'it is a principle that serves some of the most basic morally legitimate interests of individuals.'[110] Adherence to the principle of territorial integrity becomes a morally legitimate interest of the state since it is in the interest of protection of individual security, right and expectations as well as in the integrity of political participation. Both these interests are secured by an effective legal order and effective jurisdiction of laws which depend on stability of the existing state.

Contd. from previous page

in a territory to form its own state if that group constitute a majority in that territory, the state it forms will be able to carry out effectively its legitimating functions (justice and security etc.) and the new state formed does not impair the parent state's capacity to carry out its own legitimating functions. See, Christopher Wellman, A Defense of Secession and Self-Determination, 24(2) PHILO. & PUB. AFFAIRS 161 (1995).

109. The arguments advanced here are largely drawn from the moral philosopher Allen Buchanan who contends that secession as a manifestation of self-determination can never be justified, but that the burden is on the separatists to demonstrate their territorial claim by showing that they have suffered injustice. Similar positioning is also taken by the legal theorist, Lea Brilmayer.

110. *Supra* note 95, at 35.

Even though both primary and remedial right to secession violate the principle of territorial integrity as strictly understood by international lawyers, remedial right should be accepted nonetheless. Since 'the principle of territorial integrity must not serve as a shield for tyrants, autocrats and dictators, it must not become a cloak behind which human deprivations are justified, condoned and perpetuated,'[111] secession should be recognized when it is the only remedy available to the oppressed groups.

Creating space for remedial right entails devising its reconciliation with the principle of territorial integrity. This necessitates a marked shift in the interpretation of principle of territorial integrity – from an absolutist interpretation (which makes no distinction between legitimate and illegitimate states) to a progressive interpretation. According to the progressive interpretation, principle of territorial integrity of existing states is only applicable to 'legitimate' states.[112] With this interpretation Remedial Right Only theories seem to be more consistent with well-entrenched, morally progressive principles of international law. Primary Right theories, on the other hand, by recognizing a primary right to secede for any group within a state, in the absence of injustices directly contradict the principle of territorial integrity of existing states, on its progressive interpretation.

Yet another objection to Primary Right theories is that their acceptance would give 'perverse incentives' to the existing state, while Remedial Right Only Theories create laudable incentives'. For instance, the existing states would have an incentive to refrain from treating their citizens unjustly in order to reap the protection against disintegration. States would have an incentive to continue as legitimate, rights-respecting states – protection of their territorial boundaries.

111. B.C. Nirmal, The Right to Self-Determination in International Law 250 (1999).

112. There cannot be a unanimous opinion about what constitute a legitimate state. But broadly it can be agreed that states are not legitimate if they (i) threaten the lives of significant portions of their population by a policy of ethnic or religious persecution and (ii) exhibit institutional racism that deprives a substantial portion of the population of basic economic and political rights.

In contrast, in an international order where a primary right to secede is recognized, states in an attempt to avoid their own dissolution would have an incentive to take steps which would prevent groups from becoming claimants of the right to secede (so that essential conditions of primary right to secede as suggested like Beran and Wellman do not succeed). This in turn might lead to perpetration of injustice. States, for instance, would have an incentive to ensure that no region becomes economically and politically self-sufficient so that no region can claim to be capable of performing the legitimating functions of a state. Incentives regarding immigration would also be equally perverse as the states would restrict the movement of people to prevent potential secessionist majority from setting in economically thriving regions. On the same rationale, potentially secessionist group would try to concentrate in prosperous regions and displace others from that region.

The Principle of National Self-Determination, as supported by Margalit and Raz, also suffers from similar and perhaps graver problem of perverse incentives. Right to national self-determination of all 'encompassing groups' might lead to aggressive nation-building programs by the state which are 'designed to obliterate minority group identities – to eliminate all "encompassing groups" within their borders save the one they favour for constituting "the nation" and to prevent new encompassing groups" from emerging.'[113] Primary right to secede in this sense would be a devastating blow to ethnic and cultural pluralism and the benign aspiration of multiculturalism. Diversities would be eliminated under the nationalist drive of homogenization and one *hegemonic* national identity would be imposed by the state on all diverse groups constituting nations in themselves obliterating all other identities that constitute their being – all for the sake of safeguarding their territorial boundaries.

Since Remedial Right Only Theories place significant constraints on the right to secede, (when not ruling out

113. *Supra* note 95, at 56.

secession entirely) they not only constrain the chances of violence that ensues post-secession[114] but also constitute a lesser threat to the territorial integrity of existing states. Primary Right Theories in contrast are a direct and more profound threat to territorial integrity of state (even just states!).

Remedial Rights Only Entrenched in International Law

The complete aversion to the secession by states does not find support in the international legal instruments. No doubt the value of domestic sovereignty and territorial integrity is given utmost importance in international order[115] to the extent that the central governments are allowed to preserve their territorial integrity, *i.e.* a state is entitled to oppose secession by all lawful means (by following the rules of international human rights and humanitarian law).[116] But international law does not offer any ultimate guarantee against separation and this is substantiated in practice by the principle of effectiveness and in theory by the 'safeguard clauses' of some international instruments.

The Friendly Relations Declaration has an implicit recognition of what may be called a remedial right to secede.[117] Though the *proviso* to the Declaration is mostly invoked by central governments of the states to assert their right to sovereign unity, the much forgotten and underplayed latter part of the proviso divulges some interesting points:

114. In many situations secession exacerbates the ethnic conflicts which in turn lead to secessionist movements – when another ethnic group becomes a minority in the new state or when some members of the seceding group are left behind in the parent state that now become more vulnerable to the discrimination of the majority.

115. Noteworthy in this regard are arts. 2(7) of the UN Charter, Principle 6 of Declaration on the Granting of Independence to Colonial Countries and Peoples and 'saving clauses' in several other Declarations.

116. *Supra* note 38, at 48-50.

117. Vienna Declaration and Programme of Action adopted by the World Conference on Human Rights on 25 June 1993 also contains a similar reference, though in a slightly different language:
'In accordance with the Declaration on Principles of International Law concerning Friendly Relations and Cooperation Among States in accordance with the Charter of the United Nations, this shall not be construed as

Contd. on next page

'Nothing in the foregoing paragraphs shall be construed as authorizing or encouraging any action which would dismember or impair, totally or in part, the territorial integrity or political unity of sovereign and independent States conducting themselves in compliance with the principle of equal rights and self-determination of peoples as described above *and thus possessed of a government representing the whole people belonging to the territory without distinction as to race, creed or colour'* (emphasis supplied).

In the above 'saving clause', though it is underscored that the value of territorial integrity is of paramount importance to the state (by putting the requirement of not disrupting the territorial integrity of the states at the beginning of the provision), 'since the possibility of impairment of territorial integrity is *not totally excluded,* it is logically admitted.'[118] A state availing recourse to the saving clause must satisfy the two conditions specified therein. First, it must be conducting itself in compliance with the principle of equal rights and self-determination of peoples, and second, it must be possessed of a government that represents the whole people belonging to the territory. 'Although secession is implicitly authorized by the Declaration', Cassese cautions, 'it must, however, be strictly construed, with all its exceptions'.[119] Hence, secession can be warranted if racial or religious groups are persistently denied participatory rights, their fundamental rights are trampled continuously and there is no likelihood of a peaceful settlement within the existing framework of the state. It is interesting to note that the Declaration seems to be linking the external self-determination with the internal self-determination since '(e)xtreme and unremitting persecution

---

Contd. from previous page

authorizing or encouraging any action which would dismember or impair, totally or in part, the territorial integrity or political unity of sovereign and independent States conducting themselves in compliance with the principle of equal rights and self-determination of peoples and thus possessed of a Government representing the whole people belonging to the territory without distinction of any kind.'

118. Antonio Cassese, Self-Determination of Peoples: A Legal Reappraisal 119 (1996).

119. *Id.*

and the lack of any reasonable prospect for peaceful challenge may make secession legitimate'.[120]

At the risk of repetition, remedial right to secede (as against a primary right) must be recognized within the jurisprudence of self-determination. But even that remedial right must be a right of the last resort. There should first be an effort to explore the less extreme forms of self-determination or the internal rights of self-determination to resolve the dispute between secessionists and the parent-state.

At the same time it should not be forgotten that secession is 'an extremely conservative response to state authority'[121]. Rather than challenging the dominant conception of the nature of state authority and the international order that takes the states to be its fundamental elements, secessionists uncritically accept the contemporary model of state that is rooted in territorial sovereignty and merely fight for breaking a state to make more states! This approach takes a very myopic view of the problem – a group of people is not happy in X state, so let's give them a new Y state-by 'assum(ing) that the problem is a particular state, not the character of the state itself'.[122] Thus, secessionists hardly take a radical stand against the dominant structure. Secessionists also fail to explore innovative models of political community and truly liberate themselves from the theory and practice of the contemporary notions of state authority.[123]

5. Concluding Remarks

The controversy surrounding the right of self-determination covers issues of epic proportions. This chapter has touched upon only a few of them and has reached four broad conclusions.

First, Right of self-determination is a continuing right of the people. It is as relevant to peoples in independent

120. *Id.*
121. *Supra* note 65.
122. *Id.*
123. Buchanan asserts that every internal right of self-determination is a more fundamental challenge to the dominant notion of state authority than secession as it rejects the idea of state sovereignty in its purest form (i.e. there is only one legitimate legislative authority).

and sovereign countries as it was in dependent/colonial territories. This calls for an immediate re-consideration by India to the reservation made to article 1 of ICCPR which limits the article's application to colonial territories only. The present discourse that seeks to limit it to the colonial context only is advanced by states whose main interest is to maintain themselves (which means every inch of their land) even at the cost of human beings who inhabit them. Second, the contemporary meaning of self-determination is not restricted as the right of peoples/nations to sovereign independence. It is the right of all 'peoples' to determine their political future and to pursue their economic, social and cultural development freely. Politically, it is manifested not only through independence (secession) but also through self-government, local autonomy, federalism or any other form of participation in the government. Thus, self-determination includes external, internal as well as economic self-determination.

Third, right to secede from an independent and sovereign state cannot altogether be rejected as an unlawful manifestation of right to self-determination. If a state perpetuates gross injustice on a part of its population, the sufferers can legitimately assert their right to secede from the parent state. This, no doubt, dilutes the territorial integrity of the state which is of the paramount value, but 'justice must be done, even if heavens fall'. If a state inflicts misery on its own men and women, justice demands that they be given a right to secede from that state.

But this should not be taken as conferring recognition to the secessionist claims even against 'just' states.[124] The argument that one people make one nation and so deserve one state, would only result in more *shadow lines* on land

124. Hence, the categorical right to secede granted in the Constitution of Ethiopia becomes questionable. Its proponents, however, contend that 'the Constitution should not impose the Ethiopian identity on any people' and '(t)he right to association vests only through the consent of the people and no authority should impose it as a duty'. See, Derege Demissie, *Self-Determination including Secession* v. *The Territorial Integrity of Nation States*, A Prima Facie case for Secession, 20 Suffolk Transnat'l L Rev 165 (1996).

that would breed exclusion and separation. The great stories behind creation of new nation states are more than stories of successful attainment of independence, they are also grand narratives of displacement, dispossession and lost identities. The right of self-determination thus needs to transcend the logic of nationalistic fervor and centre itself within the *morality of inclusion* that forms the bedrock of multicultural societies. This paves way for the final conclusion of the paper.

Fourth, right to self-determination must be understood in the context of *postnational* politics.[125] Today the world is made up of diasporas, refugees, guest workers, transnational intellectuals and illegal aliens- all increasingly unrestrained by spatial boundary and territorial sovereignty; this is the situation of *postnational* where borders seemed to have dissolved. The politics of secessionism thus seems to be too obsolete to face the challenges of the *postnational* situation as secessionists fail to see the crisis that the nation-state (obsessed with territory and homogeneity) is bound to face in the multicultural and globalizing world.

Secession being an extremely conservative response to the model of modern state, is certainly not the highest limit of right to self-determination. What is needed is a radical shift in approach - from politics of exclusion to politics for inclusion. The struggle calls for discovering innovative alternatives to nation-form which would challenge the very exclusionary root of nation building and secure a multicultural existence of inclusion to all peoples. Self-determination has to be re-conceptualized to harmonize it with the *postnational* politics; it might mean weakening the dominant state model and turning the borders porous for the flow of people, ideas, cultures and love.

---

125. Aditya Nigam, Empire, Nation and Minority Cultures: The Postnational Moment, XLIV (10) ECO & POL. WKLY. 57 (March 7, 2009).

CHAPTER III

Sovereignty

P. Puneeth

1. Introduction

BESTOWING 'SOVEREIGNTY' on the Independent India is one of the objectives envisaged in the preamble of the Constitution. This chapter analyzes, briefly, how far and to what extent the Constitution protects India's sovereignty, which does not, in the first place, have any fixed meaning or content. The chapter also throws light upon the challenges to India's sovereignty in the era of globalization.

2. The Concept of Sovereignty

The concept of sovereignty, which is one of the four essential attributes of a state, does not have timeless or universal meaning. It has held different meanings in different times and in different places. Different theorists have also attributed different meanings to it. Lassa Oppenheim has rightly observed thus:[1]

> There exists perhaps no conception the meaning of which is more controversial than that of sovereignty. It is an indisputable fact that this conception, from the moment when it was introduced into political science until the present day, has never had a meaning which was universally agreed upon.

1. Lassa Oppenheim, International Law 66 (1928).

Historically, as stated by Richard N. Haass,[2] a sovereign State has been attributed with four main characteristics: "First, a sovereign state is one that enjoys supreme political authority and monopoly over the legitimate use of force within its territory. Second, it is capable of regulating movements across its borders. Third, it can make its foreign policy choices freely. Finally, it is recognized by other governments as an independent entity entitled to freedom from external intervention."

The general perception is that the evolution of the concept of sovereignty *vis-à-vis* states, as it is understood today, began with the 1648 Peace Treaties of Westphalia, which also established the legal basis of modern statehood. It is basically an agreement among Europe's rulers to recognize each other's right to rule their own territories free from outside interference.[3] "Westphalian Constitution", in the words of Anthony Mcgrew,[4] "...welded together the idea of territoriality with the notion of legitimate sovereign rule. Westphalian sovereignty located supreme legal and political authority within territorially delimited states. *Sovereignty involved the rightful entitlement to exclusive, unqualified, and supreme rule within a delimited territory.*"

Though the concept of sovereignty has had varied meanings across history, the supreme authority within a delimited territory has always been its core content. That means, the sovereign state is the one above, and there is no other actor to compel it to act in specific ways. It has the monopoly over the legitimate use of force and the power to govern within the delimited territory without answerability to any outside agency.

This concept of sovereignty, in terms of exclusive, unqualified and supreme authority to rule within a

---

2. Cited in John H. Jackson, "Sovereignty – Modern: A New Approach to an Outdated Concept" 97 American Journal of International Law 782 (786) (2003).

3. Anthony Mcgrew, "Globalization and Global Politics" in John Baylis, Steve Smith, *et al* (eds.), The Globalization of World Politics: An Introduction to International Relations 15 - 33 (OUP, 2008).

4. *Id.* at 24. Emphasis supplied.

delimited territory, does not hold the field any longer. In the contemporary era, the nature and contents of sovereignty have undergone tremendous change owing to two main factors – the emergence of national constitutions and the emergence of large body of transnational law. The constitutions, by prescribing limitations on the power of the state, deny state the unqualified and absolute power to rule. The emerging transnational law, by setting standards for the domestic governance and constraining the states to incorporate them into their legal systems, also denies the states their sovereign authority to evolve policies on their own for the governance of their respective countries.

3. Sovereignty of India under the Constitution

The Constitution, enacted for the purpose of the governance of independent India, has resolved, very firmly, solemnly and in explicit terms, to constitute the nation into a sovereign, socialist, secular, democratic republic. Provisions have also been made in various operative parts of the Constitution to enliven these objectives set out in the preamble. Since, these expressions – sovereign, socialist, secular, democratic republic – are not defined anywhere in the Constitution, their true characters and contents need to be understood having regard to the operative provisions of the Constitution.

Though framers of the Indian Constitution have firmly resolved to bestow sovereignty on independent India, it is evident on the perusal of the entire scheme of the Constitution that they never intended to confer on any individual or institution the *exclusive, unqualified and the supreme authority to rule* within the territory of India. The Constitution of India has established federal polity for the governance of the country. It has embodied, in essence, the theory of separation of powers and assigned different functions to different organs of the government. Institutional checks and balances are also envisaged to ensure that every organ of the government works within the boundary earmarked for it. Thus, the sovereign authority has been divided between the centre and the units, in the first place, and further between the three dominant organs of the government. Further, since the Constitution embodies the principles of constitutionalism, there are inherent limits to the power of the state. It guarantees certain fundamental rights, which are essentially limitations on the power of the state. It lays down roadmap, in the form of directive principles of state policy, for the progress of the country. These directive principles are considered to be fundamental in the governance of the country and they bind the state. The state does not have an absolute, unfettered and unguided authority to make laws for the governance of the country. It is under constitutional obligation to apply directive principles in making laws and respect fundamental rights in all its endeavours. Thus, India's internal sovereignty is subject to constitutional limitations.[5]

However, India's sovereignty is not subjected to any external authority under the scheme of the Constitution of India. Though, it imposes an obligation on the state to endeavour to "foster respect for international law and treaty obligations", it does not in any way curtail the power of the union or the state, as the case may be, to legislate on any subject in conformity with constitutional limitations notwithstanding the obligations undertaken under international law. But, how far in the era of globalization, India can remain immune from the influence of external forces in making laws or devising policies for the governance of the country needs to be examined.

4. Impact of Globalization on India's Sovereignty

The process of globalization has brought in its wake profound transition. Although globalization was initially seen as an economic phenomenon, it is noticeably all pervasive today. It may not be an exaggeration to state that globalization is impacting, directly or indirectly, on almost all aspects of human life. It is bringing about fundamental transformations in various fields. The developments that are taking place in the era of globalization have consequences, *inter alia*, on the nation-states, their sovereignty and legal systems established within their domestic jurisdictions. It is

5. *Synthetics and Chemicals Ltd.* v. *State of Uttar Pradesh,* (1990) 1 SCC 109: AIR 1990 SC 1927: JT 1989 (4) SC 267; *Charan Lal Sahu* v. *Union of India,* (1990) 1 SCC 613: AIR 1990 SC 1480.

feared that the phenomenon of globalization undermines the state sovereignty as it minimizes the ability of governments to control their own economies and societies.[6]

Global integration, interconnectedness and interdependence, taking place in the era of globalization, have resulted in diminishing states' authority to have exclusive say with respect to several matters within their jurisdiction. Matters of domestic concern such as health, education, environment, economics and protection of human rights within the domestic jurisdiction, etc., have now become matters of international concern and, thus, fall within the ambit of international law.[7] There is a large body of international law, or more appropriately called transnational law, emerging in the form of international treaties, covenants, conventions, agreements, etc., which deal with such issues of domestic concern. Sovereign independent states are increasingly constrained to incorporate norms and standards set out in such international instruments into their domestic legal framework. However, the process of formal incorporation of such standards into domestic legal framework does not provide any meaningful role for the states. Sovereign independent states are, thus, virtually compelled to act as administrative units to implement policy decisions taken at the global level.

Today, it is noticeable that much of the contents of the laws enacted for the domestic governance are increasingly supplied by the global regulatory norms and standards set out in international treaties, covenants, conventions, agreements etc., More and more such international instruments are emerging in order to address the issues and challenges thrown-up by globalization.[8] Proliferation of such international instruments is seen mainly in three areas:

6. Lawrence M. Friedman, "Frontiers: National and Transnational Order" in Karl-Heinz Ladeur, *supra* note 2 at 25, 33. Also *see* Anthony Mcgrew, *supra* note 8 at 15.

7. *People's Union for Civil Liberties* v. *Union of India,* (1997) 3 SCC 433: 1997 AIR SCW 1234: AIR 1997 SC 1203.

8. *See* P. Puneeth, "Impact of Globalization on Nation-States and Sovereignty" in Deepa Kansra, Rabindra Kr. Pathak *et al* (eds.), Rethinking Law: Emerging Issues and Challenges 112-122 (2013).

(i) international human rights law;

(ii) international economic law, and

(iii) international environmental law. But, they are not confined to these three areas only.

In the contemporary era of globalization, nation-states do not enjoy the *exclusive, unqualified and supreme authority to rule* within the delimited territory. Their choices and preferences in formulating policies and enacting laws for the governance of the country are constrained by the norms and standards set out in the international instruments. Thus, in the present era, none of the states can maintain even their external sovereignty to the fullest extent.

It is in this context that one needs to examine how far India, which is legally proclaimed to be sovereign in the preamble of the Constitution, can maintain its external sovereignty in the contemporary era of globalization. It may be noted that the impact of globalization varies from country to country. As far as India is concerned, it is axiomatic to state that the great tides and currents of globalization have not allowed India to remain unaffected. Not only its economy, as it is evident from the liberalization, privatization and globalization policy adopted since 1991, the impact of globalization is seen in very many other fields as well. The globalization is not without consequence to the India legal system.

The process of globalization has led to the emergence of many international instruments in the form of treaties, covenants, conventions, etc. They are basically intended to address issues and challenges arising out of globalization. Many invariably touch upon the issues of domestic concern. Ever since India has got independence and the Constitution has been brought into force, the Government of India has been entering into several such treaties, agreements and has also been a signatory to many international covenants and conventions in the exercise of its executive power. It has been estimated that on an average 150 agreements are concluded by India every year including amendments, extensions of existing agreements, etc.[9] However, unlike in America, they do not automatically become part of the law of the land. Legislations need to be enacted in certain cases to incorporate them into domestic legal system. In fact, there are several legislations enacted in India to give effect to such international instrument. However, the important point to be noted is that the need for formal incorporation does not provide meaningful autonomy to India to devise the policy in areas covered by such instruments. In the era of globalization, India like any other country, is increasingly constrained to incorporate them. Thus, it cannot claim to have complete autonomy from external influences in formulating policies for the governance of the country.

5. Concluding Remarks

Though the framers of the Indian Constitution have firmly resolved to bestow 'sovereignty' on the country, it is evident from the scheme of the Constitution that they have certainly not intended to make India sovereign in the Westphalian sense. The sovereignty of India is subjected to the constitutional scheme. In addition, as the above discussion elucidates, in the contemporary era of globalization, India's external sovereignty, like the other countries, is also facing threats from global forces. Thus, the preambular objective of making India a sovereign, in whatever limited sense it is envisaged in the Constitution, cannot possibly be achieved in the era of globalization.

---

9. K. Thakore, "National Treaty Law and Practice: India" 27 Stud. Transnat'l Legal Pol'y 103 (1995).

CHAPTER IV
Socialism

*Deepa Kansra**

Socialism has troubled many. From an ideology labelled as non-existent in the capitalist world, it has caught the imagination of Latin American countries amidst massive poverty and inequality. The socialism of the 21st century, as popularized in Latin America is a deviation from the rhetoric of the socialist ideology; all means of production with the state.[1]

The socialist ideology states that the strength of socialism lies in its ability to satisfy the aspirations of the people in completely oppressed and exploitative conditions. In the past, socialism fulfilled several political aspirations. For instance, utopian socialists visualized "change to a new social order coming about, not as a result of conflict of economic interests, but as the result of discovery of the truth regarding the workings of natural or moral law."[2] The Marxian socialists contended that class conflicts between the two dominant

* The finer details of the chapter are provided in India and the Dynamics of Socialism in the Global Order (Deepa Kansra), 2012. ISBN 978-81-7273-637-8

1. 21st Century Socialism as promoted by the Latin American countries is reclaiming the values associated with socialism; love, solidarity, equality between men and women. The adjective 21st century is added to differentiate the new socialism from the errors and deviations present in the model of socialism that was. Marta Harnecker, "Five Reflections about 21st Century Socialism", Online University of the Left, available at http://ouleft.sp-mesolite.tilted.net/?p=746
2. Harry Laidler, "Socialism", Vol. 25 The Encyclopedia Americana: International Edition 196 (1969).

economic classes- the workers and the capitalists was destined to lead to a classless society based on proletarian aspirations. Fabian Socialism- saw socialism coming "through gradual peaceful progress as a result of reaction of the society to private monopoly, the progress of political economy and the application of democratic principles."[3] Historically, as socialism communism, a revolutionary creed, sought to overthrow the bourgeoisie to establish power of the industrial proletariat. The Communist premise differed from all the previous movements in that it overturned the basis of earlier relations of production and intercourse, and subjugated them to the power of the untied individuals.[4]

To date, socialism cannot be restricted under a single or simple formulation.[5]

1. Socialism in India

The Indian experience with socialism has been complex. However, the textual allegiance to the socialist ideology under the Indian constitution has had a strong impact on the workings of the various institutions; legislative, executive and the judicial.

On attaining independence in 1947, India absorbed the liberal ideals in the form of a parliamentary democratic structure, the directive principles of state policy, fundamental rights, the separation of powers, independence of the judiciary, universal suffrage, and economic planning. The most revolutionary ideas that characterized the moral and political victory of India came to be associated with the ideals of nationalism and socialism. As rightly expressed in this regard, "Swaraj was not only anti-imperialist; it was giving birth to socialism".[6] The very values of justice, democracy and equality were drawn expressly to signify a significant socialist change with the goals of upliftment and emancipation, in order to overcome the horrors of the past. The 'phase witnessed

3. *Ibid.*
4. Christine Sypnowich, The Concept of Socialist Law, 14 (1990).
5. Donald S. Busky, Democratic Socialism: A Global Survey, 11 (2000)
6. Gail Omvedt, Reinventing Revolution: New Social Movements and the Socialist Tradition in India, 6 (1993).

a transition from the pattern of revolutionary organization closely associated with communism,[7] towards a constructive democratic approach to social economic problems'.[8]

The objective of curing the divisions and inequalities in the Indian society were sought to be achieved by the political force of the socialist ideology,[9] which was to be successful in espousing the cause of liberation on a large scale. The most expressive agenda had been by the Congress party's commitment to socialism at the Karachi Session early in 1931, "which was both a declaration of rights of man and a humanitarian socialist manifesto."[10] The socialist objectives were widely approved, but the 'means' to achieving change were still debatable.[11] The socialist divide concerning the manner of achieving change was one of the reasons as to why socialism did not expressly find place under the Indian Constitution until 1976.

2. The Directive Principles of State Policy

Post independence, in the earliest of Constitutional interpretations, the Directive Principles of State Policy (DPSP) under Part IV to the Indian Constitution were identified most closely with the socialist ideology.

The DPSP enlist the most specific reforms that must be brought about by the state, in specific by the policy of the government. The goals are the provision for adequate means of livelihood, the 'ownership, control and distribution' of the

---

7. The power of revolutionary Communism had a specific role to play. It not only aimed at changing the very essence of the state by introducing a fundamental social transformation from a capitalist state to that of a socialist. See Gennady Belov, What is the State?, 25 (1986).
8. Vishwanath Prasad Varma, Modern Indian Political Thought 471 (1967).
9. Malcolm Hause, "India under the Impact of Western Political Ideas", in S.P Aiyer and Srinivasan, Studies in Indian Democracy 3 (1965).
10. S.H. Patil, "Democratic Socialism: An Ideology of the Indian Constitution", 27(1-4) Journal of Constitutional and Parliamentary Studies 89 (1993).
11. The objective was "to create a socio-economic revolution in India... in order to end the exploitation of the masses; political freedom must include the real economic freedom of the starving millions." However, learning from the experiences of Russia, the Congress was divided into three groups as to the strategy of action. The division was between, "conservative elements and the Communist elements in the Congress. The third force was democratic socialism." *Ibid.*

material resources of the community to subserve the common good, equal pay for equal work, healthy environment of work and living for the impoverished persons, public assistance to the people in cases of unemployment, old age, sickness and disablement, and raising the level of nutrition to improvement of living of the people.[12] The defining feature of Part IV is placed in Article 37, which states that "the provisions contained in this Part shall not be enforceable by any court, but the principles therein laid down are nevertheless fundamental in the governance of the country and it shall be the duty of the state to apply these principles in making laws." Part IV of the Constitution was found to make reference to the 'purpose' strategy of socialism.

In addition, fundamental rights under Part III reflect upon the basic essential tenets of the socialist ideology. Yet again, Part III reflects the basic obligations of the three primary institutions of the legislature, executive and the judiciary.[13] The proposed model of governance under the Indian Constitution is subject to the specific or underlying governing principles of checks and balance, separation of powers, and the sanctity of fundamental rights and the DPSP.

Over the years, the strategy for bringing about socio-economic change in pursuance of the DPSP has added strength and vigour to the democratic process. Much of the decisions post independence, for instance the abolition of zamindari system reflected a strong opposition to capitalism. The dominant attitude after independence was that the capitalism system was to be resented for its attachment to colonial exploitation.[14]

In its true character, the Indian welfare state reflects a commitment to socialism for achieving a complete transformation of the society on the lines of equality and justice, along with the provision of basic necessities of food,

12. Articles 36-51 are the specific provisions under Part IV of the Constitution.

13. For instance, the Supreme Court (article 32) and the High Court (article 226) are responsible to address the violation of fundamental rights or other legal rights by the state.

14. *Supra* note 8 at 73.

clothing, shelter, education and dignity. The state is the ultimate caretaker of the future of India and its people, and so is it legitimate for the state to undertake various patterns of planning and governance under the guidance of the Constitution.

However, the strength of ideological commitments depends largely on the model and practice of governance. As highlighted by Christine Sypnowich, a socialist jurisprudence must begin with an understanding of the ambivalence of legal ideology, which, in its very role as legitimating force, offers moral values...[15] In other words, governance and socialism share an association which must at all times be preserved.

In the context of India, there is a need to understand the level of compatibility between socialism and democracy/ governance.

3. The 42nd Amendment

The 42nd (Amendment) Act, 1976 introduced the expression 'Socialist' in the Preamble. The objective of achieving a socio-economic revolution, which would end poverty and ignorance and disease and inequality of opportunity, led to the adoption of the said amendment.[16]

The amendment introduced a phase which witnessed the clash of 'legislative socialism', with that of 'socialism of the court'. The amendment was thus interpreted as creating a duty on all state organs to move towards a socialist order.[17] In the words of the apex court, it is a socialist state which the Preamble directs the centers of power Legislature, Executive and Judiciary to strive to set up."[18]

Also stated was that socialism ought not to be treated as a mere concept or an ideal. Socialism ought to be practiced

15. Christine Sypnowich, The Concept of Socialist Law, 49 (1990).

16. It is often indicated that the 42nd Amendment was to deal with the continued interference of the courts, which acted as an obstacle to socialist endeavors by the policy makers.

17. The amendment was subsequently also challenged by a non-profit organization, the Good Governance India Foundation. See Malathi Nayak, India's Socialist Mandate to be challenged in the Supreme Court, at *http://www.livemint.com/2007/12/06001031/India8217s-socialist-mandat.html*, December 6 (2007). (Last Visited 13.5.09)

18. *D.S. Nakara* v. *Union of India*, AIR 1983 SC 130: (1983) 1 SCC 305: 1983 (1) SCJ 188.

in every sphere of life and be treated by the law courts as a constitutional mandate.[19] The amendment paved way for a fresh pragmatic and humanistic approach to socialism.[20] A series of cases such as *Randhir Singh* v. *Union of India,*[21] (equal pay for equal work), *D.S Nakara* v. *Union of India,*[22] (pension in old age), *G.B. Pant University of Agriculture and Technology, Nainital* v. *State of Uttar Pradesh,*[23] (regularization

19. *H.S.E.B* v. *Suresh,* AIR 1999 SC 1160: 1999 AIR SCW 892: (1999) 3 SCC 601.
20. Compared to the earlier dogmatic approach to socialism, the case of *Excel Wear* v. *Union of India,* (AIR 1979 SC 25: 1978 Lab IC 1537: (1978) 4 SCC 224) threw light on the new ideological perspective. In brief the facts were; the petitioner, Excel Wear a registered partnership firm applied to the state as it was finding it difficult almost impossible to carry on business, in response the state refused for closure for the reason that it would be prejudicial to public interests. The petitioners contended that the right to close down business was an integral part of right to carry on the business guaranteed under 19(1)(g) of the Constitution. The restriction almost amounts to negation or destruction of the right. The respondent on the other hand only asserted that the restriction was reasonable in the interest of the public. However, the petitioners requested that since the expression socialist has been inserted in the Preamble, the tests of reasonableness therefore must change and be necessarily different from the dogmatic...texts laid down earlier. The court responded; "the difference pointed out between the doctrinaire approach to the problem and the pragmatic one is very apt and may enable the courts to lean more and more in favour of nationalisation and state ownership after addition of the word socialist...But so long as the private ownership of an industry is recognized and governs a overwhelmingly large proportion of our economic structure, is it possible to say that principles of socialism and social justice can be pushed to such an extreme so as to a very large extent the interest of another section of the public namely the private owners of the undertakings." (Para 24). The petition was allowed.
21. *Randhir* v. *Union of India,* AIR 1982 SC 879: (1982) 1 SCC 618: 1982 (1) SCJ 283. The court expressly established the principle of equal pay for equal work as a constitutional goal. "It is a constitutional goal capable of attainment through constitutional remedies, by the enforcement of constitutional rights... Now thanks to the rising social and political consciousness and the expectations roused as a consequence and the forward looking posture of this court, the underprivileged also are clamouring for their rights and are seeking intervention of the court."
22. *D.S Nakara* v. *Union of India,* AIR 1983 SC 130: (1983) 1 SCC 305: 1983 (1) SCJ 188. "The basic framework of Socialism is to provide a decent standard of life to the working of people especially provide security from cradle to the grave...This is a blend of Marxism and Gandhism leaning heavily towards Gandhian Socialism."
23. *G.B. Pant University of Agriculture and Technology, Pantnagar, Nainital* v. *State of Uttar Pradesh,* AIR 2000 SC 2695: 2000 AIR SCW 2870: 2000 Lab

Contd. on next page

of services), *Samatha* v. *State of Andhra Pradesh*,[24] (rights of the tribals) are enough to establish this proposition.

The Amendment to the Constitution reflected upon a new set of concerns for the courts and the government. The constitution has since then been interpreted to have been reduced to "virtual invisibility"[25], transforming from a socialist society to a capitalist one.

In 1991, the world witnessed the collapse of the Soviet Union. The impact of such an occurrence also led to noticeable changes in India.[26] From an agenda for the social-economic-political development, India began marching more rigorously towards economic growth. The Indian experience with socialism was thereon exposed to several challenges.[27]

4. Socialism and Progress Post 1991

The imperialist association with capitalism did not prevent India as well as other nations from inviting Western investment and aid. In the words of Paul Sigmund, the rationale was basically that economic planning in India did show that nationalization will not assure the rationalized development of the economy that India seeks. The Indian experience seemed to demonstrate that as an economy

---

Contd. from previous page

IC 2893. In reference to the facts, the regularization of the services of the workers in the cafeteria was essential to bring them in parity with other employees of the University. For the reason that, " there cannot possibly be any doubt that the socialist concept of the society as laid down in Part III and Part IV of the Constitution ought to be implemented in the true import of the Constitution."

24. AIR 1997 SC 3297: 1997 AIR SCW 3361: (1997) 8 SCC 191. In reference to the protection afforded to the tribals in light of Article 38, 39 and 46, the court under para 97 stated; "it is an established rule of interpretation that to establish Socialist Democratic Republic, the basic structure under the Rule of Law, a pragmatic, broad and wide interpretation of the Constitution make social and economic democracy with liberty, equality of status and fraternity a reality to 'we, the people of India' who would include the Schedule Tribes".
25. Sarbani Sen, Popular Sovereignty and Democratic Transformations, 1 (2007).
26. Raja Mohan, India's New Foreign Policy Strategy. Draft paper submitted presented at a Seminar in Beijing by China Reform and Carnegie Endowment of International Peace, Beijing. May (2006).
27. *See* Rajni Kothari, "Soviet Developments in Wider Perspective", 71 Mainstream, Annual (1991).

expands, an entrepreneurial class of investors emerges which can invest and utilize the new surpluses more efficiently than government planners.[28] In 1991, the New Economic Policy (hereinafter NEP) pushed this proposition to another limit. The policy relaxed "many restrictions on private investment, inflow and investment of foreign capital, international trade and foreign exchange."[29] But the deal of the matter was the inflow of a new age philosophy of free market and capitalism.

In response to such developments V.R. Krishna Iyer expressed; "we have a new democracy run from afar be strong capitalist proprietors influencing the political process and humoring the glitterati and winning parties Right, Left and Centre through a monoculture of globalization, liberalization, marketisation and privatization plus anti-socialism...Herein lies the contradiction between the Constitution and the elections held under the Constitution."[30]

The trend necessarily is a matter of concern, especially when the spirit of Indian Constitution has neither been pro-capitalist, nor has it been interpreted in that manner. The developments were however absorbed because many believed that the NEP was not necessarily in contradiction with the Constitution. In this regard, even the courts adopted a hands off policy.[31] In the case of *Balco Employees Union* v. *Union of India*,[32] the court went to the extent of stating that in cases involving policy decisions in economic matters, the principles of natural justice have no role to play.[33]

28. Paul E. Sigmund, The Ideologies of the Developing Nations, 19 (1964).
29. Mahendra P. Singh, "Constitutionality of Market Economy", 276 Delhi Law Review 18 (1996).
30. V.R Krishna Iyer, Rhetoric versus Reality: Essays on Human Rights, Justice, Democratic Values, 51 (2004).
31. In *Delhi Science Forum* v. *Union of India*, AIR 1996 SC 1356: 1996 AIR SCW 953: (1996) 2 SCC 405, the court said; "the national policies in respect of economy, finance, communications, and trade...have to be decided by the Parliament and the representatives of the people...They cannot be tested in court of law."
32. (2002) 2 SC 333: AIR 2002 SC 350: 2001 AIR SCW 5135.
33. The mirage of workers rights was shattered by the decision of the court in the case. The court refused to look into the process of disinvestment

Contd. on next page

One of the strongest assertion of the modernist economic strategy came by way of the Special Economic Zones (hereinafter SEZ). Although the issue itself deserves to be a separately studied and analyzed, it serves as the right example in exposing the evils that modernity may bring in the form of totalitarian tendencies of the democracy. The SEZ Act, 2005 was passed under the foreign trade policy 2004-2009, which legitimized the agenda for establishing SEZ. The SEZ crisis raised a whole lot of vital concerns in relation to acquisition of land for private players, the loss of national income owing to massive tax exemptions, the loss of land to thousands of persons, the non-existence of any adequate compensatory measures, the use of coercive force to impose policy of the government and the exposure of a weak democracy etc. [34]

Many of those exploring the reality of economic globalization have emphasized the negative impact of such trends on the poor and vulnerable citizens. Also, "a prevailing theme emerging from a key discourse on economic globalization is that the poor in developing countries will inevitably be incapable of mitigating the overbearing forces of globalised capitalism."[35] The impact of capitalism in India

Contd. from previous page

because it was a matter of policy involving complex factors. In addition, the court also stated that while it was expected of a responsible employer to take all aspects into consideration including welfare of the labour before taking any policy decision, there is no principle of natural justice which requires prior notice and hearing or consultation prior to the taking of the decision. "As a matter of good governance and administration whenever such policy decisions are taken, it is desirable that there should be wide range of consultations including considerations any representations which may have been filed, but there is no provision in law which would require a hearing to be granted before taking a policy decision." *Id* at para 57.

34. The use of excessive force by the state is totalitarian and undemocratic, the reason being; "it is not an advance in civilization but retrogression. It has been adopted by peoples who are politically and socially immature. They have not grasped the fact that the essential condition for an advanced civilization is tolerance, and that society...of different views...can live together in peace...The achievement of the state involves the use of force." See Clement R. Attlee, "Democratic Socialism versus Totalitarian Communism and Fascism", in William Ebenstein, Modern Political Thought: The Great Issues, 597 (1960).

35. Jonathan Jones, "India's Democracy has a Heartbeat", available at *http://www.indiaseminar.com/semsearch.htm* (2009). Last visited on 27.3.09.

has certainly unleashed a more profit motivated agenda of governance, reforms and land acquisition.

5. The Realm of Public Purpose

The socialist trend in India is also written as pidgin[36] socialism. It means that, the socialist idea originated in the West, but after its importation into India it underwent significant transformation, more so a repacking of the original package.[37] In other words, the Indian socialism has got "imprisoned in a modernist ideological package which put severe limits on the way it could relate to India and the way Indians could relate to it".[38]

The new trend of privatization has introduced new forms of economic and social alienation by the process of land acquisition and displacement. The utility of the Land Acquisition Act, 1894[39] and the Rehabilitation and Resettlement Bill, 2007[40] require utmost attention. The two reflected upon the exercise of power of eminent domain that has been used extensively since independence.

In the more recent times, the hope is expressed in the proposed Land Acquisition and Rehabilitation and Resettlement Bill, 2011 which seeks to balance the need for facilitating land acquisition for various public purposes

36. The term 'Pidgin' is a language born out of cultural contact, although borrowing heavily from its parent language.

37. Yogendra Yadav, "Future of Pidgin Socialism", 407 Seminar, 20 (July 1993).

38. *Id* at 23.

39. The Act is an expression of the doctrine of eminent domain, which invests power in the state to take over private land for a public purpose, which may include for the residential purposes of the poor or helpless etc. The coercive nature of taking over is toned down by compensating persons with interest in the land....The expansion of the power and its use to effect mass displacement and, more recently, to hand so acquired to corporations, has added urgency to understanding the scope of land acquisition and displacement.

40. The Bill aims to provide a social impact assessment of the schemes and plans that are likely to affect the families by way of displacement. The assessment will involve participation and a transparent process to evaluate the problems to be faced by the concerned persons. The assessment will take place in case displacement affects a specific number of families as mentioned in the Act. The Act makes no provision for publishing the report of the social impact assessment.

including infrastructure development, industrialization and urbanization, while at the same time meaningfully addressing the concerns of farmers and those whose livelihoods are dependent on the land being acquired.[41] The bill is an attempt to fill in the legislative gap in the area of rehabilitation, resettlement and compensation for loss of livelihoods.

The salient features of the proposed Bill are;

(a) It puts in place a new institutional mechanism to ensure that the R&R provisions are implemented effectively as part of land acquisition. (Dispute Resolution Authorities for both Centre and States).

(b) The Bill will enjoy primacy over all other specialized laws that deal with land acquisition. (Highways, SEZ etc.)

(c) It includes private companies that purchase land directly from the farmers and others.

(d) Social Impact Assessment made mandatory if area acquired is more than 100 acres. Under section 4, the Bill also requires a public hearing at the affected area, to incorporate the views of the people in the SIA.

(e) Land returned to original owner if not used for the concerned purpose for 5 years.

(f) All documents to be made available in public domain and on the website.

(g) Disciplinary proceedings against government officer guilty of *malafide* action against the provisions of the Act.

(h) Under the Bill, an affected family includes under section 2(c), a family whose land or other immovable property has been acquired or which is involuntarily and permanently displaced from their land or immovable property; a landless family, which includes agriculture labourer or artisans, which has been working in the affected area and whose primary source of livelihood has been affected by land acquisition in such area; tribals and other traditional forest dwellers, who

41. The Ministry of Rural Development, Government of India (July 27th 2011).

have lost any traditional rights recognized under the Scheduled Tribes and Other Traditional Forest Dwellers (Recognition of Forest Rights) Act, 2006.

(i) Under section 2(y), there is requirement of a written consent of 80% of the people affected by the acquisition of land for industry/Companies.

The draft Land Acquisition and Rehabilitation and Resettlement Bill, 2011 is to be tabled in Parliament in the winter session, after getting the nod from the Group of Ministers that have spoken of requiring consent of 2/3rd land losers, while acquiring land for public private partnership and private projects.[42]

The Bill with the provision for compensation, resettlement, and stakeholder's participation has wide socio-political dimensions.

The experiences worldwide have also indicated that in the absence of equitable property rights there is a high likelihood of social unrest. Reports of the UN and independent experts based on empirical evidence are indicative of a strong link between property rights, freedom, and prosperity.

6. Initiatives for Land Reforms

With the objective of securing land reforms, several initiatives have also been undertaken by civil society participants. Identifying land reforms as an essential and extremely important component of any paradigm of development, Ekta Parishad constituting one of the biggest organizations, has been fighting for the land rights of the rural poor and the deprived sections at the grass roots. From 2008-2010, the organization trained community leaders and various organizations for peaceful movements and Satyagraha.

---

42. NDTV, "Group of Ministers clears Land Acquisition Bill", (16th October 2012) Available at http://www.ndtv.com/article/india/group-of-ministers-clears-land-acquisition-bill-280631 (Last visited 31.10.2012). Also see, India Today, "Land Acquisition Bill cleared, to be Tabled in Winter Session" (16th October 2012). Available at http://indiatoday.intoday.in/story/land-acquisition-bill-cleared-to-be-tabled-in-winter-session/1/225045.html

In 2012, there was the formulation of the Jan Satyagraha. The special strengths of the Jan Satyagraha are; (a) it has been able to incorporate a very wide range of problems and concerns relating to land struggles and the marginalized communities. (b) it has made available valuable information on the latest situation of land grabbing, displacement, deprivation and other injustices.[43]

At the global platform, the most recent pledges to pursue land reform by securing land as an asset were made at the International Conference on Agrarian Reform and Rural Development of FAO, convened in Porto Alegre, Brazil, in March 2006. The Final Declaration adopted at the Conference encourages the holding of a national and inclusive dialogue to ensure significant progress on agrarian reform and rural development and the establishment of appropriate agrarian reform "mainly in areas with strong social disparities, poverty and food insecurity, as a means to broaden sustainable access to and control over land and related resources". The Governments represented at the Conference also recommended that the FAO Committee on World Food Security adopted a set of reporting guidelines in order to monitor the implementation of the Declaration. The preparation of the Voluntary Guidelines on Responsible Governance of Tenure of Land and other Natural Resources, led by FAO, is the single most important attempt to follow up on the commitments made at the Conference, and the Declaration of the World Summit on Food Security, held in 2009, underlines that link. It is too early to assess the Guidelines in the light of what they promise to achieve.[44]

---

43. Bharat Dogra, "Land Reforms and the Significance of Jan Satygraha", Vol. L No. 40 Mainstream 7 (September, 2012).
44. There is deliberation on the adoption of an optional protocol to promote the right to property as a human right, particularly in poor developing countries with questionable human-rights records. An optional protocol on the right to property would allow individuals to complain that their ESC rights have been violated. See Jacob Mhangama, "Individual Liberty, Free Markets and Peace", Cato Policy Report (2011). Available at http://www.cato.org/pubs/policy_report/v33n3/cprv33n3-1.html

As for the status of property in India, the expanding horizons of the democratic polity require the immediate incorporation of a rationale approach and structure in the existing development model.

7. Concluding Remarks

The proponents of socialist critique continue to deny the role of socialism in bringing about any change in the modern day governance. Francis Fukiyama highlights the weakness of the socialist ideology. According to Fukiyama, 'the problem with socialism lies in its difficulty to change with time. Accordingly, socialism must change with the world and yield results by taking into consideration the reality of capitalism and globalization. The socialist problem as furnished by Fukiyama has been witnessed in the past; when the socialist economies like that of the U.S.S.R grew faster than the capitalists in the 1950's and 60's, but subsequently failed miserably with the change in economic activity. It was because with the increase in economic complexities, the State centralized machinery to deal with the problems was leading to delay, distortion and manipulation of the economic affairs. And as information became more and more detailed and complex, State did not have the requisite skill and technique to deal with the matters.'[45]

In the modern times, the State continues to hold a dominant control over the affairs of the country. A look at the democratic politics in India provides an understanding of the constraints in the realization of socio-economic justice. It is true that the continuous expansion in the ideological vacuum, as to where does the allegiance lie whether pro-capitalist or pro-socialist, has led to the emergence of widespread discontent, exclusion and disintegration. There is a need to inspire the society for generating the desire for change and development.

---

45. Francis Fukiyama, "Will Socialism Make a Comeback? Globalisation Protests show New Potential". Available at *http://www.net4dem.org/cyrev/archive/issue7/articles/Fukiyama/fukiyama.pd* (Last visited 10.4.09).

To improvise on the socio-political realities, building a model of socialist development would require raising of the consciousness of the people through participation in all spheres of economic, social and political life, coupled with a committment of the State to respond to the awakened populace.

CHAPTER V

Secularism

Amit Bindal[1]
Latika Vashisht

The Indian democracy has always been projected and celebrated as a multi-cultural/linguistic/religious one. The Indian constitutional framework establishes a secular democratic space that accords freedom of religion to all persons[2] as well as religious denominations[3] and entrenches

---

1. The finer details of this chapter are also discussed under "Conceptualizing Religion in the Public Sphere: Essential Practices Test and Beyond" in Deepa Kansra, Rabindra Pathak, Bhrigu Vishkarma (Eds.), Re-Thinking the Law: Emerging Issues and Challenges, Authors Press (2013) ISBN 978-81-7273-686-6.
2. Article 25 of Constitution of India reads: Freedom of conscience and free profession, practice and propagation of religion:
   (1) Subject to public order, morality and health and to the other provisions of this Part, all persons are equally entitled to freedom of conscience and the right freely to profess, practise and propagate religion
   (2) Nothing in this article shall affect the operation of any existing law or prevent the State from making any law
      (a) regulating or restricting any economic, financial, political or other secular activity which may be associated with religious practice;
      (b) providing for social welfare and reform or the throwing open of Hindu religious institutions of a public character to all classes and sections of Hindus
      Explanation I: The wearing and carrying of *kirpans* shall be deemed to be included in the profession of the Sikh religion
      Explanation II: In sub clause (b) of clause reference to Hindus shall be construed as including a reference to persons professing the Sikh, Jain or Buddhist religion, and the reference to Hindu religious institutions shall be construed accordingly.
3. Article 26 of Constitution of India reads: Freedom to manage religious affairs Subject to public order, morality and health, every religious denomination or any section thereof shall have the right:

Contd. on next page

the rights of religious and linguistic minorities.[4] Despite these constitutional guarantees and protections, the Indian democracy has witnessed various state sponsored pogroms of communal violence targeting the religious minorities. The year 2012 marks 10 years to one of the most atrocious communal riots that broke in Godhra in the state of Gujarat in March 2002.[5] The massacre of Muslims in the Godhra riots was the breaking point of rising Hindu fundamentalism in India.[6] While the perpetrators of Godhra continue to hold state power, sanctioned by "free and fair elections", it becomes imperative to question the efficacy and effectiveness of the constitutional promise of secularism in India.

Secularism under the Indian Constitution is quite distinct from the western liberal idea of "wall of separation". The constitution of India provides a guaranteed fundamental right to 'profess, practice and propagate' religion to 'every person'. The framers have carefully and meticulously subjected the freedom of religion to 'public order, health and morality'. article 25 of the Constitution of India guarantees individual right to freedom of religion whereas the ensuing article, article 26, deals with freedom of religion as a collective right or denominational right.

Indian secularism does not mean non-interference with religious affairs; it rather *requires* intervention from the state. However, the intent of such positive state intervention is to make religions inclusive and to protect and uphold the right to freedom of religion of the hitherto excluded and stigmatized groups. However, the secular spirit of

---

Contd. from previous page

(a) to establish and maintain institutions for religious and charitable purposes;

(b) to manage its own affairs in matters of religion;

(c) to own and acquire movable and immovable property; and

(d) to administer such property in accordance with law.

4. Articles 29 and 30, Constitution of India.
5. Upendra Baxi, 'The Second Gujarat Catastrophe' (August 24, 2002) 37 (34) Economic and Political Weekly 3519.
6. Ratna Kapur, Makeshift Migrants and Law: Gender, Belonging and Postcolonial Anxieties (Routledge, 2010) Chapter 6.

the Constitution mandates the state to observe neutrality towards all religious groups and communities. These twin concurrent goals of secularism that envisage a neutral as well as interventionist state are unique to the Indian model of secularism and mark a radical shift from the liberal idea of a secular state. Neutrality and interventionism may appear to be conflicting but it is the duty of the power keepers in state and judiciary to strike the balance that checks that neutrality does not acquire majoritarian overtones and intervention does not produce subaltern subjects.

1. Interpreting Religious Freedom

The Supreme Court of India in the initial decade of the working of the Constitution of India was confronted with the task of interpreting the extent and scope of freedom of religion. This was no easy task as the balance was required to be struck between giving religion its due and the constitutional promise of secular Indian state in the post Independent India. The Constitution itself has permitted an interventionist state as far as 'secular activities' associated with religion are concerned.[7] Therefore, it was important to clearly determine the definition of 'secular activities' where the state intervention is permissible, and distinguish it from 'religious activities' that are guaranteed freedom by the constitution. The Supreme Court evolved the doctrine of essential practices test to achieve this goal. It basically meant that those practices of various religions that are absolutely essential in their religion would be granted protection under the fundamental right (to the extent that no ordinary legislation can take them away or abridge them). In other words, the core of religion, which the judiciary saw as 'essential practices' of the religion came to be seen as a constitutionally protected rights under the Indian Constitution. This was the basic idea behind the essential practices test.

Though the concept had a benign goal and laudable purpose but the complexities for full realization of the doctrine came up with the birth of the doctrine itself. Through

7. Article 25(2), Constitution of India.

the said doctrine, the court assumed the role of discovering 'true' or 'essential core' of religion as well as rationalization of religious practices. This led to the issue whether it is within judicially manageable standards to do so since finding the core of religion has been a task, not fully accomplished even by those who have given their lives to theology! Thus, while the courts in their limited powers attempted to find out the 'true core of religion', in reality this exercise became a subtle process of assimilation of minorities by denying them constitutional protection. And the essential practice test, from "core practices" came to be implemented as the test for "true religion" amongst many religions.

After independence, the essential practices test was first expounded in *Commissioner, Hindu Religious Endowments, Madras* v. *Sri Lakshimindra Thirtha Swamiar of Sri Shirur Mutt.*[8] The state made a legislation to control some activities, which were hitherto controlled by Brahmins and priests, and take them in their own control. The State legislation made for the purpose of acquiring control over the 'secular' activities of the Religious Endowments, namely, Madras Hindu Religious and Charitable Endowments Act, 1951. Such state control through law was challenged as an attack on the constitutionally guaranteed right to freedom of religion. The petitioner (who was the *mathadhipati i.e.* head of the religious group) challenged the legislation on the ground that it violated article 26 of the Constitution of India. Although many provisions of the enactment were struck down by Court on different counts, it upheld the *inspection of accounts* and *even inspection of temples by the State authorities* since, according to the court, it did not interfere with the essential aspects of religion.

To define the scope of 'secular activities', Justice B.K. Mukherjee resorted to *'essential principles test'*. It was held that for defining social welfare content the judiciary can distinguish essential from the non-essential activity. Dealing with as to what constitutes matters of religion within article 26(2)(b), the Court observed:[9]

8. AIR 1954 SC 282: 1954 SCJ 335: 1954 SCR 1005 (hereafter Swamiar case).
9. *Id.* at para 17 (emphasis supplied).

> A religion undoubtedly has its basis in a system of beliefs or doctrines which are regarded by those who profess that religion as conducive to their spiritual well-being, but it would not be correct to say that religion is nothing else but a doctrine of belief. A religion may not only lay down a code of ethical rules for its followers to accept, *it might prescribe rituals and observances, ceremonies and modes of worship which are regarded as integral parts of religion, and these forms and observances might extend even to matters of food and dress.*

Quite clearly the definition of religion, though well meaning, defined religion in a much broader manner to include rituals and observances, ceremonies and modes of worship as integral part of it. Commenting further on what would constitute an essential practice of the religion, the court said:[10]

> What constitutes the essential part of a religion is primarily to be ascertained with reference to the doctrines of that religion itself. If the tenets of any religious sect of the Hindus prescribe that offerings of food should be given to the idol at particular hours of the day, that periodical ceremonies should be performed in a certain way at certain periods of the year or that there should be daily recital of sacred texts or oblations to the sacred fire, all these would be regarded as parts of religion and the mere fact that they involve expenditure of money or employment of priests and servants or the use of marketable commodities would not make them secular activities partaking of a commercial or economic character; all of them are religious practices and should be regarded as matters of religion within the meaning of article 26(b).

By expounding the notion that essential practice are to be culled out from the 'doctrines of that religion itself', the court usurped upon themselves the task of scrutinizing religious books and texts, practices and customs in order to

10. *Id.* at para 20.

find out what constitutes 'essential' to a particular religion. How awfully this daring attempt turned out to be due tc the sheer incapacity of judiciary as an institution to interpret religious texts is something that the rest of this chapter will attempt to elucidate.

2. The Historical Evolution of the Doctrine

Ronojoy Sen points out that the essential practices doctrine was "a derivative discourse of the colonial-era doctrine of 'justice, equity and good conscience'."[11] An important mission of the colonial regime-orientalists as well as utilitarians- was to achieve uniformity and certainty of Hindu and Muslim laws. This entailed *brahmanization* and rationalization of law leading to the consolidation of a 'uniform high-culture law' through codes and case law that preferred *brahmanical*, 'high-culture classic texts' to local customs and popular religious practices.[12]

Sen's point can be illustrated from the case of *Ratilal* v. *State of Bombay*.[13] Bombay legislature passed the Bombay Public Trusts Act, 1950. The legislation was passed with a view to properly regulate and improve provisions for the administration of the public and religious trusts in the state of Bombay. The petitioners challenged the constitutional validity of the legislation as they saw any form of regulation as tampering on their religious freedom under Article 26. Relying upon the case of *Swamiar*, Justice Mukherjee stated:[14]

> Religious practices or performances of acts in pursuance of religious belief are as much a part of religion as faith or belief in particular doctrines...No outside authorities has any right to say that these are not essential parts of religion and it is not open to

---

11. Ronojoy Sen, Articles of Faith (Oxford University Press, 2010) 246.
12. *Id.* at 42-45. On the problematic of Brahmanization and universalization of Hindu Law, also *see* Madhu Kishwar, 'Codified Hindu Law: Myth and Reality' (Aug. 13, 1994) 29 (33) Economic and Political Weekly 2145-2161.
13. AIR 1954 SC 388: 1954 SCJ 480: 1954 SCR 1055.
14. *Id.* at 14.

> the secular authority of the State to restrict or prohibit them in any manner they like under the guise of administering the trust estate.

The court seemed to be granting complete autonomy to the religious denominations to determine what practices are essential to it. Such complete freedom given to the religious authorities was nothing less than what Sen refers to as *brahamanisation* of the culture.

In *Durgah Committee,*[15] what is particularly interesting is the radical interpretative turn it brought about in the understanding of essential practices doctrine, through an *obiter* observation. The court went a step ahead of *Devaru* and redefined the essential practices doctrine by "taking up the role of sifting superstition from 'real' religion"[16] and thus, 'rationalizing religion':[17]

> Whilst we are dealing with this point it may not be out of place incidentally to strike a note of caution and observe that in order that the practices in question should be treated as a part of religion they must be regarded by the said religion as its essential and integral part; otherwise even purely secular practices which are not an essential or an integral part of religion are apt to be clothed with a religious form and may make a claim for being treated as religious practices within the meaning of article 26. Similarly, even practices though religious may have sprung from merely superstitious beliefs and may in that sense be extraneous and unessential accretions to religion itself. Unless such practices are found to constitute an essential and integral part of a religion their claim for the protection under article 26 may have to be carefully scrutinized; in other words, the protection must be confined to such religious practices as are an essential and an integral part of it and no other.

15. AIR 1961 SC 1402: (1961) 2 SCA 171: (1962) 1 SCR 383.
16. Ronojoy Sen, above n 12, 55.
17. AIR 1961 SC 1402: (1961) 2 SCA 171: (1962) 1 SCR 383 (34).

Justice Gajendragadkar further crystallized the new avatar of essential practices test in *Shastri Yagnapurushdasji.*[18] In this case the *Satsangis* claimed that they formed a distinct religion being followers of a specific sect called *Swaminarayan* sect and sought protection from the Bombay Harijan Temple Entry Act. This statute was enacted to ensure that all the peoples including the Harijans should be allowed to enter the temple of this sect. The issue before the court was whether the *Swaminarayan* sect represented a distinct and separate religious sect unconnected with the Hindus and Hindu religion, and whether their temples were outside the purview of the said Act.

The issue in a nutshell was that if the *Swaminarayan* sect is included within the meaning of 'Hindus' then they must throw open their doors for everyone as the Bombay Act provided. This is because article 25(b) clearly mandates that nothing can prevent the state from making any law "throwing open of Hindu religious institutions of a public character to all classes and sections of Hindus". Alternatively, they could have side stepped the requirement of the Act if they were not a Hindu denomination.

The Court delved into the history of *Swaminarayan sect. Swaminarayan* was the follower of *Ramanuja* who practised the worship of Lord Krishna, and was a Hindu saint. After this survey, the Court held that *Satsangis* were a part of Hindu religion. In this context, it must be clearly understood that the Court expanded the meaning of Hinduism and described it as all-encompassing. The Court made reference to the famous passage from *Bhagwadgita* (one of the Hindu religious texts) which propounds the idea that divine manifestations in different forms take place at different times to purify the corrupted practices of religion. The court said:[19]

> "When we think of the Hindu religion, we find it difficult, if not impossible, to define Hindu religion or even adequately describe it. Unlike other religions in the world, the Hindu religion does not claim any one

18. AIR 1966 SC 1119: (1966) 2 SCWR 109: (1966) 3 SCR 242.
19. *Id.* at para 29.

prophet; it does not worship any one God; it does not subscribe to any one dogma; it does not believe in any one philosophic concept; it does not follow any one set of religious rites or performances; in fact, it does not appear to satisfy the narrow traditional features of any religion or creed. It may broadly be described as a way of life and nothing more."

Further the court noted:[20]

"If we study teachings of these saints and religious reformers, we would notice an amount of divergence in their respective views; but underneath that divergence, there is a kind of subtle indescribable unity which keeps them within the sweep of the broad and progressive Hindu religion."

Once, defining 'Hinduism' in such broad terms, the Court didn't find any difficulty in assimilating the concerned sect within the fold of Hindu religion. Thereby, the impugned Act was made applicable to them as well as to their temples. Thus, the use of expression *way of life* describing Hinduism must be understood in this context. The Court in *Yagnapurushdasji* as rightly pointed out by Jacobsohn was doing "an elaborate effort to interpret Hinduism in a useful way, namely to felicitate the realization of some of the ameliorative aspects of the Constitutional commitment to secularism."[21] Thus, as Jacobsohn pointed out, this broader definition of the expression 'Hindu' was illustrative of ameliorative secularism. But it must be borne in mind that *Yagnapurushdasji* undoubtedly has become the pioneering case defining Hinduism as a religious category which has been appropriated later to grant constitutional protection to the political project of *Hindutva*[22] in the *Hindutva* judgments.

20. *Id.* at para 38.

21. Gary Jeffery Jacobsohn, The Wheel of Law (Oxford University Press, 2003) 206.

22. Hindutva is a political appeal of the Hindu Right Wing parties in India. The essentials of Hindutva are a common nation, a common race and a common civilization. Though religion does not figure in this definition (since essentials of Hindutva are premised on nationality), in India this

Contd. on next page

Senior Supreme Court lawyers Dr. Rajeev Dhavan and Fali S. Nariman sum up the scope of essential practices test as 'a three step inquiry':[23]

> judges are now endowed with a three step inquiry to determine, in tandem, whether a claim was religious at all, whether it was essential for the faith and, perforce, whether, even if essential, it complied with the public interest and reformist requirements of the Constitution.

There is no doubt that the doctrine vested wide powers in the court. Derrett arguing against this newly invented preposition by the Court observed:[24]

> The Courts can disregard as non-essentials anything that is not proved to their satisfaction...and they are not religious leaders or in any relevant fashion qualified in such matters...The Constitution doesn't say 'freely to profess, practice and propagate the essentials of religion,' but this is how it is construed.

Undoubtedly this power vested in the court has played out to either exclude or to assimilate the minority religious communities within the majoritarian framework. The court's reasoning became exclusionary on many occasions as it assumed majoritarian overtones in its attempt to chisel out the secular practices of a particular religion. This has operated to deny constitutional protection to the minority practices by terming them 'secular' and 'non-essential' and thus, falling

---

Contd. from previous page

political project functions to exclude and alienate all religions which are not of Indian origin. Islam and Christianity are the "Others" within this conceptualization. See Arvind Sharma, 'On Hindu, Hindustan, Hinduism and Hindutva' (2002) 49(1) Numen 1-36.

23. Rajeev Dhavan and Fali Nariman, 'The Supreme Court and Group Life: Religious Freedom, Minority Groups and Disadvantaged Communities' in B.N. Kirpal and others (eds), Supreme But Not Infallible (Oxford University Press, 2000) 260. Dhavan and Nariman in their critique stated: "The judges are unequipped to deal with such issues . . . virtually assumed a theological authority . . . with a power greater than that of a high priest, maulvi and dharmashastri."

24. J.D.M. Derrett, Religion, Law and the State in India (New York Publishers, 1968) 223-224.

within the zone of state regulation. For instance, the court held that the sacrifice of a cow on the festival of Muslims, *Eid*, was not essential to Islam, because there was an option of a cow, a camel or six goats, and thus, the practice could be restricted by law banning the slaughter of cows.[25] In yet another controversial case, which will be discussed later in length, it was held that offering prayers in a mosque is not an essential practice of Islam.[26] On the other hand it can also be seen how the test has been used to assimilate the minorities within the dominant Hindu framework. This assimilative drive has acquired two dimensions. First, as Ronojoy Sen points out:[27]

(There) has been the marked disinclination of the Court to accept more recent religious groups as 'proper' religion or even religious denomination. Consequently, the religious practices of these groups have not been able to pass the essential practices test. Of course, given the all-encompassing definition of Hinduism in *Yagnapurushdasji*, it is unlikely any sect within Hinduism is ever going to get the court's approval as a separate religion.

This tendency was apparent in *S.P. Mittal* v. *Union of India*,[28] where the Auroville Act was challenged by the followers of Sri Aurobindo. The majority speaking through Justice R.B. Misra held that Aurobindo society did not constitute a religious denomination[29] and the teachings of Sri Aurobindo only represented his philosophy and not a religion. Similarly, in *Jagadishwarananada* v. *Police Commissioner, Calcutta*,[30] while accepting that *Ananda Margis* (can be roughly translated as those following the path of

25. *Mohd. Hanif Quareshi* v. *Bihar*, AIR 1958 SC 731: 1958 SCJ 975: 1959 SCR 629. Also see *State of West Bengal* v. *Ashutosh Lahiri*, AIR 1995 SC 464: (1995) 1 SCC 631: 1995 (1) SCJ 213.
26. *Ismail Faruqui* v. *Union of India*, (1994) 6 SCC 360: AIR 1995 SC 605: 1995 (96) STC 344.
27. Ronojoy Sen, articles of Faith (Oxford University Press, 2010) 58.
28. AIR 1983 SC 130: (1983) 1 SCC 305: 1983 (1) SCJ 188.
29. It may be noted that Justice Chinnappa Reddy gave his dissenting view wherein he relied upon *Swamiar* case to hold that Aurobindo was a religious teacher and he gave a new religious doctrine and practice.
30. AIR 1984 SC 51: 1983 Cr LJ 1872: (1983) 4 SCC 522.

bliss) were a religious denomination, the court resorted to essential practices doctrine to rule that *tandava dance* (a form of dance which is attributed to Lord Shiva) was not an essential practice of Anand Margis since Anand Marga as a religious order is of recent origin and the *tandava dance* as a part of religious rites is still more recent.[31]

The second, and recognizably erroneous, dimension of the assimilative move of the essential practices doctrine was manifested in the recent case of *Rajesh Himmatlal Solanki* v. *Union of India through Secretary*[32] where the court relied on the doctrine of essential practices to hold that Bhoomi Puja (foundation laying religious ceremony) is a secular practice as it benefits everyone without distinction of caste, religion etc. The next section of the paper attempts to analyze a few decisions of the Supreme Court and High Courts of India to unveil the multiple conceptions of secularism that are embedded in the judicial narratives interpreting freedom of religion and equality of all religions.

3. Religion in Public Sphere: Contemporary Contestations

December 6th, 1992 marks a fateful day in the political history of independent India. This is because it was this day when the Hindu fundamentalists along with the support of right wing nationalist parties destroyed the Babri Mosque at Ayodhya. It is very important and instructive to carefully scrutinize the conception of secularism expounded in the case of *Ismail Faruqui* v. *Union of India,*[33] [popularly known as Babri

---

31. This decision was contested by the single bench of Calcutta High court (AIR 1990 Cal 336: 1990 (2) Cal LT 212) where Justice Bhagabati Prasad Banerjee noted that "the concept of *tandav* dance was not a new thing which is beyond the scope of religion...If the courts started enquiring and deciding the rationality of a particular practice then there might be confusion and the religious practice would become what the courts wish the practice to be." In the similar tone Justice A.R. Lakshamanan wrote his dissent in *The Commissioner of Police* v. *Acharya Jagdishwarananda Avadhuta,* (2004) 12 SCC 782-83: "If these practices were accepted by the followers of such spiritual head as a method of achieving their spiritual upliftment, the fact that such practice was recently introduced cannot make it any the less a matter of religion."
32. Writ Petition (PIL) No. 2 of 2011 (hereafter Himmatlal Solanki's case).
33. (1994) SCC 6 360: 1994 AIR SCW 4897: 1995 (96) STC 344.

Masjid Demolition Case] A simple reading of the majority judgment, delivered by Verma, J. makes it abundantly clear that the notion of secularism propounded by him remains firmly rooted within the liberal democratic framework. This analysis becomes particularly interesting because Justice Verma remained silent in the *S.R. Bommai* decision[34] where 7 out of 9 judges elaborately articulated their conceptions of secularism and secularism was held to the basic structure of Indian Constitution. Jacobsohn correctly points this out discreetly when he writes that: "Though part of nine-member unanimous Court in Bommai, Justice Verma was one of the only two justices who did not use the occasion to write about secularism and the constitution."[35]

It is in *Babri Masjid Demolition* case where the notion of secularism is extensively discussed by Justice Verma. The conception of secularism expounded by Justice Verma remains firmly rooted in the notions of political liberalism such as tolerance and plea for assimilation of the minority communities within the frame set by the majority communities. Such a conception based on the liberal notion of tolerance is inadequate to deal with the problem posed by neo-right wing fundamentalism. This is the reason why this notion, due to its inherent philosophical limitations, remains appropriable by the Hindu right wing parties for their vested political interests to spearhead their agenda of Hindu nationalism. The

---

34. *S.R. Bommai* v. *Union of India*, AIR 1994 SC 1918: 1994 AIR SCW 2946: (1994) 3 SCC 1. The case was the important decision where the Supreme Court, for the first time, declared secularism as part of basic structure of the Constitution which cannot be taken away even by a Constitutional amendment. The case, *inter alia*, dealt with the issue whether emergency declared in the states by the centre in the states which were openly supporting demolition of Babri Mosque justified. In a classic decision the Supreme Court, by majority, emergency in the states ruled by Hindu right wing parties which were supporting the demolition of mosque. Justice Verma wrote a separate opinion taking a "narrower" view about judicially manageable standards.

35. *Supra* note 21 at 199-200. Also *see* Upendra Baxi, 'Understanding Constitutional Secularism in 'Faraway Places': Some Remarks on Gary Jacobsohn's 'The Wheel of Law', Indian Journal of Constitutional Law (2007). Available at <http://www.indlaw.com/display.aspx?E676257C-EA84-4718-9661-6EB1E6AD34B3> (visited on 13/2/2012).

following discussion unfolds the limits of the philosophy of political liberalism in understanding the constitutional politics of Indian secularism.

The majority decision in *Babri Masjid Demolition* case, validates Acquisition of Certain Areas at Ayodhya Act, 1993, the legislation enacted by the Parliament which acquires the disputed land. The legislation was attacked to be anti-secular as it was slanted in favour of the Hindu community on various counts. It provided for abatement of all pending suits and proceedings thereby depriving the Muslim community from any judicial remedy for their entitlements.[36] Further, the maintenance of status quo actually ended up allowing the Hindus to continue to worship on the disputed site whereas the Muslims were totally excluded from that area. This was mischievous so far as it was a discriminatory act against the Muslim community in spite of the catastrophic demolition of the Babri Masjid by the hysterics of political right wing forces propagating the philosophy, almost in a vulgar form, of Hindu nationalism.

This was the backdrop under which the Supreme Court had to decide upon the constitutionality of the legislation enacted by the Parliament. All these challenges to the enactment were deeply situated in the proper understanding of the notion of constitutional secularism. The court opens up the decision by comparing the notion of secularism to equality. This form of juxtaposition of equality and secularism is very much emblematic of the writings of Hindu nationalists. In the very beginning of the discourse on secularism the court extolled the virtue of tolerance as the cornerstone of Indian secularism. Citing Dr. Shankar Dayal Sharma from the famous Zakir Hussain Memorial lectures, the court observed:[37]

---

36. Section 4(3) of Acquisition of Certain Areas at Ayodhya Act, 1993 provided for abatement of all suits and legal proceedings thus the Muslim community was deprived of their claim over the land due to adverse possession for almost over 400 years since 1528 AD when the mosque was constructed. *See* S.P. Sathe, Judicial Activism in India (Oxford University Press, 2006).

37. (1994) 6 SCC 360 (34).

We in India, however, understand secularism to denote 'Sarva Dharma Samabhaav': an approach of tolerance and understanding of the equality of all religions. This philosophical approach of understanding, coexistence and tolerance is the very spirit of our ancient thought.

This followed a discourse from Vedic literature and then some discussions from other religious sources. However, it is curious that the first quote which was selected from the *Bommai* decision was none other than the discourse on tolerance:[38]

> As stated above, *religious tolerance* and equal treatment of all religious groups and protection of their life and property and of the places of their worship are an essential part of secularism enshrined in our Constitution. We have accepted the said goal not only because it is our historical legacy and a need of our national unity and integrity but also as a creed of universal brotherhood and humanism. It is our cardinal faith. Any profession and action which go counter to the aforesaid creed are a *prima facie* proof of the conduct in defiance of the provisions of our Constitution.

Later the preference for the conception of political liberalism as the philosophy that dominated the conceptualisation of the idea of constitutional secularism became apparent from the citations from the work of John Rawls in the very next paragraph of the judgment:[39]

> In a pluralist, secular polity law is perhaps the greatest integrating force. A cultivated respect for law and its institutions and symbols; a pride in the country's heritage and achievements; faith that people live under the protection of an adequate legal system are indispensable for sustaining unity in pluralist diversity. Rawlsian pragmatism of 'justice as fairness' to serve as an 'overlapping consensus' and deep-seated agreements on fundamental questions of basic

38. *Id.* at para 151.
39. *Id.*, at para 38.

structure of society for deeper social unity is a political conception of justice rather than a comprehensive moral conception.

The reasoning of the Supreme Court in holding that the mandate of status quo that has been adopted by the enactment is not discriminatory is noteworthy. The court almost constructed the Hindu community as the victim or the loser in the Parliament's decision to effectuate the status quo as, in the view of the court, it was the Hindu devotees who were worshipping the idols and it was only the Hindu devotees whose worship was interrupted due to the act of demolition on 6th December, 1992.[40] This was because the Muslim community was anyway not offering any worship on the site at that point in time.

Thus, it comes as no surprise when the court, almost reversing the contention of the petitioners, ends up finding the Hindu community as the losing one in the entire event and the status quo that has been enacted by the passing of the enactment by the Parliament becomes a kind of price that the Hindu community has to pay and it has to 'bear the cross on its chest' in the form of the mandate of status quo!

The provision does not curtail practice of right of worship of the Muslim community in the disputed area, there having been *de facto* no exercise of the practice or worship by them there at least since December, 1949; and it maintains *status quo* by the freeze to the reduced right of worship by the Hindus as in existence on 7-1-1993. However, confining exercise of the right of worship of the Hindu community to its reduced form within the disputed area as on 7-1-1993, lesser than that exercised till the demolition on 6-12-1992, by the freeze enacted in section 7(2) appears to be reasonable and just in view of the fact that the miscreants who demolished the mosque are suspected to be persons professing to practise the Hindu religion. The Hindu community must, therefore, bear the cross on its chest, for the misdeed of the miscreants reasonably suspected to belong to their religious fold.[41]

---

40. *Id.*, at para 46.
41. *Id.*, at para 53.

In a strange logic the provision, whose constitutionality has been challenged as anti-secular as it slants in favour of the Hindu community turned out to be a provision which victimises the Hindu community! Both the dissenting judges thought otherwise. Indeed, the majority acceded to the acquisition of the disputed land by the government as constitutionally permitted by evoking the doctrine of eminent domain which the court equated as the sovereign power of the government. However, the minority judges, evoking radical conception of secularism observed that "to condone the acquisition of a place of worship in such circumstances is to efface the principle of secularism from the Constitution."[42] Justice Verma, interpreting article 25 of the Constitution, observed that the right guaranteed under this Article is not absolute. Evoking the doctrine of essential practises[43] the court observed that:[44]

> A mosque is not an essential part of the practise of the religion of Islam and namaz (prayers) by Muslims can be offered anywhere, even in the open.

The manner in which the previous precedents were avoided is appalling. Justice Verma did not take note of the

---

42. *Id.*, at para 140.
43. *Id.*, at para 78. The doctrine of essential practices was evoked by the Supreme Court: "While offer of prayer or worship is a religious practice, its offering at every location where such prayers can be offered would not be an essential or integral part of such religious practice unless the place has a particular significance for that religion so as to form an essential or integral part thereof. Places of worship of any religion having particular significance for that religion, to make it an essential or integral part of the religion, stand on a different footing and have to be treated differently and more reverentially."
44. *Id.* at para 82. Also *see* H.M. Seervai, Constitutional Law of India (N.M. Tripathi Publishers, 1983) 929.

    Eminent constitutionalist H.M. Seervai explains: "An individual Muslim has the right to profess his religion. He may do so by offering prayers at home or in a public place. But he has equally a right to offer prayers in a mosque...Religion has both a personal and institutional side. No doubt men can pray in their homes...but throughout the ages men have worshipped in temples, churches, mosques and the like. In practice the personal right is inseparable from the institutional right."

following observations made by an earlier bench of Supreme Court in *All India Imam Org.* v. *Union of India*:[45]

> "Essentially the mosque is a center of community worship where Muslims perform ritual prayer and where historically they also gathered for political, social and cultural functions. (2) The functions of the mosque is summarised by the 13th Century Jurist Ibn Taymiyah as a place of gathering where prayer was celebrated and where public affairs were conducted, (3) All mosques are where Muslims men on an equalitarian basis rich or poor, noble or humble, stand in rows to perform their prayers behind the Imam."

In the same case the court further said that "Mosques are wakf and are required to be registered under the Act over which the Board exercises control. Purposes of their creation is community worship. Namaz or Salat is the mandatory practice observed in every mosque '(Among the Five Pillars (arkan; *e.g.*; rukn) of Islam, it holds the second most important position, immediately after the declaration of faith (shahadah)".[46] These remarks are squarely against the logic of *Ismail Faruqui* case but Justice Verma failed to even make a reference of this decision while reaching his conclusion. This speaks volumes about the fact how the essential practices test is completely dependent on the subjective assessment of individual judges.

An examination of the minority judges opinion further stresses upon the conclusion reached above. The minority justices (both in judicial minority as well as belonging to minority sects)[47] in *Babri Masjid Demolition* case conceptualised

---

45. AIR 1993 SC 2086: 1993 AIR SCW 2092: (1993) 3 SCC 584. Though this case pertained to grant of dignified emoluments to the Imams, the court made pertinent observations about the importance of mosque in Islam.

46. *Id.*, at para 5.

47. This is immensely valuable to note that the both the two judges who dissented from the view taken by majority that offering of *namaj* is not an essential practice in Islam were non-Hindu judges-Justice A.M. Ahmadi being a Muslim and Justice Barucha, a Parsi. This is in no way to impute non-impartiality to the judges but merely the fact that the test is all-too-subjective in nature.

the notion of secularism in an altogether different manner. A notion of secularism which cannot be taken away to maintain public order and thus they found the acquisition of the disputed site, which was a place of worship, by the government as contra-constitutional. The minority opinion clarified that it is only an individual's right to profess, practise and propagate religion under article 25 that is subjected to the requirement of public order. The court further observed that "Secularism is absolute" and "the State may not treat religions differently on the grounds that public order requires it".

In *Dr. Ramesh Yeshwant Prabhoo* v. *Prabhakar Kashinath Kunte,*[48] the court discussed at length the vexing question whether appeal to *Hindutva* in elections amounts to 'corrupt practice'. The question was of immense importance as the Representation of People's Act provides that no political party can rely on communal appeal during elections.[49] The three-judge bench speaking through J.S. Verma, J. answered the question in the negative. The court observed:[50]

> No precise meaning can be ascribed to terms 'Hindu', 'Hindutva', and, 'Hinduism'; and no meaning in the abstract can confine it to the narrow limits of religion alone, excluding the context of Indian culture and heritage ... *'Hindutva'* is related more to the way of life of the people in the sub-continent. It is difficult to appreciate how ... [It] fall within the prohibition ...

48. 1995 SCALE 1: AIR 1996 SC 1113: 1996 AIR SCW 652 (hereafter Prabhu's case).
49. Section 123(3), The Representation of People's Act, 1951. This provision is very much specific to the Indian context. This is in a multi-religious nation like India, hate-speech/communally charged speech, which is commonplace in an electoral context cannot be justified as a facet of freedom of speech and expression. In this very case the constitutionality of section 123 was challenged as violating freedom of speech and expression. However, the Supreme Court upheld the validity of this section holding that the section puts a justified restraint on the constitutionally protected right to freedom of speech and express.
50. *Supra* note 48.

Thus, *Hindutva* got rescued from being caught within the coils of the proscribed section as the court equated the same to *way of life* of the people. The Court followed the logic that what is too universal can't be confined to contours of what may be naively described as 'religious appeal'. Indeed, in describing *Hindutva* as a *way of life* the court extensively and heavily relied upon Justice Gajendragadkar's opinion in *Yagnapurushdasji* where the expression *way of life* was equated with "Hinduism". The key passage quoted from the judgment by Justice Verma reads:[51]

> When we think of the Hindu religion, we find it difficult, if not impossible, to define Hindu religion or even adequately describe it. Unlike other religions in the world, the Hindu religion does not claim any one Prophet; it does not worship any one God; it does not subscribe to any one dogma; it does not believe in any one philosophic concept; it does not follow any one set of religious rites or performances; in fact, it does not appear to satisfy the narrow traditional features of any religion or creed. It may broadly be described as a way of life and nothing more.

One only read to ask a naïve question here: In the context of elections when a political party appeals using a symbolism or semantics having a clear religious undertone, would an ordinary voter understand the peripheral form or the deeper meaning associated with the symbol or linguistic semantic? The court's probing into the deeper meaning of *Hindutva* completely ignores the contextual specificity of this appeal. This uniqueness of 'Hinduism' as described in *Yagnapurushdasji* helped the court to reach to the conclusion that there is much more in Hindu religion than merely religion. *Yagnapurushdasji* was completely misunderstood and wrongly taken recourse to in a decision dealing with electoral setting. Although heavy reliance was made on this case, it is interesting to note that *Yagnapurushdasji* was never related in any manner whatsoever to corrupt practices under election law. The case illustrates that how reliance on precedents

51. *Id.*

which were decided in wholly different context can cause a major obfuscation in the judicial process.

4. Tolerance and Politics

The Supreme Court in its various decisions has endorsed and relentlessly attempted to spread the discourse of tolerance as an elixir to solve to issues of conflicting secularism. The ready-to-offer solution to various political issues has been an insistence on the spirit of tolerance to be inculcated in the masses. The idea of tolerance has been conceptualised as an unquestioned good which can solve many politically contested issues of the contemporary politics. This overemphasis on the notion of tolerance has a tendency to visualise the contemporary political problems as not something that has to be *overcome* rather something to be tolerated. As Wendy Brown insightfully puts it:[52]

> The retreat from more substantive visions of justice heralded by the promulgation of tolerance today is part of a more general depoliticization of citizenship and power and retreat from political life itself. The cultivation of tolerance as a political end implicitly constitutes a rejection of politics as a domain in which conflict can be productively articulated and addressed, a domain in which citizens can be transformed by their participation.

Depoliticization of the issues which were hitherto understood as political into issues of conflict of culture where citizens need to be tolerant is the latent ideological imperative that drives the discourse of tolerance. Thus, political issues of exploitation, racism and injustice are reduced and depoliticised into cultural issues which can be solved by 'promulgation of tolerance'. However, the overemphasis on tolerance only reflects upon the failure of the post-political liberal project's failure to deal with the political issues of injustice head-on. As Huntington puts it in his classic work that in the post-Cold war epoch the 'iron curtains of ideology' are replaced

52. Wendy Brown, *Regulating Aversion: Tolerance in the age of Identity and Empire* (Princeton University Press, 2006) 223-224.

by 'velvet curtains of culture'[53] The discourse of tolerance in a way neutralises, or more aptly, naturalises violence and exploitation as something that is cultural or natural or given state of existence. Thus, instead of fighting against the cultural and religious violence the remedy becomes one of compromise by the tool of tolerance.

Brown focuses on the self-referring paradoxes that inform the very concept of tolerating intolerance. She argues that there exists a certain privileging of cultures in the very act of preaching tolerance between cultures. The dominant liberal multicultural discourse presupposes that true tolerance is possible only in the western individualist culture. This, in turn, legitimises even military interventions on the intolerant other. This form of cultural hierarchy is clearly manifested in the decisions of the courts while constructing the narrative of tolerance.

Another decision advocating secular tolerance is *Hinsa Virodhak Sangh* v. *Mirzapur Moti Kuresh Jamat.*[54] The Municipal Corporation, State of Gujarat, having regard to sentiments of the members of Jain community, passed a resolution to close down all the municipal slaughter houses and banned the sale of non-vegetarian food for nine days during a Jain festival. This in effect meant that the non-vegetarians have to practice vegetarianism for a period of nine days in the state of Gujarat. The Supreme Court, overruling the decision of the Gujarat high court, upheld the constitutionality of the resolution. Although the court observed that "What one eats is one's *personal affair* and it is a part of his *right to privacy* which is included in article 21 of our Constitution as held by several decisions of this court,"[55] but since the same is circumscribed for a 'limited period' (and thereby, not disproportionate) the court upheld the restriction. The court went into a detailed discussion on the cultural practices and historical antecedents

53. Samuel Huntington, *The Clash of Civilizations* (Simon and Schuster, 1998).

54. (2008) 5 SCC 33: AIR 2008 SC 1892: 2008 AIR SCW 2117.

55. *Id.*, at para 27 (emphasis supplied). Article 21 of Constitution of India guarantees right to life and personal liberty.

and relied upon practices of Mughal Kings to emphasize the spirit of tolerance and notions of diversity in a multicultural country like India. Finally, the court reiterated that, '... it is a short restriction for a few days and surely the non-vegetarians can remain vegetarian for this short period".[56] This is a categorical instance of privileging one culture over another in the name of tolerance. As aptly pointed out by one writer:[57]

A *voluntary* decision to participate in the practices of other communities may evidence commendable goodwill, but it is beyond the requirement of tolerance. But *forcing* someone through legal sanction to participate in the practices of another community can only mean intolerance. The impugned law forces everyone else to refrain from eating meat because Jains don't eat meat for religious reasons. Wouldn't it be the same thing to require non-Christians to fast during Lent, non-Muslims to refrain from eating pork and non-Jews to eat only Kosher food?...(of course, in this religious maze, an atheist is not even counted).

Here it is interesting to note that how the discourse of tolerance ends up being camouflaged as an ideological category.[58] Tolerance itself becomes an ideology that operates to mystify the real problems of racism or violence. Following observations made by Justice Bharucha in his otherwise radical dissent in *Ismail Faruqui* mandate a mention here:[59]

> Before we pass final orders, some observations of a general nature appear to be in order. Hinduism is a tolerant faith. It is that tolerance that has enabled Islam, Christianity, Zoroastrianism, Judaism, Buddhism, Jainism and Sikhism to find shelter and support upon this land. We have no doubt that the moderate Hindu

56. *Id.*, at para 72.
57. Tarunabh Khaitan, 'Vegetarianism, tolerance and discrimination', The Hindu (26th May 2008).
58. *See* Slavoj Zizek, 'Tolerance as an Ideological Category' *Critical Inquiry* (Autumn 2007) *available at* <http://www.lacan.com/zizek-inquiry.html> (As visited on 13/2/2012)
59. *Supra* note 26 at para 156.

> has little taste for the tearing down of the place of worship of another to replace it with a temple. It is our fervent hope that that moderate opinion shall find general expression and that communal brotherhood shall bring to the dispute at Ayodhya an amicable solution long before the courts resolve it.

The judge has suggested Hinduism as a benign religion that *enabled* the non-Hindu alien traditions *to find shelter and support upon this land*. This tolerance discourse has reinforced the "us-them" binary that characterizes the liberal tradition. Such "culturalisation of politics" furthers the majoritarian agenda when visualised from the perspective of secularism in India. Almost all the debates couched in terms of tolerance reduce the issue to forceful assimilation of the minorities in the cultural frame of majority community obfuscating the real issues of minority rights and identity. Even fundamental rights guaranteed under article 21 can be eclipsed to foster the spirit of tolerance!

5. Concluding Remarks

Elie Wiesel, in the Foreword to a book on history of Jewish Holocaust states: "The danger lies in forgetting. Forgetting, however, will not effect only the dead. Should it triumph, the ashes of yesterday will cover our hopes for tomorrow."[60] The historical narrative of the evolution of essential practices test is significant to understand the failings of Indian secularism. In their quest of unveiling the true core/essentials of religion the judges were guided by their subjectivities which in turn were shrouded in the discourse of majoritarianism. The neutrality of the judiciary that emerges from an induced forgetfulness of the unsecular, exclusionary and violent realities of the past will ever define secularism as freedom of religious minorities possible only within the dominant socio-political framework.

It is evident from the workings and application of essential practices test that it has hardly been able to articulate a conception of secularism that is free from the liberal discourse

60. Sylvia Rothchild (ed) Voices from the Holocaust (New American Library, 1981) 4.

of tolerance. While noting that "(e)ven certain practices adopted by the person professing a particular religion may not have anything to do with the religion itself,"[61] the courts have interestingly concluded that a *dharma* related activity is a secular activity. For instance, commenting on the foundation laying ceremony the court in *Himmatlal Solanki's* case said:[62]

At the time of excavation of such earth or at the time when a building is to be constructed by adding physical burden, *offering of the prayer to the earth to pardon or to graciously bear the burden or the damage, if any, to make the construction successful, which is to be used for betterment of the institution of the High Court, such an action can be termed as for the betterment of all persons connected thereby directly or indirectly, irrespective of their caste or religion or community.* Therefore, such offering of the prayer to the earth at the time of foundation laying ceremony cannot be termed as non-secular action if "manav dharma" is to be understood in its real sense in furtherance to the principles of secularism to be observed by our nation.

The clear logic of the court was: Since the Foundation Laying Ceremony (Bhoomi Puja) was for the benefit of the construction, which in turn would benefit all the persons alike, it became a secular activity. Going by this logic religious prayers become secular activities as they are for the benefit of the entire humanity! Kapur aptly captures the problem with such judicial discourse when she points out that "the Supreme Court not only conflates the idea of a 'core' or 'essential' ingredient of a religion with the Hindu term dharma, it also uses the term dharma to include all those good feelings and sense of `brotherhood' unity, and friendship for the integration of Bharat (India)"[63] And thus, "there is an increasing convergence between notions of nationalism and Hindu majoritarianism in and through the discourse of secularism."[64]

---

61. *Id.* at para 13.
62. *Id.* at para 17 (emphasis supplied).
63. *Supra* note 5 at 16.
64. *Id.*

From a careful review of the repertoire of cases relating to religion under Indian constitution, the dangers of judiciary arrogating upon itself the role of interpreters of theological texts come out starkly. The Indian experience reinforces the fact that hermeneutics of religious texts is by far beyond judicially manageable standards. Further, it is important to reiterate another important point regarding conception of secularism in a multicultural society. Undoubtedly, celebration of religious events with a sense of communitarian togetherness displays the strength of a multicultural society. However, there is a very subtle distinction between voluntary celebration of religious events and excessive ritualization. When the latter inhabits the public space then majoritarianism creeps in the name of tolerance. This is where we need to realize and unmask the limits of liberal discourse of tolerance. Within the Indian context, it is the poor theoretical understanding of this issue that has led to the judicial discourse of secularism bordering on soft-*hindutva*. The danger is imminent in the post-modern multicultural societies where the quench to give religion its place can also result in threatening the valuable ideals of secularism.

CHAPTER VI

Democracy

Deepa Kansra

Political ideals that gain currency in a culture tend to become moribund with the passage of time and to suffer the fate of dogmas and dead metaphors: they lose the power they originally had to speak to us, to open up new pathways for thinking, and to inspire.[1]

Democracy has been hailed as a *global phenomenon* and the most popular feature of modern political thought.[2] Several

1. Paul Fairfield, Why Democracy 1666 (2008).
2. The significant leap in the promotion and acceptance of democracy is said to be a resultant of six principles of sufficient universal acceptance;

   (a) Democracy is an absolute good *i.e.*, desirable for its own sake and an important component of individual and social welfare, (b) higher levels of economic development are usually associated with increased democratization, (c) free markets are a necessary and sufficient prerequisite for economic growth (and development) (d) economic growth enhances social welfare, so that there is a positive feedback from free markets to democracy, *via* the growth and welfare enhancing effects of free markets, (e) democracy is also growth, may be regarded as self-sustaining, (f) democracy is an important impetus for marketisation, so democracy, growth and free markets may be regarded as constituting a virtuous cycle, each lending strength to the other.' *See* D.M. Nachane, Liberalization, Globalization and the Dynamics of Democracy in India, 25-56 International Journal of Development and Conflict: Demo Issue 26 (2010).

   According to Nico Krisch, "In the early 1990's...the international sphere seemed to move from anarchy to order, with new institutions and courts structuring the emerging landscape and common values providing a principled framework for it. The spread of constitutional democracy at the domestic level seemed to be reinforced and secured by an increasingly robust and fair international legal order." *See* Nico Krisch, Beyond Constitutionalism: Pluralist Structure of Postnational Law 3 (2010).

notable efforts have been made by the global community to promote and extend democracy to cover billions of people, with their varying histories, cultures, and disparate levels of affluence.[3]

In 2007, the United Nations General Assembly (GA hereinafter) resolved to support the efforts of governments to promote and consolidate new or restored democracies. The GA in this regard stated that democracy is a universal value based on the freely expressed will of people to determine their own political, economic, social and cultural systems and their full participation in all aspects of their lives. The GA also found it relavant to highlight that, while democracies share common features, there is no single model of democracy and that democracy does not belong to any country or region, and reaffirming further the necessity of due respect for sovereignty, the right to self-determination and territorial integrity.[4] In 2005, the United Nations Democracy Fund was created in order to implement projects aimed at enhancing democratic practice, promoting human rights, encouraging participation of all groups in democratic processes.[5]

In contrast to its growing popularity, democracy has also been closely looked at with suspicion by experts-academic, political and otherwise. The skeptics sense reluctance on the part of the leaders, politicians, experts, theorists to define democracy on terms of what happens in a democracy.[6]

---

3. Amartya Sen, "Democracy as a Universal Value", *Journal of Democracy* 10.3 (1999).
4. UNGA, 62nd Session.

   Available at http://www.un.org/ga/search/view_doc.asp?symbol=A/RES/62/7(Last visited 10.3.2012).

   In this regard, reference can also be made to the United Nations Universal Declaration of Human Rights (UDHR 1948) that states; the will of the people shall be the basis of the authority of the Government. The International Covenant of Civil and Political Rights (ICCPR 1966) provides for the right to expression, right to participate in public affairs, right to association, and the right to vote.
5. UNDF-United Nations Democracy Fund. *See* http://www.un.org/democracyfund/
6. *Skeptics* is a general term referring to the scholars/experts who challenge the popularized notions of democracy. As often argued by the skeptics, the current political arrangements are leading to fragmentation of

Contd. on next page

Skeptics assert "that the meaning of democracy is contested with no universal definition that is applicable."[7]

1. Defining Democracy

In simplest of terms, democracy has been referred to as the rule of the people, or a form of government in which the 'demos'- the people, rule with power in the hands of many rather than just a few or one.[8] In other words, *demos* can be translated as 'the people' and *kratos* as 'power'; democracy has a root meaning of the power of the people.[9]

In order to preserve the power of the people, democracy is based on the values of liberty and equality. The components as 'free speech, political equality, liberty, toleration, empathy, efficiency'[10] are crucial to the workings of a democracy.

The definitions of democracy often quoted reflect on the evolving and significant character of democracy. The Office of the United Nations High Commissioner for Human Rights[11]

Contd. from previous page

societies, and inflexible forms of decision making. *See* Will Kymlicka, "Citizenship in an Era of Globalization: Commentary on Held" in Ian Shapiro, Casiano Hacker (eds.), Democracy's Edges 112 (1999); James Bohman, Public Deliberation: Pluralism, Complexity and Democracy 1 (2000); Cherif Bassiouni, "The Future of Human Rights in the Age of Globalization", Vol. 40 No.1-3 Denver Journal of International Law and Policy 38 (2011-2012).

7. Michael Clarke, "The Contested Meaning of the International Norm of Democracy", Vol. 2 No. 2 In-Spire Journal, 2 (2008). Also available at *www.in-spire.org* (Last visited 10.12.2011).
8. A quick reference must be made to concept of direct democracy and indirect democracy. In the former, 'the political system in which the people directly make determining political decisions... An indirect democracy is a political system in which the people make the determining political decisions to an important extent directly at elections...with many of the decisions actually made by the elected representatives'. Tom Paine opined that ancient democracies increased in population, expanded in territory, for which direct democracy became inconvenient. A system of representation was a remedy for this. *See* Barry Holden, The Nature of Democracy 27-30 (1974).
9. Josiah Ober, "The Original Meaning of Democracy: Capacity to do Things, Not Majority Rule", 15 No. 1 Constellations Volume 3 (2008).
10. Burt Neuborne, "Making the Law Safe for Democracy: A Review of the Law of Democracy Etc.", 97 Michigan Law Review 1578 (May 1999).
11. 23 April, 2003, available at *UN Doc E/CN.4/2003/L.11/Add.4.* (Last visited 10-3-2012).

states that the respect for human rights and fundamental freedoms and the principle of holding periodic and genuine elections by universal suffrage are essential elements of democracy.[12]

The United Nations Commission on Human Rights (replaced by the Human Rights Council in 2006) defined democracy in comprehensive terms as 'a system of governance that encompasses procedures and substance, formal institutions and informal processes, majorities and minorities, mechanisms and mentalities, laws and their enforcement, government and civil society'.[13]

---

12. The African Union's Charter on Democracy, Elections and Governance (adopted in 2007) includes as principles: 'Respect for human rights and democratic principles; Access to and exercise of state power in accordance with the constitution of the State Party and the principle of the rule of law; Promotion of a system of government that is representative; Holding of regular, transparent, free and fair elections; Separation of powers; Promotion of gender equality in public and private institutions; Effective participation of citizens in democratic and development processes and in governance of public affairs; Transparency and fairness in the management of public affairs; Condemnation and rejection of acts of corruption, related offenses and impunity; Condemnation and total rejection of unconstitutional changes of government; Strengthening political pluralism and recognizing the role, rights and responsibilities of legally constituted political parties, including opposition political parties, which should be given a status under national law.' *See* The Office for Promotion of Parliamentary Democracy, "Democracy Revisited: Which Notion of Democracy for EU's External Relations", 12 (2009). Available at *http://www.europarl.europa.eu/oppd* (Last visited 10-12-2011).
13. Some of these elements are explained in greater detail in another declaration by the Human Rights Commission, which states; the rights entailed in a democracy include, *inter alia,* the following: (a) The rights to freedom of opinion and expression, of thought, conscience and religion, and of peaceful association and assembly; (b) The right to freedom to seek, receive and impart information and ideas through any media; (c) The rule of law, including legal protection of citizens' rights, interests and personal security, and fairness in the administration of justice and independence of the judiciary; (d) The right of universal and equal suffrage, as well as free voting procedures and periodic and free elections; (e) The right of political participation, including equal opportunity for all citizens to become candidates; (f) Transparent and accountable government institutions; (g) The right of citizens to choose their governmental system through constitutional or other democratic means; (h) The right to equal access to public service in one's own country.

Robert Dahl (Political Scientist) refers to a few criteria's to highlight as to what democracy provides opportunities for;[14] (a) Effective Participation (b) Equality in Voting (to eliminate the possibility of majority imposition of choices) (c) Enlightened Understanding (knowledge about policy and outcomes) (d) Control of the Agenda (policies must be open to change or deliberation) (e) Inclusion of adults.[15]

As evident from the above definitions, democracy is desirable to people for a variety of reasons; it acknowledges freedom, knowledge, participation, and wellbeing. The definitions signal towards the heart of a democracy as *the people, the rule, institutions, political freedom* and the *constitutional prescriptions*. The above definitions identify democracy as a political force that involves the governed and the governing, with enough strength provided to both for achieving an objective of social solidarity and political wellbeing.

Under the democratic set-up, the strength exercised over the governed by the governing is often characterized as the state power or state monopoly over legislation and violence for sustaining a system characterized by rights, rules, institutional mechanisms etc.[16] Brian Tamanaha in this regard states that in a democracy citizens create the laws under which they live (political liberty); government officials take actions against citizens in accordance with these laws (legal liberty). In the first respect they rule themselves; in the second they are ruled by the laws which they set for themselves. Citizens, therefore, are at no point subject to the rule of another individual.[17]

---

14. Robert Dahl, On Democracy 37 (2000).
15. To John Calhoun: "Democracy is not majority rule. Democracy is diffusion of power, representation of interests, and recognition of minorities. Aron: A democratic regime is one...in which the peaceful rivalry for the exercise of power exists constitutionally." Bobbio: "A democratic regime is first and foremost a set of procedural rules for arriving at collective decisions in a way which accommodates and facilitates the fullest possible participation of interested parties." *See* Robert Grey, *Democratic Theory and Post Communist Change*, Appendix 2.1 Selected Definitions of Democracy (1997).
16. Bhikhu Parekh, "The Modern Conception of Right and Its Marxist Critique" in Upendra Baxi (ed.) The Right to be Human 1-22 (1987).
17. Brian Tamanaha, On the Rule of Law: History, Politics, Theory 36 (2004).

However, in lieu of definitive features of democracy, what is open to deliberation is what constitutes *rule*, and the *people*?[18] "Does talk of the people simply imply some homogeneous will amongst all members of a given community, capable of expression in universally agreed political decisions?"[19] In context, how is *will of the people* expressed? What are the mechanisms to question democratic decision making? What standards ascertain the *legitimacy of democratic actions*? What are the moral and legal standards governing the actions of decisions makers?

The questions of this genre are multiple and complex.[20] As rightly expressed, "thinking of democracy as the exercise of political power where policies and the agents charged with implementing them are directly or indirectly determined by popular voting, leaves open the question of whether this is the best way or even a good way to motivate government."[21]

To Barry Holden, elections although are necessary to entail representatives of the people's interests, the essential characteristics of such persons is the manner of their selection,

---

18. Traditionally, the people in 'ancient Greece-only included a minority of the society among the decision makers. Aliens, slaves and women were excluded...Also a reference to people as the middle classes that were linked to property, membership of society and a consequent right to political participation...Since then, the whole task of democratic theory has been to enlarge the proportion of society involved in decision making.' *See* Barry Holden, *The Nature of Democracy* 14-15 (1974).
19. Jack Lively, Democracy 9 (1975).
20. A democratic set-up in terms of institutional mechanisms is one dimension of democracy. The expression 'formal democracy' is more so in reference to a political system that features regular fair elections, accountability, effective guarantees of freedom. However, the mere identification of democracy with the formal structural requirements is a faulty perception and must be disregarded. In the words of Maxwell Chibundu, "the legitimacy conferred by democracy flows not from its recognition of the ideal of embodiment of supreme and ultimate authority in the people... In particular democracy relies on periodic elections that are grounded on rationale deliberative processes rather than on haphazard assertions of power by the general populace." *See* Maxwell O. Chibundu, "Political Ideology as a Religion: The Idolatry of Democracy", Available at *http://ssrn.com/abstract=10223718*, 143 (2007).
21. Frank Cunningham, Theories of Democracy: A Critical Introduction 15 (2002).

not their behaviour or characteristics...[22] So does the definition of democracy include an understanding to what occurs after elections or whether it ascertains what qualifies as constructive or democratic behavior of the representatives? A consensus has thus emerged that the meaning that can be attributed to democracy is broader than the fact of appointment of the centres of governance. It assumes a holistic sanctity that must be capable of regulating itself through virtues unique to a functional democracy.

In this regard, Robert Dahl refers to the two ways of theorizing on democracy; the method of maximization, and the descriptive method. The former labeling the goal of democracy and the institutions necessary to achieve it, and the latter in reference to the varied practices of democracy that enable the identification of common characteristics and the conditions necessary for performance.[23] In order to discard a dysfunctional approach to democracy, it must necessarily be construed in light of the two classifications; democracy as norm and democracy in practice.

2. The Indian Democracy

The constitutive element of democracy in India- the Constitution of India, embodies a philosophy that can be summarized in three strands: "protecting and enhancing national unity and integrity, establishing the institutions and spirit of democracy, and fostering a social revolution to better the lot of the mass of Indians".[24]

---

22. Our understanding of democracy lies in the fact that elections are conceived to help bring about representation on several grounds. (a) The idea that election will ensure that only persons will be chosen who say that they will advance the interests of the electors, (b) That electors will ensure that representatives will behave in an appropriate way after elections. (c) That because of insecurity of tenure, a representative will refrain from promoting legislation that will adversely affect him when he loses his special status as a representative. *Supra* note 8 at 33.
23. Richard Krouse, Polyarchy and Participation: The Changing Democratic Theory of Robert Dahl, Vol. 14 (3) Polity 442 (1982).
24. Granville Austin, Working a Democratic Constitution: A History of the Indian Experience 16 (2003).

Speaking historically, under the colonial rule, the living conditions in India had reflected a great deal on the character of society the people wanted to build on attaining independence. On attaining its independence in 1947, India absorbed liberal ideals in the form of a parliamentary democratic structure, the directive principles of state policy, fundamental rights, the separation of powers of the three institutions, independence of the judiciary, universal suffrage, economic planning etc. The 'phase witnessed a transition from the pattern of revolutionary organization closely associated with communism,[25] towards a constructive democratic approach to social economic problems'.[26]

The establishment of democracy in India, a society characterized by myriad diversity in language, religion, ethnicity and economic interest was both a difficult and risky enterprise.[27] The liberal provisions in the form of democratic institutional structure of the legislature, executive and the judiciary, Part III-Fundamental Rights (hereinafter FR's), adult suffrage, and Part IV- Directive Principles of State Policy (hereinafter DPSP), were drafted in a manner conducive to reforms and growth. The attributes were seen as meaningful and absolutely essential to 'encroach uncontrolled exercise of power.'[28]

With the incorporation of several principles and rules, it was also acknowledged that liberal democracy by itself was not a flavor for change and progress. The Indian democracy had to be coupled with the zeal of the rational, powerful and right-minded citizenry of the society. For instance, the mechanism of "regular and effective elections, based on universal adult franchise, of all important offices and institutions at the central, regional, and local levels of the

25. The power of revolutionary Communism had a specific role to play. It not only aimed at changing the very essence of the state by introducing a fundamental social transformation from a capitalist state to that of a socialist. *See* Gennady Belov, What is the State?, 25 (1986).

26. Vishwanath Prasad Varma, Modern Indian Political Thought 471 (1967).

27. M. Manisha, Sharmila Deb (Eds.), Indian Democracy: Problems and Prospects, xii (2009).

28. *Supra* note 8 at 527.

political system, are referred to as the most significant factors to explain the success of India's democracy. These features also supported by an independent Election Commission, an independent judicial system that is pro-active in the defense of human rights and marginal social groups."[29]

Several endearing dimensions of the Indian democracy also rest upon the implicit norms-principles, which guide the conduct of institutions. A few of the notable features of the Indian democracy are spelled out as follows.

3. The Characteristics

The working of the Indian democracy over the years has reflected a path of pragmatism, with a few strands of conflicts and disagreements. All along, the democratic processes have been flexible and constantly guided by rules and fundamental principles.

Although the Preamble of the Indian Constitution highlights India as a democratic polity, the meaning of what is democracy can be found in the judicial interpretations of the apex court in India. More so, a discussion on democracy in India has primarily been directed by the Supreme Court, while interpreting significant laws and developments. The court has added greater meaning and dimensions to *what is democracy* in India or what are its characteristic features which must be preserved.

A few of the interpretations are highlighted in the cases below.

In *Mohinder Singh Gill* v. *Chief Election Commissioner*,[30] the court stated;

(Democracy) is a continual participative operation, not a cataclysmic, periodic exercise...Although the full flower of participative government rarely blossoms; the minimum credential of popular government is an appeal to the people after every term for the renewal of their confidence. So we

---

29. Subrata Misra, "Democracy's Resilience-Tradition, Modernity and Hybridity in India", March (2011). Available at *http://hir.harvard.edu/comment/reply/2802#comment-form* (Last visited 12-11-2011).

30. AIR 1978 SC 851: (1978) 1 SCC 405: (1978) 2 SCR 272.

have adult franchise and general elections as constitutional compulsions.

In *Secretary, Ministry of Information and Broadcasting* v. *Cricket Association of Bengal,*[31] the court stated that;

Democracy cannot exist unless all citizens have a right to participate in the affairs of the polity of the country. The right to participate in the affairs of the country is meaningless unless the citizens are well informed on all sides of the issues, in respect of which they are called upon to express their views. One-side information, disinformation, misinformation and non-information, all equally create an uninformed citizenry which makes democracy a farce when medium of information is monopolized either by a partisan central authority or by private individuals or oligarchy organizations...

In *G.V.K Industries* v. *Income Tax Officer,*[32] it was stated by the court that;

Our Constitution charges the various organs of the States with affirmative responsibilities of protecting the interests of, the welfare of and the security of the nation...The power of judicial review are granted in order to ensure that such power is being used within the bounds specified in the Constitution...The very essence of constitutionalism is also that no organ of the State may arrogate to itself powers beyond what is specified in the Constitution.

In *Nandini Sundar* v. *State of Chhattisgarh,*[33] the court stated that;

It is critical for the Government to recognize that dissent or expression of dissatisfaction is a positive feature of democracy, that unrest is often the only thing that actually puts pressure on the government to make things work and for the government to live up to its own promises.

---

31. (1995) 2 SCC 161: AIR 1995 SC 1236: 1995 AIR SCW 1856.
32. (2011) 4 SCC 36: 2011 AIR SCW 2047.
33. (2011) 7 SCC 547: AIR 2011 SC 2839: 2011 AIR SCW 4141.
    In response to a Writ Petition filed in 2007 alleging widespread violation of human rights in the State of Chhattisgarh on account of the on-going extremism/insurgency, and the counter-insurgency offensives launched by the State of Chhattisgarh.

In *Kesavananda Bharati* v. *State of Kerala,*[34] the Supreme Court of India held democracy to be a part of the *basic structure* under the Indian Constitution. Democracy, according to the Court, is a fundamental pillar of the Constitution that cannot be amended, repealed or abrogated. It is beyond the constituent power of the Parliament to tamper with the democratic features of the Constitution. Therefore, no constitutional amendment would be valid if it sought to destroy or deprive the Constitution of its democratic foundations.

In *Swaran Singh* v. *Standing Council,* [35] the court highlighted that;

This is the age of democracy and equality. No people or community should be today insulted or looked down upon, and nobody's feelings should be hurt. This is also the spirit of our Constitution and is part of its basic features.

In *People's Union for Civil Liberties* v. *Union of India* the court stated;[36]

---

34. (1973) 4 SCC 225: AIR 1973 SC 1461.

35. (2008) 12 SCR 132: AIR 2008 SC (Supp) 441.

In reference to the Scheduled Castes and Scheduled Tribes (Prevention of Atrocities Act), 1989, the so-called upper castes and OBCs should not use the word 'Chamar' when addressing a member of the Scheduled Caste, even if that person in fact belongs to the 'Chamar' caste, because use of such a word will hurt his feelings. In such a country like ours with so much diversity – so many religions, castes, ethnic and lingual groups, etc. – all communities and groups must be treated with respect, and no one should be looked down upon as an inferior. That is the only way we can keep our country united...we have to take into account the popular meaning of the word 'Chamar' which it has acquired by usage, and not the etymological meaning. If we go by the etymological meaning, we may frustrate the very object of the Act, and hence that would not be a correct manner of interpretation. (Para 22-23)

36. AIR 2003 SC 2363: 2003 AIR SCW 2353: (2003) 4 SCC 399.

The decision of the court was in reference to the power of the Election Commission of India under Article 324 of the Constitution of India. The Association for Democratic Reforms had filed a writ petition in 1994 before High Court of Delhi for direction to implement the recommendations made by Law Commission in its 170th report and to make necessary changes under rule 4 of Conduct of Elections Rules, 1961 regarding debarring a candidate from contesting election if charges have been framed against him/her by a Court in respect of certain offences and necessity for candidate to furnish details of criminal cases, if any, pending

Contd. on next page

The right to get information in democracy is recognized all throughout and it is natural right flowing from the concept of democracy...

In *People's Union for Civil Liberties* v. *Union of India*,[37] it was highlighted that;

In a democratic republic, it is the will of the people that is paramount and becomes the basis of the authority of the Government. The will is expressed in periodic elections based on universal adult suffrage held by means of secret ballot. It is through the ballot that the voter expresses his choice or preference for a candidate. Voting is formal expression of will or opinion by the person entitled to exercise the right on the subject or issue... The right to vote for the candidate of one's choice is of the essence of democratic polity. This right is recognized by our Constitution and it is given effect to in specific form by the Representation of the People Act. The Constituent Assembly debates reveal that the idea to treat the voting right as a fundamental right was dropped; nevertheless, it was decided to provide for it elsewhere in the Constitution.

The court added great dimensions to the freedom of expression and the right to vote by referring to it as a constitutional right. Freedom of voting as distinct from right to vote is thus a species of freedom of expression and

---

Contd. from previous page

against him. It also suggested that true and correct statement of assets owned by the candidate should also be disclosed. The issue before the Supreme Court was whether Election Commission is empowered to issue directions as ordered by High Court and whether a citizen has right to get relevant information about prospective candidates.

Also in *Superintendent of Police* v. *R. Karthikeyan*, AIR 2012 Mad 84, the High Court of Madras stated, India has adopted a democratic form of Government and no democratic Government can survive without accountability and the basic postulate of accountability is that the people should have information about the functioning of the Government. It is only when the people know how the Government is functioning, they can fulfill the role which democracy assigned to them and make democracy a really effective participatory democracy. Right to information is basic to any democracy. A vibrant citizenry is a prerequisite for survival of democratic society and governance...

37. AIR 2003 SC 2363: 2003 AIR SCW 2353: (2003) 4 SCC 399.

therefore carries with it the auxiliary and complementary rights such as right to secure information about the candidate which are conducive to the freedom.[38]

In the more recent case of *Sahara India Real Estate Corp. Ltd.* v. *Securities and Exchange Board,*[39] the court stated that;

It must not be forgotten that no single value, no matter exalted, can bear the full burden of upholding a democratic system of government. Underlying our Constitutional system are a number of important values, all of which help to guarantee our liberties, but in ways which sometimes conflict. Under our Constitution, probably, no values are absolute. All important values, therefore, must be qualified and balanced against, other important, and often competing, values.

In *Minerva Mills Ltd.* v. *Union of India,*[40] Bhagwati, J. said "judicial review is an integral part of our constitutional system and without it, there will be no government of laws and the rule of law would become a teasing illusion and a promise of unreality. I am of the view that if there is one feature of our Constitution which, more than any other, is basic and fundamental to the maintenance of democracy and the rule of law, it is the power of judicial review..."

In light of the various decisions of the court, a few features or objectives of the Indian democracy can be carved out;

- To uphold the Constitution and the law without fear or favour.
- Adult franchise and general elections.
- Equality in law.
- Dissent or expression of dissatisfaction.
- The power of judicial review.
- The right to information.
- The rule of law.
- The right to vote.
- The inclusion of citizens in the decision making processes of the State.

---

38. *Ibid.*
39. (2012) 8 SCALE 541.
40. AIR 1980 SC 1789: (1980) 3 SCC 625: 1980 Ker LT 573.

It is thus evident that democracy in India has expanded beyond the electoral process in order to accommodate newer connotations related to institutional behavior and aspects of social justice.

4. The Functional Parameters

In terms of quality, the Indian democracy has added stronger mechanisms for ensuring credibility and responsiveness of institutions. In other words, it has been functional and dynamic. The following are a few functional dimensions.

4.1 Political Freedom and Representative Democracy

The ties between democracy and the citizens have assumed great importance in India. The democratic culture has acknowledged both the personal entitlement of people to try to persuade and the advantage of inserting all potentially relevant considerations into decision making.[41]

More specifically, the concept of political representation has become the most important facet of contemporary democratic theory and practice in India. Representation as an ideal is referred to "as crucial in constituting democratic practices...in addition democratic theorists are increasingly appreciating the contributions of representation to the formation of public opinion and judgment, as well at its role in constituting multiple pathways of social influence within and often against the state."[42] It is that a 'regulatory rights-enforcement approach to the principle of general adult suffrage is meaningless. It must be replaced by an *organizational* approach. Instead of granting its subjects an enforceable right to vote the state must organize and operate an actual system of elections.[43] Voting does not by itself

---

41. Balmiki Prasad Singh, "The Future of Democracy", Vol L No. 35 *Mainstream* 16 (August 2012).
42. Nadia Urbinati and Mark Warren, "The Concept of Representation in Contemporary Democratic Theory", Vol. 11: 387 Annual Review of Political Science 388 (2008).
43. Sack Peter, "Legal Technology and Quest for Fraternity: Reflections on Preamble of Indian Constitution" 32:3 Journal of the Indian Law Institute 304 (1990).

involve empowerment and effective participation. In other words, "an election in which the electorate can only choose or reject a single list of candidates is not democratic on the sense of the word..."[44]

In the context of India, democracy for several years been associated with the electoral process, for which the right to vote has cautiously been defined and interpreted to maintain its essence. However, democracy today also implies the requirement for high caliber of politicians, the availability of choices among rival political parties and leaders, a consensus among them on overall direction of national policy, and specifically political leadership which is accountable to the people.[45]

With the expanding horizon of the Indian democracy, there are visible attempts at ensuring congruence of "people's interest and legislative policy" by mechanisms such as "referendum" and "initiative."[46] In terms of meaning, the citizen initiated referendum is essentially an instrument whereby citizens, by a direct vote, can decide whether a legislation passed by Parliament should be accepted or repealed...The citizen initiated referendum provides a structural mechanism, whereby people's protests and opposition can have a direct impact on policy. The mechanism can also be utilized to bring forth a new legislation or constitutional amendment, whereby putting the proposal on the political agenda.[47]

In order to innovate and flourish, the Indian democracy must be capable of re-defining the nature of politics and

44. *Supra* note 8 at 9.

45. *Supra* note 42 at 17.

46. Prashant Bhushan, Marlena, Atishi, "Initiatives and Referendums: The Next Step in Indian Democracy", Vol. XLVII No. 34 Economic and Political Weekly 34 (August 2012).

The authors make specific reference to incidents in India which reflected a sense of people's participation and consultation having impact on decision making and policy.

47. *Ibid.*

The authors also discuss the increasing global acceptance of such means of representative democracy. Referring to the case in Switzerland (2000), wherein a Electricity Market Law for liberalization and deregulation of the electricity market was rejected for non-acceptance from the citizens.

reforms and not be tied to any given definition. In addition, the reforms must give effect to the status of individuals as autonomous rights-bearers, entitled to play a role in determining both their rights as citizens and the political rules they have to play by.[48]

One such endeavor is evident in the State of Gujarat, wherein the government passed the Gujarat Local Authority Law (Amendment) Bill in 2009, making voting compulsory in elections to local self government bodies such as Municipalities and Panchayats. The Statement of Objects and Reasons of the Gujarat Bill are as follows:—

It is observed that due to low turnout of voters to discharge their duty by exercising their right to vote, the true spirit of the will of the people is not reflected in the electoral mandate…

In this regard, a survey on 260 subjects of all socio-economic and educational backgrounds, conducted by the Research Foundation for Governance in India (Analysis of Compulsory Voting in Gujarat) indicates the following facts; (a) Voter engagement in local politics is a problem. It prejudicially affects political accountability and responsibility towards political mandates. (b) Reasons for not voting include- disinterest in politics, mark of protest against the government, lack of awareness etc.

The Research Foundation puts forth substantial arguments in favor and against compulsory voting. (a) In Favor- Compulsory voting will enable people to be aware of their local bodies. (b) Not in Favor- compulsory voting is no guarantee for efficient governance. Also, is the State equipped to punish each and every person who does not perform his/her civic duty? For a few, the scheme is also expressed as coercive and unreasonable for the citizens,[49]

---

48. Richard Bellamy, Constitutionalism and Democracy xi (2006).
49. 'Other countries that go by compulsory voting are Australia, Peru etc. In the former voters may either explain their reasons for not voting, or pay fine. In Peru, the citizens must carry proof of their voting to avail social services provided by the State'. *See* Report of Research Foundation for Governance in India. Available at *http://www.rfgindia.org/publications/Analysis%20of%20Compulsory%20Voting%20in%20Gujarat.pdf* (Last visited 8-11-2011).

for they require a competent set of candidates, than a stick beating law on political reforms. A survey conducted by the HT-CNN IBN confirmed the public demand for honest and accountable leadership. As expressed; "if one were to confuse faith in democracy with faith in politicians, the results of our survey would be rather depressing...One (such) reform proposed recently was the *right to recall.*"[50]

As evident, the Indian legal discourse is certainly paving way for political reforms. One may expect significant changes pertaining to the right to vote, the right to negative vote, the right to recall or even compulsory voting.[51]

4.2 Public Interest Litigation

Public Interest Litigation (PIL) has been the greatest contribution by the Indian courts to understanding the functional contours of the Indian democracy.

According to S.P. Sathe, PIL emerged and grew when the court liberalized its procedure with a view to facilitating access to the common man and increasing public participation in the judicial process as a means to control other bodies of government. This required radical change in the traditional paradigm of the judicial process. The traditional legal theory of judicial process envisioned a passive role for the courts. It postulated: (1) The courts merely found the law or interpreted it, but did not make it; (2) if the courts made the law, they did so only to fill in the gaps left by statute, and then only to the extent necessary for the disposal of the matter; (3) a court will not decide a question of law unless the decision is absolutely necessary for the disposal of the matter before

50. Abhijit Patnaik, "Will the Honest Netas, Please Stand Up", The Hindustan Times at 13 (28th November, 2011).

51. In *N.P. Ponnuswami* v. *Returning Officer, Namakkal Constituency*, (1952) SCR 218 the court observed that the right to vote or stand as a candidate for election was not a civil right but a creature of statute or special law and must be subject to the limitations imposed by it. In *Jyoti Basu* v. *Debi Ghosal*, (1982) 1 SCC 691: 1982 (1) SCJ 245 the court held that "a right to elect, though fundamental to democracy... neither a fundamental right nor a common law right. It is pure and simple, a statutory right." Also *see* in *Anukul Chandra Pradhan* v. *Union of India*, (1997) 6 SCC 1; *Union of India* v. *Association for Democratic Reforms*, (2002) 5 SCC 294: AIR 2002 SC 2112: 2002 AIR SCW 2186; *PUCL* v. *Union of India*, (2003) 4 SCC 399: AIR 2003 SC 2363: 2003 AIR SCW 2353.

it; (4) after a matter is dealt with by a court and it has given its decision, such a decision is binding on the parties and the same matter cannot be raised again before the same court or a court of concurrent jurisdiction; (5) only a person who has suffered an injury or whose right is violated can approach the Court and initiate the judicial process; and (6) a person who has a cause of action and *locus standi* to raise an issue before a court of law must do so within a prescribed time limit provided by law.[52]

PIL in India has been a part of the constitutional litigation by the independent judiciary armed with the power of judicial review. The power to enforce the Fundamental Rights is conferred on both the Supreme Court and the High Courts. The courts can test not only the validity of laws and executive actions but also of constitutional amendments. It has the final say on the interpretation of the Constitution and its orders, supported with the power to punish for contempt, and can reach everyone throughout the territory of the country.[53]

Since its inception, the Supreme Court has delivered judgments of far-reaching importance involving not only adjudication of disputes but also determination of public policies and establishment of rule of law and constitutionalism.

In the case of *S.P. Gupta* v. *Union of India*,[54] the Supreme Court of India held that;

> Where a legal wrong or a legal injury is caused to a person or to a determinate class of persons by reason of violation of any constitutional or legal right . . . and such person or determinate class of persons is by reasons of poverty, helplessness, or disability or socially or economically disadvantaged position, unable

52. S.P. Sathe, "Judicial Activism: The Indian Experience", Vol. 6: 29 Journal of Law and Policy 63-64 (2001).
53. Surya Deva, "Public Interest Litigation in India: A Critical Review", Issue 1 Civil Justice Quarterly 23 (2009).
54. AIR 1982 SC 149: 1982 Raj LR 389: (1981) Supp SCC 87 (210); *See* also *PUDR* v. *Union of India*, AIR 1982 SC 1473: (1982) 2 SCC 494: (1982) 2 SCWR 202; *Bandhua Mukti Morcha* v. *Union of India*, AIR 1984 SC 802: (1984) 3 SCC 161: 1984 Lab IC 560.

to approach the Court for any relief, any member of the public can maintain an application for an appropriate direction, order or writ.

In *Sheela Barse* v. *Union of India*,[55] the Supreme Court was of the view that the court is not merely a passive, disinterested umpire or onlooker, but has a more dynamic and positive role with the responsibility of organizing of the proceedings, moulding the relief and, equally important, is supervising the implementation thereof.

In *Guruvayoor Devaswom Managing Committee* v. *C.K. Rajan*,[56] the court made known few governing principles of PIL. (a) The court in exercise of powers under article 32 and 226 of the Constitution of India can entertain a petition filed by any interested person in the welfare of the people who are not in position to knock the doors of the court. (b) issues of public importance, enforcement of fundamental rights of a larger number of public *vis-à-vis* the constitutional duties and functions of the State, if raised, the court can treat a letter or telegram as a PIL upon relaxing procedural laws as also the law relating to pleadings. (c) The dispute between two warring groups purely in the realm of private law would not be allowed to be agitated as public interest litigation. (d) The court in special situations may appoint a commission, or other bodies for the purpose of investigating into the allegations and finding out facts...(e) ordinarily the High Court should not entertain a writ petition by way of PIL questioning constitutionality or validity of a statute or a statutory rule.

Tracing the development of PIL in India, "in the first phase which began in the late 1970s and continued through the 1980's the PIL cases were generally filed by public-spirited persons (lawyers, journalists, social activists or academics). Most of the cases related to the rights of disadvantaged sections of society such as child labors, bonded laborers, prisoners, mentally challenged persons, pavement dwellers, and women. The relief was sought against the action or inaction on the part of executive agencies resulting in

55. AIR 1988 SC 2211: JT 1988 (3) SC 765: (1988) 4 SCC 226.
56. (2003) 7 SCC 546: AIR 2004 SC 561: 2003 AIR SCW 6039.

violations of Fundamental Rights under the Constitution. Post 1990's, in comparison to the first phase, the filing of PIL cases became more institutionalized in that several specialized NGOs and lawyers started bringing matters of public interest to the courts on a much regular basis. The breadth of issues raised in PIL also expanded tremendously from the protection of environment to corruption-free administration, right to education, sexual harassment at the workplace, relocation of industries, rule of law, good governance, and the general accountability of the Government... the third phase the current phase, which began with the 21st century is a period in which anyone could file a PIL for almost anything...From the judiciary's point of view, one could argue that it is time for judicial introspection and for reviewing what courts tried to achieve through PIL.[57]

In order to maintain the credibility of PIL as an instrument for the access of justice several attempts have been made time and again.[58] In this regard, Mehta argues that to the extent

57. Surya Deva, "Public Interest Litigation in India: A Critical Review", Issue 1 Civil Justice Quarterly 27-29 (2009).

58. An attempt to curb the misuse of the PIL was made, though not strictly on the part of the Government, in 1996 when a private member Bill was introduced in the Rajya Sabha, the Upper House of the Indian Parliament. The Public Interest Litigation (Regulation) Bill had proposed that petitioners filing frivolous PIL cases should be "put behind bars and pay the damages". However, the Bill which raised concerns of interfering with judicial independence could not receive the support of all political parties. As the Bill lapsed, this attempt to control the misuse of PIL failed. In addition, the Supreme Court has compiled a set of "Guidelines to be Followed for Entertaining Letters/Petitions Received by it as PIL". The Guidelines, which were based on the full-court decision of December 1, 1988, have been modified on the orders/directions of the Chief Justice of India in 1993 and 2003. The Guidelines provide that ordinarily letter/petitions falling under one of the following 10 categories will be entertained as PIL: bonded labour matters, neglected children, non-payment of minimum wages, petitions from jails complaining of harassment, death in jail, speedy trial as a fundamental right, etc., petitions against police for refusing to register a case, harassment by police and death in police custody, petitions against atrocities on women, in particular harassment of bride, bride-burning, rape, murder, kidnapping, etc. petitions complaining harassment or torture of persons belonging to scheduled caste and scheduled tribes, petitions pertaining to environmental pollution, disturbance of ecological balance, drugs,

Contd. on next page

rule of law signals for making available a forum of appeals, one can argue the Supreme Court of India has done a decent job.

In reference to PIL, there has also been a margin of criticism. As often stated, "the unelected judges have effectively replaced the notion of the separation of powers among three governmental branches with a unitarian claim of formal judicial supremacy. The concept of the rule of law is supposed to legitimate this claim, but whether judicial supremacy either as such or as exercised by the Indian Supreme Court actually upholds the rule of law remains an open question."[59] The competing claims in support and against the exercise of power of the courts have further led to developments *vis-à-vis* judicial power and policy making.

The following are a few notable decisions in PIL:

> In *People's Union for Democratic Rights* v. *Union of India,*[60] a letter addressed to the Supreme Court was treated as a writ petition to look into the blatant violations of labour law in India while undertaking construction works for the Asian Games. The petitioners claimed that the various authorities to whom the execution of the different projects was entrusted engaged contractors for the purpose of carrying out the construction work of the projects and they were registered as principal employers under section 7 of the Contract Labour (Regulation and Abolition) Act, 1970. These contractors engaged workers through Jamadars who brought them from different parts of India particularly the States of Rajasthan, Uttar Pradesh and Orissa and paid to these

Contd. from previous page

food adulteration, maintenance of heritage and culture, antiques, forest and wildlife and other matters of public importance, petitions from riot-victims and family pensions. The PIL Cell has been entrusted the task of screening letters/petitions as per these Guidelines and then placing them before a judge to be nominated by the Chief Justice of India. See *Id* at 39.

59. Pratap Bhanu Mehta, "The Rise of Judicial Sovereignty", Vol. 18:2 Journal of Democracy 72 (April 2007).

60. AIR 1982 SC 1473: (1982) 2 SCC 494: (1982) 2 SCWR 202.

Jamadars the minimum wage of Rs. 9.25 per day per worker and not to the workmen direct. The Jamadars deducted Rupee one per day per worker as their commission and then paid the workers. There was also violation of Contract Labour (Regulations and Abolition) Act, 1970, which was leading to exploitation and unhealthy conditions of work.

The court stated- public interest litigation which is strategic arm of the legal aid movement and which is intended to bring justice within the reach of the poor masses, who constitute the low visibility area of humanity, is a totally different kind of litigation from the ordinary traditional litigation which is essentially of an adversary character where there is a dispute between two litigating parties, one making claim or seeking relief against the other and that other opposing such claim or resisting such relief. Public interest litigation is brought before the court not for the purpose of enforcing the right of one individual against another as happens in the case of ordinary litigation, but it is intended to promote and indicate public interest which demands that violations of constitutional or legal rights of large number of people who are poor, ignorant or in a socially or economically disadvantaged position should not go unnoticed and unredressed... Public interest litigation is essentially a cooperative or collaborative effort on the part of the petitioner, the State or public authority and the Court to secure observance of the constitutional or legal rights, benefits and privileges conferred upon the vulnerable sections of the community and to reach social justice to them. The court in this regard directed the Delhi Administration to ensure that wages were to be paid directly from the contractors to the workers, with no commissions being deducted by the Jamadars.

In *Bachpan Bachao Andolan* v. *Union of India*,[61] the petition was filed in public interest under article 32 of the Constitution in the wake of serious violations and abuse of children who were forcefully detained in circuses, in many instances, without any access to their families under extreme inhuman

61. AIR 2011 SC 3361: 2011 AIR SCW 5169: (2011) 5 SCC 1.

conditions. As reported, there were instances of sexual abuse on a daily basis, physical abuse as well as emotional abuse. The children are deprived of basic human needs – food and water. The petitioner is engaged in a social movement for the emancipation of children in exploitative labour, bondage and servitude. Bachpan Bachao Andolan has been able to liberate thousands of children with the help of the judiciary and the executive as well as through persuasion, social mobilization and education. The petitioner indicated that for the first time the petitioner came to know about the plight of children in Indian circuses way back in 1996. At that time, the petitioner had rescued 18 girls from a circus performing in Vidisha District of Madhya Pradesh. This was possible after a complaint made by a 12-year-old girl, who managed to escape from the circus premises. Her complaint was that she and several other Nepalese girls had been trafficked and forced to stay and perform in the circus where they were being sexually abused and were kept in most inhuman conditions; also stating, that there are no labour or any welfare laws, which protect the rights of these children. Children are frequently physically, emotionally and sexually abused in these places. The most appalling aspect is that there is no direct legislation, which is vested with powers to deal with the problems of the children who are trafficked into these circuses. The Police, Labour Department or any other State Agency is not prepared to deal with the issue of trafficking of girls from Nepal holding them in bondage and unlawful confinement. There is perpetual sexual harassment, violation of the Juvenile Justice Act and all International treaties and Conventions related to Human Rights and Child Rights where India is a signatory.

In this order we are limiting our directions regarding children working in the Indian Circuses. Consequently, the court directed;

(i) In order to implement the fundamental right of the children under article 21A it is imperative that the Central Government must issue suitable notifications prohibiting the employment of children in circuses within two months from today.

(ii) The respondents are directed to conduct simultaneous raids in all the circuses to liberate the children and check the violation of fundamental rights of the children. The rescued children be kept in the Care and Protective Homes till they attain the age of 18 years.

(iii) The respondents are also directed to talk to the parents of the children and in case they are willing to take their children back to their homes, they may be directed to do so after proper verification.

(iv) The respondents are directed to frame proper scheme of rehabilitation of rescued children from circuses.

(v) We direct the Secretary of Ministry of Human Resource Development, Department of Women and Child Development to file a comprehensive affidavit of compliance within ten weeks.

In *Azad Rickshaw Pullers Union* v. *State of Punjab*,[62] the Punjab Cycle Rickshaw, or Regulation of Rickshaws Act of 1975 was in question, which provided that licenses to ply rickshaws could be given only to those owners who run the rickshaws. Licenses could not be given to those who owned the rickshaw but rented them to other persons. The Act threatened the unemployment of a number of rickshaw pullers who did not own their rickshaws, and threatened to leave many rickshaws owned by the non-driving owners idle. The Act was struck down and a scheme was provided by the court whereby the rickshaw pullers could apply for loans to the Punjab National Bank to acquire the rickshaws.

In *Centre for PIL* v. *Union of India*,[63] the Supreme Court allowed two writ petitions challenging the legality of the appointment of P.J. Thomas as Central Vigilance Commissioner on the basis of the recommendation of the high powered committee (HPC) constituted under the proviso to section 4(1) of the Central Vigilance Commission Act, 2003. The apex court reiterated the settled position that though the Government was not accountable to the Courts in respect of

62. AIR 1981 SC 14: 1981 SC Cri R 43: (1981) 1 SCR 366.

63. (2011) 3 SCALE 148: AIR 2011 SC 1267: 2011 AIR SCW 1690.

policy decisions, it was accountable for the legality of such decisions. If a duty was cast under the proviso to section 4(1) of the said Act on the HPC to recommend to the President the name of the selected candidate, the integrity of that decision making process had to ensure that the powers were exercised for the purposes and in the manner envisaged by the said Act, otherwise such recommendation will have no existence in the eye of law.

The apex court, while disposing of the petition passed the several directions, including the following:

(1) In cases of difference of opinion amongst the members of the HPC, the dissenting member of the committee should give reasons for the dissent and if the majority disagrees with the dissent, the majority shall give reasons for overruling the dissent as to bring fairness-in-action.

(2) All the civil servants and other persons empanelled should be outstanding civil servants or persons of impeccable integrity.

(3) The empanelment should be carried out on the basis of rational criteria, which would have to be reflected by recording of reasons and/or noting akin to reasons by the empanelling authority.

(4) The selection committee should adopt a fair and transparent process of consideration of the empanelled officers.

4.3 Civil Society

The expansion of democracy has to a great extent been a resultant of a vigilant civil society in India.[64] Constitutional experts refer to this change as an evolution of democracy from being "vote-centric to "talk-centric".[65] In this regard, John Dryzeck (Scholar) refers to it as deliberative turn in democratic theory. A more deliberative democracy would bring greater benefits for the society at large as well as the

64. *See* Simon Chesterman, Michael Ignatieff and Ramesh Thakur (Eds.), Making States Work: State Failure and the Crisis of Governance (2005).
65. Will Kymlicka, Contemporary Political Philosophy: An Introduction 290 (2002).

groups within. The credit for expecting such results lies in the dynamism of constitutionalism.

In specific, Constitutionalism provides for structures, forms, and apparatuses of governance and modes of legitimization of power. But constitutionalism is not all about governance; it also provides contested sites for ideas and practices concerning justice, rights, development, and individual associational autonomy. Constitutionalism provides narratives of both rule and resistance.[66]

Deliberative democracy satisfies the following essentials[67]:

(a) The reason giving requirement that affirms the need to justify decisions made by citizens and their representatives. Deliberative democracy also makes room for many other forms of decision-making (including bargaining among groups, and secret operations ordered by executives), as long as the use of these forms themselves is justified at some point in a deliberative process. Its first and most important characteristic, then, is its *reason-giving* requirement.

(b) Mutual Respect – that implies the moral basis for this reason-giving process satisfies that persons should be treated not merely as objects of legislation, as passive subjects to be ruled, but as autonomous agents who take part in the governance of their own society, directly or through their representatives. In deliberative democracy an important way these agents take part is by presenting and responding to reasons, or by demanding that their representatives do so, with the aim of justifying the laws under which they must live together.[68]

The deliberative turn in democracy also explains the increasing presence of civil society action within political

66. Prabhakar Singh, "Constitutionalism in International Law during the Times of Globalization: A Sociological Appraisal", Indian Yearbook of International Law and Policy 237 (2009).

67. Amy Gutmann, Dennis Thompson, Why Deliberative Democracy 3 (2004).

68. *Supra* note 71 at 4.

and social spheres. The task of communicating is often associated with the civil society; recognized as a functional and responsive entity. The civil society is closely associated with 'the masses', a 'popular upsurge', 'movement from below', it is capable of varied and relative interpretations. As advocated, the civil society is responsible for 'fundamentally reducing the role of politics in society by expanding free markets and individual liberty, or a missing link in the success of social democracy.'[69] The notion of civil society brings to life the concept of 'deliberative democracy', 'participatory process' and a 'talk-centric system of laws'.[70]

69. Micheal Edwards, "Civil Society", Encyclopedia of Education (2005). Available at *http://www.infed.org/association/civil_society.htm* (Last visited 11-8-2011).

70. In reference to the South African case of *Minister of Health* v. *Treatment Action Campaign,* (2002) on social rights, the impact of social movements can be drawn. The Treatment Action Campaign (TAC), a social movement led the long struggle to push the South African government to provide life-saving anti-retroviral treatment to hundreds of thousands of HIV/AIDS sufferers in the nation's public healthcare system. It prevailed despite the obdurate resistance of the nation's President and most of the African National Congress leadership. TAC made the polity and not the courts its chief sphere for rights claims. It raised broad politico-constitutional claims and pursued broad programmatic changes and institutional innovations outside the courts, while pursuing a narrow legal-constitutional strategy. TAC built up hundreds of local branches and a poor people's social movement among HIV/AIDS sufferers. Treatment Literacy combined with rights education enabled poor South Africans with HIV/AIDS to participate in and make demands on their own treatment and care. TAC also helped shape the Constitutional Court's own understanding of the judicial role in adjudicating and realizing constitutional social rights by collaborating with civil society and state actors. TAC's chief sphere for rights claims has been the polity, coalition-building, policy proposals and political initiatives, publicity and lobbying campaigns. All these activities have done more good than the litigation strategy. *See* William E. Forbath, "*Realizing a Constitutional Social Right Cultural Transformation, Deep Institutional Reform, and the Roles of Advocacy and Adjudication*" Available at http://ssrn.com/abstract=1292879 (Last visited 5-8-2011).

Also, in the 1990's the Chikla Bachao Andolan movement in India, a movement of fishermen, who resisted the Integrated Shrimp Farm Project (ISFP) a joint venture between the Tata Iron and Steel Company (TISCO, a private sector firm) and the State Government of Orissa for prawn cultivation and export. The project threatened the livelihood of the fishing communities living around the lake, people who for generations had farmed the lake with age-old knowledge of ecology and resource sustainability. The collective resistance put up by otherwise-competing

Contd. on next page

In terms of functionality, civil society enhances deliberation and aims at rectifying errors in governance.[71] It fills in the gaps that may emerge within the electoral apparatus.[72] With the need for civil action and participation, doubts are often raised as to the relationship of civil society with the state, functionality and impact it may have on the process of law.[73] The growing popularity of the public space "highlights the ambiguity of the term 'civil society..."[74] For that very reason, democratic theory explores the changing patterns of democratic culture *vis-à-vis* civil society.

Contd. from previous page

groups, desperate voices within the rural communities and student groups and other community organizations led to significant results in favour of the fisherman. The movement raised important questions about government policy formulation, historical resource use and control, and issues of equity and access of the marginalized versus the power elites. *See* Rajesh Tandon and Ranjita Mohanty, "Does Civil Society Matter: Governance in Contemporary India", 7:2 February, The International Journal on Not for Profit Law (2005).

71. Historically, from the democratic transitions of the late 1980s and early 1990s and the end of the Cold War, democracy promotion became a key element of foreign policy and development assistance. From the 1980s, 'civil public had dramatically transformed itself into the political public, asserting its right not only to hold state power accountable, but its right to dismiss states that failed to respond to the political aspirations of their people... notably people had the competence to chart out a political discourse on the kind of polity they wanted to live in.' The phase with the decline of the Cold War added momentum for the transition of voluntary groups within the political landscape. In the history of Africa, Latin America, and in other parts of South Asia the widespread criticism of representative institutions has made it easier for the public space to be utilized. For instance, National Endowment for Democracy claims to be building civil society in Venezuela but is only supporting groups mobilized against President Hugo Chavez, or politicians on both sides of the Atlantic continue to be engaged in a forced march to civil society in the Middle East, it is clear that the ways in which these ideas are interpreted does have a real impact on the lives of real people in the here and the now. Neera Chandokhe, "The Civil and the Political in the Society: The Case of India" in Peter Burnell and Peter Calvert, "Civil Society in Democratization" 143 (2004).
72. Purvi Dass, "Global Democratic Governance: Role of Civil Society Organizations", Available at http://www.civicus.org/pg/world-democracy-day/1127-global-democratic-governance—role-of-global-civil-society-organisations (Last visited 15-7-2011).
73. *Supra* note 71 at 143.
74. Peter Burnell and Peter Calvert, Civil Society in Democratization 7 (2004).

As discussed, the experiences in India indicate that civil society hysteria is closely associated with the fact of crisis of the developmental state.[75] The civil society is the platform for deliberation, and inevitably crucial to democracy, for addressing exclusion or suppression within the political space. Recent literature "outlines a model of 'associational democracy' in which state and civil society organizations are both part of a single, new regulatory framework that transforms both."[76] Deliberation plays an important role in the model of governance.[77] 'The associational democratic project proceeds in three steps. With the first, it advocates devolution of public policy prerogatives to local secondary associations. Secondary associations are civil society organizations, that is, social groups intermediate between the economy and the formal institutions of the state.[78]

The increasing presence of civil society actions, coupled with the demands for political inclusiveness highlight that the essential facet of any right discourse in a democracy has to be linked to the process of socialization and deliberation, which is an ongoing process.

In India, the success of democracy has to be ascertained in reference to how constructively it permits and responds towards the establishment of a social relation between the

75. Jean-François Bayart links 'civil society' with the notion of antagonism between state and society, restricting the term to those social organizations which embody 'society in its relations with the state insofar as it is in confrontation with the state...Hugh Roberts equates civil society with 'political society' in the sense of a particular relationship between state and society based on the principles of citizenship, rights, representation and the rule of law." *Ibid* at 9.
76. Lucio Baccaro, "Civil Society meets the State: A Model of Associational Democracy", International Labour Organization- International Institute for Labour Studies, Discussion Paper 138 (2002).
77. The requirements for deliberation are extremely stringent. According to Habermas communicative action (deliberation) requires truthfulness, moral appropriateness, and sincerity of communication. Also, deliberation takes place in an "ideal speech situation" in which power differences are levelled. According to Rawls 1993 (49), participants in deliberation are "reasonable," that is, "ready to propose principles and standards as fair terms of cooperation and to abide by them willingly, given the assurance that others will likewise do so. *Id* at 11.
78. *Id* at 4.

people. First and foremost democratic efficiency can be seen in terms of ability and opportunity to participate in effective deliberation on part of those subject to collective decisions. Deliberation now is understood to be the essence of democracy, much more than constitutional rights, electoral process, self government etc. Civil society in particular offers the opportunity to deliberate and operates essentially as an 'independent domain,'[79] and in a non-coercive fashion.[80]

On a practical note, civil society needs a healthy and encouraging environment to perform and excel.[81] The state must allow for a platform through which the needs of the people can be put forth and discussed.[82] The deliberative turn of Indian democracy has had a meaningful bearing on law and rights. With an increase in demand for good governance and people's participation, the right to information been defended and realized within statutory or legal bounds. The citizens and the civil society have utilized the right to know for ensuring meaningful participation and transparency in public matter.

The global pursuit towards realizing the right to information has long been active and impressive. In 2004, the UN Special Rapporteur on Freedom of Expression stated that "recognizing the fundamental importance of access to information to democratic participation, to holding governments accountable and to controlling corruption, as well as to personal dignity and business efficiency, we declare that the right to access information held by public authorities is a fundamental human right which should be given effect at the national level through comprehensive legislation...establishing a presumption that

---

79. Orly Lobel, "The Paradox of Extra-Legal Activism: Critical Legal Consciousness and Transformative Politics", Vol. 120 Harvard Law Review (2007).
80. John Dryzek, Deliberative Democracy and Beyond: Liberals, Critiques, Contestations 1 (2002).
81 *Ibid.*
82 Pranab Bardhan, "Our Self Righteous Civil Society", XLVI Vol. No. 29 Economic and Political Weekly 18 (July 2011).

all information is accessible subject only to a narrow system of exceptions".[83]

The Commonwealth Human Rights Initiative identifies the two features of the right to information as; (a) The right of the public to request access to information and the corresponding duty on the government to meet the request, unless specific, defined exemptions apply; (b) The duty of the government to proactively provide certain key information, even in the absence of a request. In addition, the lack of information undermines the functioning of a representative democracy, information may enable citizens to participate in the making and implementation of policies, access to information may also function as an anti-corruption tool.[84]

In 2012 in the case of *Namit Sharma* v. *Union of India*,[85] the Supreme Court of India stated that despite the absence of any express mention of the word 'information' in our Constitution

---

83 Special Rapporteur on the Promotion and Protection of Right to Freedom of Opinion and Expression. Available at http://www.ohchr.org/EN/Issues/FreedomOpinion/Pages/OpinionIndex.aspx.

84. The Commonwealth Human Rights Initiative, "The Right to Information: Strengthening Democracy and Participation", Available at http://www.humanrightsinitiative.org/programs/ai/rti/articles/RTI%20Paper%20-%202005%20Ombuds%20Conf.pdf (Last visited 2-10-2012).

The Human Rights Initiative also discussed the use of right to information in Delhi to that almost 90% of the food meant to be distributed to poor people under the Indian Public Distribution System (PDS), was being siphoned off by corrupt ration dealers. The NGO, named Parivartan, obtained the sales registers and stock registers of some ration dealers in October 2003 using the Delhi Right to Information Act. The records related to distribution of wheat, rice and kerosene during June 2003. The information was disseminated to supposed recipients of rations, who were aghast to see that rations had been siphoned off in their names. The ration dealers had told PDS beneficiaries that they were not receiving stocks from the government, while selling the rations on the black market. Using the records obtained under the Right to Information Act and cross-checking it against the ration cards kept by PDS beneficiaries, Parivartanís research revealed that during the month of June, out of a total of 182 families interviewed, 142 families did not receive a single grain of wheat (only 595kg of 4650kg was distributed) and 167 families did not receive a single grain of rice (only 110kg of 1820kg was distributed). With their documents in hand, Parivartan was able to confront ration dealers with proof of their corrupt practices. Parivartan has since reported that of 82 families they spoke with in follow-up interviews, all were now getting their full entitlements at correct prices.

85. Writ Petition Civil No. 210 of 2012.

under article 19(1)(a), this right has stood incorporated therein by the interpretative process by this Court laying the unequivocal statement of law by this Court that there was a definite right to information of the citizens of this country. Earlier the Supreme Court spelt out with clarity the right to information as a right inbuilt in the constitutional framework, though there existed no provision giving this right in absolute terms or otherwise.

The RTI Act in India has also been a functional asset of the Indian democracy, with the objective "to radically alter the administrative ethos and culture of secrecy and control, the legacy of colonial era and bring in a new era of transparency and accountability in governance". Similarly, the expression 'Right to Information' has been defined in section 2(j) to include the right to inspection of work, documents, records, taking certified samples of material, taking notes and extracts and even obtaining information in the form of floppies, tapes, video cassettes, etc. Greater transparency, promotion of citizen-government partnership, greater accountability and reduction in corruption are stated to be the salient features of the Act of 2005.

5. The Right to Democracy

For a long time, both local and global scholarship has been determined to explore the possibility of formulating democracy as a right.

Theoretically, the right to democracy involves the recognition of an interest in democracy, and an interest in the process of democratization in all aspects of political existence. Both the individual and the State have a stake in democracy. Current discourse on political reforms and social unrest or struggle is primarily directed to establishing democratization in all walks of life. The right to democracy seeks to ensure the presence of a functional, responsive and capable democracy, in line with its normative objectives.

The state also shows immense interest in democracy. Institutional behavior day-by-day is directed towards the task of constructing a functional democracy. To understand democracy as a right, we must be able to identify a bare minimum of its existence within a political order. The process of democratization would involve the presence of a constitution, or a similar system of basic norms which authorize the making of *determining decisions* by the people. This would also distinguish democracy from 'systems in which the people, through civil disobedience, riot, general disorders...influence political decision making to such an extent that they are in effect, making the basic determining decisions on important matters of public policy...[86]

To that extent, constitutional framework for building institutional structures is seen as a necessity for democracy. Democracy is defined as a political system wherein individuals are "entitled to determining decisions,"[87] and also make such decisions. Such abilities establish the supreme power of the people, styled as *popular sovereignty*. Thus, democracy incorporates both the 'matter and manner of laws'.[88]

In addition, *participation/inclusion* in the political arena is fundamental for democracy to flourish. In this regard Prof. Upendra Baxi deals with the *notion of access* that has often been incorporated by political theory in concepts such as representation, democracy, participation and pluralism.[89]

Access as interpreted by Baxi may be regarded as a form of interaction, which may generate access relationships and structures (or institutions). The complexity of access relations comes to full view when we ask:

(i) access by whom and *to* whom?;

(ii) access to what? (values, resources, public or private goods);

(iii) access through what? (formal/informal procedures, norms, institutions);

86. *Supra* note 8 at 9.

87. *Id.* at 10.

88. Allan Hutchinson, Joel Rios, "Democracy and Constitutional Change", Victoria University of Wellington Legal Research Papers, 13 (September 2011). Available at *http://ssrn.com/link/Victoria-U-Wellington-LEG.html*. Also available at *http://papers.ssrn.com/abstract=1714633* (Last visited January 2012).

89. Upendra Baxi, Access, "Development and Distributive Justice: Access Problems of the Rural Population", Vol. 18:3 Journal of the Indian Law Institute 375 (July-September, 1976).

(iv) access for what? (self/collectivity, manifest/latent aims); and access *in* what? (that is, in what social milieu/cultures). Access relations and institutions thus involve *roles,* rules, procedures, arrangements—in short, institutional frameworks, objectives, values, ends—in short, cultures.[90]

The ability to appraise and incorporate meaningful access would eventually determine not only the presence of a democratic culture, but also the character and course of democracy at a given point in time.

It is true that the normativity and functioning of democracy as the two dominant dimensions raise several questions; First, what are the modalities of institutional behavior? What roles are performed by the legislative, judicial and executive institutions? Second, rights are subjected to the interpretive capability of the constitutional machinery day-by-day. To what extent can interpretation be contained or dictated? What possible limitations are inherent to the process of rights interpretation? In other words, "is there a fundamental right to decide democratically the most important issues confronting us, and particularly, the content of rights we possess?"[91] Third, democracy is identified as a medium for the authentic representation of the interests and opinions of the people. Who determines the channels of communication?

What emerges from the above discussion is that democracy as a right has both substantial and procedural dimensions. In the same manner, the essence of the Indian democracy is clearly reflected in the processes and mechanisms adopted for fulfilling the objective of justice and inclusion. For its politically activated and socially vibrant pursuit of development in this age of conflict, globalization and materialism, the Indian democracy continues to capture the attention of local and global scholarship.

---

90. *Id.* at 376.

91. Larry Alexandra, "Constitutions, Judicial Review, Moral Rights and Democracy: Disentangling the Issues", Legal Studies Research Paper Series, University of San Diego (2007). Available at *http://ssrn.com/abstract=1019605.*

CHAPTER VII

Republic

Mallika Ramachandran

1. Republic: Meaning and Concept

The expression 'republic' is commonly understood as a state in which the head of state is an elected representative as opposed to a hereditary monarch. Many definitions of 'republic' describe it in these terms as well as in terms of the 'location' of power or sovereignty in such states which rests with the people or community as a whole. The *Concise Oxford Dictionary* defines the term as a "state in which supreme power is held by the people or their elected representatives or by an elected or nominated president, not by a monarch" or "a society with equality between members"; in the second sense, the term being traced to the French expression 'république' from the Latin *respublica*.[1] The *Random House Dictionary* similarly defines it as "a state where the supreme power rests in the body of citizens entitled to vote and is exercised by representatives chosen directly or indirectly by them", or "a state in which the head of government is an elected or nominated president and not a monarch."[2] Also, the *Encyclopedia Americana* describes 'republic' as "...a form of government in which sovereign power rests with the people-either with the entire body of active citizens or with a majority of it... On the basis of popular sovereignty, the government is exercised by directly or indirectly elected magistrates or representatives. Any government organised in this form is

1. Concise Oxford Dictionary, 9th Ed. p. 1168.
2. Random House Dictionary (1976) p. 1121.

considered a republic even though people may hold only formal and not actual sovereignty."[3]

D.D. Basu in his *Commentary on the Constitution* distinguishes between 'narrow' and 'wide' meanings of the term. He observes that while in a narrow sense, 'republic' is used simply in opposition to monarchy, and means a form of government under which the head of the executive is chosen by the people[4]; in a wider sense, the word "denotes a government where none holds the public power as a proprietary right, but all power is exercised for the common good where the inhabitants are subjects and free citizens at the same time."[5] The definition of the term in the wide sense thus also indicates the purpose of a republican government which is the common good of the people.

Another definition that takes into account the purpose of republican government, set out in *Aiyer's Law Lexicon*,[6] states that a republic is "a government for the protection of the citizen against the exercise of all unjust power. It is a government administered by a few, as the representatives of the people and for their benefit". It alternatively states, "a republic is an independent sovereign power in other words, a state, just as certainly and in the same sense as a monarchy, limited or absolute: and every state is a person, an artificial person, in a more extensive and far higher sense than an ordinary corporation". In fact, another commentator, Brazier is of the view that a republic is not any particular form of government but "is wholly characteristical of the purport, matter or object for which a government ought to be instituted, and on which it is to be employed, *res publica*, public affairs or the public good or literally translated the public thing".[7] Thus, in his view, a government is republican not by reason of its form but due to its purpose.

3. Encyclopaedia Americana, Vol. 23 (1969 Ed) at para 391
4. Leacock quoted in Justice Y.V. Chandrachud, Justice S.S. Subramani and Justice B.P. Banerjee (Eds), D.D. Basu, Commentary on the Constitution of India, 414 (8th Ed, Vol. 1, Wadhwa and Co. Nagpur, 2007).
5. *Id* at 415.
6. 2nd Ed, p. 1663 and 1664.
7. Rodney Brazier, "A British Republic", 61(2) Cambridge Law Journal 351-85 (2002).

Black's Law Dictionary,[8] points out that the term "contrasts on the one hand with pure democracy in which the people or community as an organised whole wield the sovereign power of government, and on the other with the rule of a person (such as a king, emperor, czar or sultan)".

Madison in *Federalist No. XXXIX* observed that a republic "is a government which derives all its powers directly or indirectly from the great body of the people, and is administered by persons holding office during their pleasure, for a limited period or during good behaviour".[9] In his view, an essential condition for such government is that it "be derived from the great body of the society, not from an inconsiderable proportion, or a favoured class of it; otherwise a handful of tyrannical nobles, exercising oppressions by delegation of their powers, might aspire to the rank of republicans, and claim for their government the honourable title of republic"[10] . However, it is 'sufficient' for such a government "that the persons administering it be appointed, either directly or indirectly, by the people; and that they hold their appointments either by tenures just specified; otherwise every government in the United States, as well as every other popular government that has been or can be well organised or well executed would be degraded from the republican character".[11]

Some characteristics or features of republics as may be seen from the aforesaid descriptions of the term are that: the term has been used to describe both 'state' as well as the form of government prevailing in a state; the head of the executive is to be chosen by election and is not a hereditary monarch;

8. 7th Ed. p. 1306.
9. James Madison, Federalist No. XXXIX, "The Conformity of the Plan to Republican Principles", (undated). It may be mentioned here as Shapiro notes that Madison defence of republican institutions was offered when he was thirty six years old and the more mature Madison rejected the republican thinking that is most famously attributed to him and was of the view that democratic competition was the best available guarantor of the values that republicans seek to protect. *See* Ian Shapiro, "On Non-Domination", 62 University of Toronto Law Journal 293 (2012).
10. *Id.*
11. *Id.*

the supreme power in such state rests in the people and is exercised through representatives; power is derived from the great body of society and not an inconsiderable proportion or favoured class; and there is equality between members, all power is exercised for the common good, and citizens are protected against unjust exercise of power.

2. Republicanism

The expression 'republicanism' has been used to describe 'adherence to or sympathy with a republican form of government' or 'the principles or theory of republican government'[12], or 'republican principles or adherence to them'[13]. In the context of political theory and philosophy, the Stanford Encyclopaedia of Philosophy takes note of two senses in which this term is used, one, a loose tradition or family of writers in the history of western political thought including Machiavelli, English thinkers like Milton, and Sydney, others such as Montesquieu and Americans like Jefferson, who emphasized common ideas and concerns such as the importance of civic virtue and political participation, the dangers of corruption, the benefits of a mixed constitution and the rule of law, as well as their reliance on classical examples particularly Cicero and the Latin historians; in the second sense, in contemporary political theory and philosophy, it refers to a specific and still contested interpretation of the classic republican tradition, particularly the works of Quentin Skinner, Philip Pettit, etc., according to which the paramount republican value is political liberty, understood as non-domination or independence from arbitrary power.[14] Tomkins also points out that republicanism "is an approach to government that has ancient, indeed classical roots, some looking to Aristotle and the Greek polis, others looking to the Roman republic of Cicero, Livy, Tacitus and Sallust".[15]

12. *See* Merriam-Webster Dictionary, available at http://www.merriam-webster.com/dictionary/republicanism.

13. *Supra* note 2 at 1121.

14. Stanford Encyclopaedia of Philosophy, "Republicanism", (2010 rev.), available at http://plato.stanford.edu/entries/republicanism.

15. Adam Tomkins, Our Republican Constitution, 57 (Hart Publishing, 2005).

Republicanism "can also be understood and institutionalised as a schema of civic action and as such would establish a constitutional linkage between principles of civic freedom and the institutions available for their formal reception and practical fulfilment"[16]. In the words of Philip Pettit, republicanism is firstly, a theory of freedom and secondly, a theory of government.[17]

3. Major Themes and Principles of Republicanism

Various scholars and commentators have identified the core themes and principles associated with republicanism. These central or core themes[18] include: anti-monarchism and popular sovereignty; the rule of law and the rule of virtue among politically active citizens; freedom as non-domination and its consequences and the institutional design of accountability.

An important component of republicanism, particularly, according to contemporary writers on the issue,[19] is the idea of freedom as non-domination. As Pettit observes, "the central theme in republican concerns throughout the ages, and which explains all other commitments, has been the desire to arrange things so that citizens are not exposed to domination... they do not live *in potestate domini...*", and domination was viewed by all republicans whether in classical Rome, renaissance Italy, seventeenth century England or eighteenth Century America 'an evil to be avoided' in organising a polity.[20] However, there is a debate between 'civil humanists' and

16. Andrew Fraser, "In Defence of Republicanism: A Reply to George Williams", 23 Federal Law Review 362 (1995) at 365.
17. Philip Pettit, "Republicanism", The Stanford Encyclopedia of Philosophy, (Spring 2003), available at http://plato.stanford.edu/archives/spr2003/entries/republicanism.
18. Philip Pettit quoted in *supra* note 15 at 365; *supra* note 15 at 57. Gey notes, that the three salient characteristics of 'civic republicanism' are the goal of civic virtue; organic concept of community; and the notion that individuals are socially constructed. Steven G. Gey, "The Unfortunate Revival of Civic Republicanism", 141 University of Pennsylvania Law Review 801 (1993).
19. As has been observed in the Stanford Encyclopaedia of Philosophy the conception of 'political liberty' as non-domination is 'absolutely central' to the contemporary civic republican program. See *supra* note 14.
20. *Supra* note 17.

'civic republicans' regarding the meaning of political liberty in the classical republican tradition.[21]

Larmore points out that at the centre of Philip Pettit's conception of republicanism is his concept of non-domination, "according to which we are free to the extent that we do not find ourselves under the domination of others, subject to their will and exposed to the vicissitudes of their desires", and which is a negative conception, though it nonetheless accords a role to democratic self rule.[22] Pettit points out that the difference between his argument and that of Quentin Skinner as concerns the element of freedom is that while according to him, freedom means non-domination, in Skinner's opinion, it means non-domination and non-interference.[23] The republican concept of freedom as non-domination challenges Hobbes' equation of liberty with licence or the unfettered ability to do what one wants.[24] Shapiro argues that non-domination is the bedrock of justice but it ranges from the 'trivial to the momentous' and it is only the most serious forms that merit the attention of the government. He rejects the negative/positive dichotomy in favour of a relational view which involves thinking about unfreedom as it relates to agents and restraining and enabling conditions, actions and systems of authorisation.[25] Bellamy is of the opinion that that republicanism offers a distinctive political and social program from the notion of freedom as non-domination, in particular a justification for a more participatory and egalitarian society which is democratic in the widest sense and a way of integrating social and political theory in a way

21. *Supra* note 14.
22. Charles Larmore, "A Critique of Philip Pettit's Republicanism", available at http://www.rationalites-contemporaines.paris-sorbonne.fr/IMG/pdf/RepublicanismLiberalism_Larmore_.pdf (last visited, 22 October, 2012).
23. Philip Pettit, "Keeping Republican Freedom Simple: On a Difference with Quentin Skinner" 30 (3) Political Theory 339 (June, 2002) at 342.
24. Mortimer Newlin Sellers, "The Origins of Republican Legal Theory", available at http://ssrn.com/abstract=1139837.
25. Ian Shapiro, "On Non-Domination", 62 University of Toronto Law Journal 293 (2012).

that emphasizes how political and social relations interact through its emphasis on power and status.[26]

It may be mentioned here as Bellamy points out, that the views of Skinner and Pettit, who look to the neo-Roman tradition of republican thought through Cicero and Machiavelli, view freedom as non-domination as opposed to the other two approaches, one, going back to Aristotle stressing the importance of civic participation for individual self realisation and the second, drawing on the enlightenment tradition of republican thought from the writings of Kant and Paine, both of which conceive freedom in terms of collective self-mastery achieved through popular sovereignty.[27] It was the work of Isaiah Berlin which brought out the two conceptions of liberty, negative liberty which has been defined as opportunity or the right to be left alone, or the absence of social interference with private actions which is the dominant conception of liberty among contemporary Anglo-American philosophers while positive liberty, which is not as easy to define, consists in the performance of certain courses of conduct or the attainment of certain objectives or the 'notion of self-mastery', or the capacity to influence the governance of one's society.[28]

A second element in republicanism is the idea of civic virtue, which includes participation by the people in society, the ideas of public spiritedness and respect for law. Tomkins explains that the realisation of freedom as non-domination requires that we as citizens engage in the political process, and reminds us of a deep and active sense of public spiritedness, which is what is essentially meant by the phrase 'civic virtue';

26. Richard Bellamy, "Republicanism: Non-Domination and the Free State", in G. Delanty and S.P. Turner, Routledge Handbook of Contemporary Social and Political Theory, (March, 2011), available at http://ssrn.com/abstract=1593042.

27. *Id. See* also Larmore who notes that Pettit's conception of freedom differs from the more prominent strand in the republican tradition that defines freedom in positive terms as individual or collective self autonomy. Larmore, *supra* note 22.

28. *See* Mathew H. Kramer, "Freedom and the Rule of Law", 61 Alabama Law Review 827 (2010), *supra* note 15 at 48; *supra* note 14; William Damon, "The Core of Civic Virtue", 2011 (3) Hoover Digest.

the determination of 'public good' being a question for the citizenry and not something imposed.[29] Civic virtue, which is a specifically political virtue, necessary for securing a society without domination, in Pettit's view, has three elements: one, the rule of law can be a reality only in a society where citizens respect the law for its own sake and not merely due to the fear of sanctions; two, citizens participate in public life making their needs and concerns heard; and, three, they must practice constant vigilance, being on the look-out for excessive concentrations of power, which never cease to be a danger.[30]

Damon stresses on the need to inculcate virtue in young people, asserting, *inter alia*, that 'a citizenry devoted in large part to moral and civic virtue' is necessary for the very survival of a free society, and points out that "when virtue loses its public footing, too few citizens accept the responsibilities necessary for sustaining liberty in that society".[31] He refers to Montesquieu's observation that in a republic, virtue may be defined as love for the laws of one's country and one's country; and notes that while the word 'patriotism' is viewed with suspicion, it need not take a chauvinistic and insular form but can go hand-in-hand with a concern for people everywhere with a respect for human rights and a belief in universal justice.[32] Gey, noting that both Cass Sunstein and Frank Michealman refer to 'civic virtue' as the animating principle of civic republicanism, feels that this concept is both the theoretical core and Achilles heel of all modern variations of civic republican theory[33]

Another component of republicanism identified by both Pettit, and Tomkins is that of anti-monarchism. Tomkins elaborates on this concept observing that the most obvious thing to say about republicanism is that it is anti-monarchic;

29. *Supra* note 14.

30. *Supra* note 22.

31. *Supra* note 28 (Damon).

32. *Id*.

33. Gey, *supra* note 18 He observes that "During the last decade, Constitutional theory has been radically altered by the infusion of ideas loosely grouped under the title civic republicanism".

in a republic, power starts with the people who delegate it upwards, and for instance in the United States, power not delegated to the United States under the Constitution remains with the States respectively or with the people, and this is the very essence of the republican ideal that the polity belongs to the people, it is a 'public thing' or *'res publica'*.[34] It has been noted however, that the distinction between monarchies and republics is not always clear and in some constitutional monarchies, almost all real political power vests in the people exercised through elected representatives, while the monarch exercises theoretical powers.[35]

According to Tomkins, also deriving from republicanism is the theme of 'the institutional design of accountability' which is concerned with the realisation of republican values in Constitutional practice and addresses the structures needed to secure a republican government making those in power accountable to those over whom and in whose name such power is exercised.[36] This element in his view is and has been 'absolutely central' to British Constitutional Practice. Zucca, reviewing Tomkins' work, observes, however, that "the very objective of maximising freedom as non-domination through political accountability does not yield any precise policy choice in situations of disagreement and must therefore be supplemented by other values".[37]

Besides these central themes, various specific principles relating to or ideas influenced by republicanism have also been taken note of. These include[38] secure government for the common good; government functioning within a written or unwritten Constitution; division of power and checks and balances; elected executive in a process that different parts of the populace with rival interests are represented; limited tenure of those in government with a requirement of periodic elections; deliberative senate, regulated popular assembly, an

34. *Supra* note 15 at 57.
35. *See* 'Republic' at http://en.wikipedia.org/wiki/Republic.
36. *Supra* note 15 at 64-5.
37. Lorenzo Zucca, "Our Republican Constitution: Adam Tomkins-Book Review", 65 (2) Cambridge Law Journal 454-6 (2006).
38. *Supra* note 24; *Supra* note 17.

independent judiciary and rule of law, equality of material possessions; government decisions to be supported by reasons relating to common interests; and existence of an active, concerned citizenry to invigilate government power, and challenge its abuses.

4. History and Development of the Concept

The concept of republicanism is most often traced back to the roman *res publica,* and the ideals appearing in the writings of Cicero, Livy etc, though even classic Greek city-states, and states in ancient India could be referred to as republics. Republican ideas influenced and were interpreted by several philosophers and writers in subsequent periods, and have once again seen a revival in the writings of contemporary theorists like Pocock, Wood, Skinner, Pettit, etc. It may be mentioned here that though republican concepts in various periods of time share common ideas, there were also many differences in the way the term has been understood and interpreted at different times.

As mentioned above, it has been noted that even the classic Greek city states of the 5th and 4th centuries could be called republics as governments in such states were ordinarily directly elected by the people. However, there were wide differences within this 'general framework' which included the 'egalitarian democracy of Periclean Athens and the aristocratic- military oligarchy of Sparta', and the 'people' were only a minority of the adult population with women, resident aliens, and slaves being given no political rights.[39]

The Romans used the term *'res publica'* to describe their state, which is a term that evades translation but is most often translated into English as 'commonwealth' or 'republic'.[40] As has been observed in the Encyclopaedia Americana, "In the political tradition of the West, prior to the American and French revolutions, the term 'republic' could refer to any state which was a commonwealth, *i.e.,* to say which was not ruled by a tyrant or despot but was governed in the

39. *Supra* note 3.

40. *Supra* note 24.

common interest rather than in the interest of a person or a clique".[41] It further notes that in this sense even a monarchy or aristocracy could be called a republic "if the government created and promoted the common interest and welfare, and the term could be applied to states in which political rights were greatly restricted".[42] It can thus be said that the purpose of the government was more relevant than the form in the understanding of the term.

'*Res publica*' was defined by Cicero as "the property of the people or populous by which he meant not any group of humans but a large group associated in pursuit of a shared sense of justice, and their own common welfare" and Cicero and Livius were of the view that "republican institutions collapsed when party conflict upset the traditional checks and balances between the senate, the magistrates, and the people of Rome".[43]

Wood observes, that the writings of the 'golden age of Roman literature', such as Cicero, Livy, Sallust, and Tacitus, who set forth republican ideals, particularly fascinated the eighteenth century, and had a lasting and powerful influence on Western Culture, and having been 'revived and refurbished by the Italian renaissance, became, "what has been variously called civic republicanism or classical republicanism and were carried into early modern Europe and made available to wider and deeper strata of the population".[44]

Machiavelli, Rousseau and Montesquieu, among others greatly influenced many subsequent thinkers on republicanism including the French and American revolutionaries and the more contemporary writers on republicanism. As Sellers points out, "Machiavelli did the most to revive the republican tradition in Italy" and the 'republican vocabulary' adopted by Montesquieu and Rousseau "influenced the subsequent republican tradition, particularly in France".[45] He further

41. *Supra* note 3.
42. *Id.*
43. *Supra* note 24.
44. Gordon S. Wood, "Classical Republicanism and the American Revolution", 66 Chicago-Kent Law Review 13 (1990) at 18.
45. *Supra* note 24.

points out that "the resistance of the Swiss, Italian cantons and the Netherlands against imperial control added practical models for republican liberty".[46]

Monstesquieu in his treatise *The Spirit of the Laws,* discussed the principles of monarchy and republicanism systematically and comparatively; weighed their advantages and disadvantages; described their 'adhesive forces' and also pointed out that modern governments were mixtures of both to some extent or another.[47] He did not agree that 'liberty was to be found only in republics' but felt that "individual liberty and security, religious toleration, the rule of law, commercial prosperity, and progress in arts, sciences and manners" could be provided by "a constitution-bound monarchy in a large scale."[48] According to Montesquieu, British liberty was 'modern, commercial and moderate, compatible with refinement and progress' but where 'commerce and the form of republicanism were joined', he saw 'corruption and decline, not the spirit of liberty.[49]

Sellers points out that Rousseau and his disciples' ideas on republicanism differed from both Roman, and Polybian antecedents as well as later American concepts, "in its greater reliance on unanimity in the public assemblies, rather than checks and balances to guard against faction".[50] Rousseau incorporated many republican ideas in his philosophy, particularly, the evil of dependency and the rule of law, and introduced the argument that people as a collective body are the rightful sovereign and can never cede their sovereignty to representatives, this argument taking republicanism in a radically new direction and breaking with the traditional doctrine.[51] Rousseau was of the view that there was a "tight

---

46. *Id.*
47. *Supra* note 44 at 16.
48. Jacob T. Levy," Montesquieu, Liberal Republicanism and the small-republic thesis", available at http://ssrn.com/abstract=739447 (last visited 17 July 2012) at 9.
49. *Id at* 6.
50. Mortimer Sellers, "Republican Influences on the French and American Revolutions", available at http://ssrn.com/abstract=1141202.
51. *Supra* note 17.

relationship among republican forms, civic virtue, personal service to state, patriotism, smallness, and the avoidance of commerce and partial private interests and insisted that governments need not assume republican forms to become republics at the level of justification".[52] However, his concept of 'civic virtue', and ideas as to the "necessary corruption of large states set an almost impossible task for French republicans, which contributed to the excesses of Maximilien Robespierre and Jacobin terror in Paris"[53].

Republican thoughts and ideas were also seen in England and the works of several English philosophers and writers. While a monarchical form of government prevails and has prevailed through much of English history, Brazier notes that in the Anglo Saxon Period, the monarch was elected by a council of wise men known as the witan who chose the most competent member of the family and could also remove the King for misgovernment.[54] Though a 'republican' form of government was established by Cromwell, and the English commonwealth denominated respublica on his state seals, the word 'commonwealth' came to be associated with parliamentary unicameralism during the English Civil War[55]. After the 1640's a Constitutional order was established by the Parliament based on the republican ideas of accountability and the neo-Roman argument voiced by some Parliamentarians also began to come centre-stage; later in 1660, it was the Constitution as amended by the Long Parliament in 1641, that was restored.[56] The English Constitution has been observed to be one of the most republican of the monarchies of Europe and most agreed that the mixture of republicanism in the English Constitution was a crucial source of its strength.[57]

52. *Supra* note 48 at 9-10.
53. *Supra* note 50.
54. *Supra* note 7.
55. *Supra* note 50.
56. *Supra* note 15 at 67-8, 95-6.
57. *Supra* note 44 at 17 Even Paine in his treatise, Common Sense, has observed that "it is the republican and not the monarchical part of the Constitution of England which Englishmen glory in, *viz.* the liberty of choosing a house of commons from out of their own body—and it is easy to see that when republican virtue fails, slavery ensues. *See* Thomas Paine, Common Sense, (1776).

Republican ideas were also considered in England in the eighteenth century when great "British writers spoke in republican tones" and the intellectual opposition to Sir Robert Walpole's long administration "inevitably drew on "classical republican values to voice its love of freedom and its antagonism to corruption" and, "placed the character of classical republicanism-integrity, virtue, and disinterestedness at the centre of public life".[58]

Republican ideas have been observed to have greatly influenced both French and American Revolutionaries. As Sellers notes, "the Roman name of 'republic' evoked first and above all the memory of government without kings" and French and American statesmen who came into conflict with their monarchs, found in Rome 'a valuable ideology of opposition' and 'the courage and vocabulary to pursue their own independence'.[59] He further points out that the principles of the republican tradition and essence of republican government which was remembered by the French and American statesmen was government for the good of the public, under the sovereign people, antithetical to monarchy and arbitrary rule, according to the rule of law, guided by the legislatures and executive; and that Rome's 'greatest and most lasting contribution' to them consisted in "a set of Constitutional mechanisms designed to secure republican liberty through the fundamental structure of the State."[60] In the American thinkers' view, what distinguished their republican Constitution from the Roman version, was 'the total exclusion of the people in their collective capacity' from any share of the government of the United States, and extending the 'representative principle' to the more 'democratic' branches of government, would be a 'remedy for the diseases more incident to republican government'[61]. It has been pointed out that only at the time of the French and American revolutions, did the term 'republic' assume the

---

58. *Id.* at 21, 22 (Wood).
59. *Supra* note 50.
60. *Id.*
61. *Id.*

connotation of a free state, with constitutionally defined and guaranteed civil rights and liberties of individuals.[62]

Subsequent conceptions of republicanism were influenced by the French and American models which created their own narratives and provided a more contemporary model of successful republican government but the influence of the Roman model and of thinkers like Cicero, Sallust, Livy and Tacitus also remained.[63] Levy notes that in the decades that followed the American Revolution, there was a steady transformation in republican theory from civic to liberal.[64] By the middle nineteenth century, America gave as free play to commercial activity and self interestedness of people as any society in history; however, classical republican ideals did not die away but "tempered the scramble for private wealth and aspirations" and continued to underlie many ideals and aspirations, including the yearning for individual autonomy, belief in equality and dislike of pretension and privilege.[65]

Another important concept that may taken note of in this regard is the term, 'civic humanism' which was coined in the context of the Weimar republic in the background of the traditions of German historical scholarship, and which is "a variant of republicanism indicating active, participatory, patriotic citizenship as well as the ethos and educational ideal that goes with it".[66] It is an approximate interpretation of the term *Bürgerhumanimus,* the first part of which (*'Bürger'*) connotes citizenship and also a bourgeois social condition and outlook as well as an urban context for the realisation of the good life, while *humanism* echoes the German reception of the heritage of classical antiquity.[67] This concept marked "the victory of secular economic, social, and political ideals versus the asceticism, religious obscurantism, and hierarchy of the Middle Ages" and announced the beginning of modern

62. *Supra* note 3.
63. *Supra* note 50.
64. *Supra* note 48 at 17.
65. *Supra* note 44 at 37.
66. 'Civic Humanism', Stanford Encyclopaedia of Philosophy (2002).
67. *Id.*

democratic thought.[68] The purpose of the commonwealth was the realisation of human potentiality and encouraging all forms of creativity and ingenuity which contribute to public welfare; the republic being a necessary medium of self realisation and republican freedom depends on civic activity.[69]

Republicanism was once again revived and studied by several contemporary theorists and writers some of whose interpretations of classical republicanism are referred to as civic republicanism or neo-republicanism. It may be mentioned here that a distinction has been drawn even among the views of the 'revivalists' who are classified as 'civic humanists' and 'civic republicans'. The interpretation of classical republicanism in the first few decades of its 'revival', including in the views of Pocock, Wood, Worden, etc, whose views were rooted in the experience of the ancient Greek polis and which understood active political participation, and civic virtue as valuable components of human flourishing is referred to as 'civic humanism'.[70] Another interpretation of classical republicanism that is prevalent among contemporary writers such as Skinner and Pettit, among others, referred to as civic republicans, is one where the paramount value of republicanism, is 'political liberty' which is understood as non-domination, or independence from arbitrary power.[71] Fallon attributes the 'republican revival' to two reasons, work of historical scholars (such as the work of Pocock, Wood, etc.) which showed the American Constitution framers 'functioned in an ideological universe which included the language and discourse of civic republicanism' and second, an intellectual dissatisfaction with liberalism.[72] According to Pinto, 'neo republicanism' is 'a normative theory of democracy', its three major common conceptions being, civic virtue, meaning *inter alia*, involvement in the community, and preference

68. *Id.*
69. *Id.*
70. *Supra* note 14.
71. *Id.*
72. Richard H. Fallon, Jr., "What is Republicanism and is it Worth Reviving?", 102 *Harvard Law Review* 1695 (1989) at 1696-97.

for public interest; political participation which involves an extended process of deliberation and discussion equally and independently by all; and a certain model of citizenship and patriotism around a civic conversation, and participation in the polis, with an emphasis on responsibility and duty.[73] Gey, who is critical of civic republicanism, feels that civic republicans give government virtually unlimited power and therefore, fail to check the tendency of absolute power to corrupt absolutely, and also writes of the dangers of granting 'citizen politicians' the ultimate power.[74] Other criticisms of republicanism include that as the term has had varied and even contradictory meanings at different periods of time, the term is all but meaningless,[75] and that it implies extensive self sacrifice and renunciation of individuality.[76]

5. India as a Republic

The Preamble to the Indian Constitution describes the country as a 'sovereign, socialist, secular, democratic republic'. India, which gained its independence in 1947, became a republic in 1950 with the adoption of the Constitution when her first President, Dr. Rajendra Prasad entered office. As Dr. Kashyap notes, India decided to remain a Member of the Commonwealth even after independence as this did not compromise her position or imply any diminution if her status as a sovereign nation or a Republic in any way.[77]

It may be mentioned here that the idea of republics was not unknown in the country prior to the adoption of the Constitution and in fact many states in ancient India had republican forms of government which were council based and not monarchical.

73. Ricardo Leite Pinto, "Neo Republicanism and Constitution Law: A Republic of Reasons", Communication to the VIIth International Congress of the Constitutional Law Associations, (Athens, 2007), available at http://www.enelsyn.gr/papers/w7/Paper%20by%20Prof.%20Ricardo%20Leite%20Pinto.pdf.

74. Gey, *supra* note 18.

75. Republicanism, available at http://en.wikipedia.org/wiki Republicanism.

76. *Supra* note 14.

77. Subhash C. Kashyap, Constitutional Law of India, 308 (Vol. 1, Universal Law Publishing Co., New Delhi, 2008).

At the stage of the drafting of the Constitution, some debate took place over the use of the word, 'republic' in the preamble. As Basu notes, at the time of circulation of the draft Constitution, "the drafting committee itself was not unanimous on the precise implication of the word 'republic' *vis-à-vis* India's membership of the commonwealth".[78] Dr. Subhash Kashyap, discussing the controversy at the drafting stage, notes that Sh. B.N. Rau, commenting on the 1948 draft, was of the view that "in the changed and still changing conception of the commonwealth, there was still room for a completely independent state inside the commonwealth, and whatever description of India might be adopted in the Preamble would not by itself suffice to define effectively its relationship to the British Commonwealth".[79] He felt that the question of India's future relationship to the commonwealth would have to be decided separately but nonetheless he was of the opinion that the term 'republic' had certain associations and its use in the preamble might imply that it was being prejudged and thus it would be wise to avoid using the term.[80] In another note in his personal capacity, Rau observed that the commonwealth had reached a stage when even a state with a republican Constitution may well be given a place within it and India may continue to be a member of the commonwealth both due to ideological affinities as well as for practical reasons.[81] However, much of this debate lost all its force when by a declaration adopted at the end of April, 1949, the government of various commonwealth countries announced their acceptance and recognition of India's continued membership even after the adoption of our republican Constitution[82].

There is not very much detailed discussion as to the meaning or interpretation of the term 'republic' in the sense

78. *Supra* note 4 at 415.
79. Dr. Subhash C. Kashyap, The Framing of India's Constitution: A Study, 129 (2nd Ed, Universal Law Publishing Co., Delhi, 2004).
80. *Id.* at 130.
81. *Id.* at 130
82. *Supra* note 4 at 415.

used in the preamble. Some commentators have defined the term as is commonly defined in dictionaries, encyclopaedias, etc discussed above. For instance, According to Prof. Kailash Rai, 'republic' indicates that the form of government is one in which the Head of State will be an elected person and not a monarch like the King or Queen in England and this term has been used to make it clear that India will not follow a system in which the Head of State will be a hereditary monarch".[83] Similarly, another commentator observes, "in a republic, all offices including the highest, that is, of the head of State are open to all citizens. There is no bar to a citizen being elected to any public office. It also means that the source of all authority under the Constitution is the people and not any hereditary ruler".[84]

Dr. Subhash Kashyap in his book *Constitutional Law of India* has discussed the concept of 'republic' as occurs in the preamble, in a detailed manner. He takes note of this basic concept of 'republic' which is "that of a state in which people are supreme, there is no privileged class and all the public offices are open to every citizen without any discrimination"[85], and refers to the words of Justice Hidayatullah: "...Democratic republic may, therefore, broadly mean a State with an elected head and a government by the representatives of the people."[86] Mention may also be made here also of Madison's view, that a republic is a government in which a scheme of representation takes place and differs from a 'democracy' in that in a republic, government is delegated to a smaller number of persons elected by the rest and it can be extended over a greater sphere of the country.[87]

According to Dr. Kashyap, "it is in the widest sense that the Preamble speaks of India being a republic". The head of

83. Kailash Rai, The Constitutional Law of India, 70 (9th Ed, Central Law Publications, Allahabad, 2010).
84. Brij Kishore Sharma, Introduction to the Constitution of India, 26 (Phi Learning Pvt. Ltd., New Delhi, 2009).
85. *Supra* note 77 at 307.
86. *Id.*
87. James Madison, Federalist No. X ,"The Union as a Safeguard Against Domestic Faction and Insurrection", (November 23, 1787).

the Union is a President who is elected for a fixed term by an electoral college of the representatives of the people. All citizens are equal in the eyes of law, there is no privileged class and all public offices are open to every citizen without any distinction of race, caste, sex or creed.[88] He also notes that all forms of republican polity have at their root, "the concept of sovereignty vesting in the people, of citizens being both the ruler and the ruled at the same time, of people ruling over themselves through their freely elected representatives, and having an elected Head of State usually called the President".[89]

Another eminent commentator, D.D. Basu, who has also discussed the narrow and wide meanings of the expression republic,[90] feels that "it may be said that the preamble to our Constitution uses the term in both these senses. For not only shall we have an elected president, instead of a hereditary King at the head of our State, but the state will also be characterised by the absence of any ruling or privileged class and all office-from the humblest to the highest-including that of the president will be open to all citizens without any distinctions of caste, religion, or sex. Thus, Indian citizens will be subjects and free citizens at the same time."[91]

Jagdish Swarup, in *Constitution of India*, notes that 'republic' "has been rather freely applied to almost any kind of State that has no monarchical headship, and has, with whatever limitations some system of election to the office of the Head of State.... The head of a republic, the President, is elected, not hereditary".[92] He distinguishes between two forms of republican government prevalent today, in one type, the 'head' having merely ceremonial functions above the conflict of parties, analogous to that of a Constitutional monarch such as the President of India, and another, represented by the

88. *Supra* note 77 at 307-08.
89. *Id.* at 308.
90. *Supra* note 4.
91. *Id.* at 415-16.
92. Dr. L.M. Singhvi (Ed), Jagdish Swarup's Constitution of India, 52-3 (Vol. 1, Modern Law Publications, Allahabad, 2006).

United States, where the President has the arduous task of combining the ceremonial offices of the State with the political activities of the head of the executive.[93]

Dr. Kashyap is of the opinion that republics usually go hand in hand with a Presidential system; however in a classic Parliamentary model, on the other hand, Parliament is supposed to be sovereign and the head of the state is usually a hereditary or non-elected dignitary. "The Constitution of India has tried to bring about a marriage between the Parliamentary and Presidential systems. India is in the unique position of being both a parliamentary democracy and a republic."[94]

Thus, as has been pointed out by commentators, and as described in the preamble, India is a democratic republic as understood in the common interpretation of the term republic, *i.e.*, where the head of the State is not a hereditary monarch, and also in the wider sense of the term, where power is not held as a proprietary right, all public offices are open to all the citizens equally and power is to be exercised for common good. The executive power of the Union of India is vested in the President, who is also the 'supreme commander' of the defence forces of the Union.[95] The President is elected by the members of an electoral college, and any citizen of the country, who has attained 35 years of age and meets the qualifications for election as a Member of the House of People is eligible to be elected as the President, and once elected the President occupies office for a term of five years. The office of the President is thus open to every citizen of the country possessing the requisite qualifications and not restricted to a select few or any favoured group.

Further, it can be said that many of the principles associated with republics and republican ideas identified by various scholars and commentators as discussed in the previous sections can in fact be found incorporated in the provisions

---

93. *Id.*

94. *Supra* note 77 at 308.

95. Article 53, Constitution of India.

of the Constitution of India such as an elected government which functions in accordance with the Constitution, limited tenures of the government and the President with periodic elections, accountability, an independent judiciary, the rule of law and equality between persons.

The Constitution specifically recognises universal adult suffrage as the basis of elections to the House of People and Legislative Assemblies of States (article 326) and also states that no person shall be ineligible for inclusion in, or to claim to be included in electoral rolls on the grounds of race, religion, caste, sex or any of them (article 325). Any citizen of India, who possesses the prescribed qualifications, will be eligible to be elected as a Member of Parliament (article 84). It may be mentioned here as Bellamy observes, that the system of equal votes, majority rule and competing parties, in contemporary democracies can be seen as offering an updated form of the republican system of mixed government, equalising power in decision making and producing balanced decisions.[96]

The President of India holds office for a term of five years from the date on which he enters office. The Constitution also prescribes the tenure for the House of People (Lok Sabha) which is five years from the date appointed for its first meeting as well as the Council of States (Rajya Sabha) in relation to which it provides that "as nearly as possible one-third of the members thereof shall retire as soon as may be on the expiration of every second year in accordance with the provisions made in that behalf by the Parliament by Law" (article 83).

The President is aided and advised by a council of ministers headed by the Prime Minister, and acts in accordance with such advice (article 74). The council of ministers is to be collectively responsible to the house of people [article 75 (3)].

The Constitution recognises the right to equality of all persons and provides against non-discrimination in various matters. Article 14 of the Constitution provides that the State

96. *Supra* note 26.

shall not deny to any person equality before law or equal protection of all laws in India. Article 15 provides, *inter alia,* that the State shall not discriminate against citizens on grounds of religion, race, caste, sex, place of birth or any of them and also provides for protection against any liability, disability, restriction or condition on ground only of religion, race, caste, sex, place of birth or any of them in matters of access to and use of various public places. Article 16(1) recognises that there shall be equality of opportunity for all citizens in matters relating to employment and appointment to any office under the State. And article 16(2) provides that no citizen shall on grounds only of religion, race, caste, sex, descent, place of birth, residence or any of them, be ineligible for or discriminated against in respect of any employment or office under the State.

The right to life and right to various freedoms with reasonable restrictions are also guaranteed by the Constitution. Article 21 provides that no person shall be deprived of the right to life or personal liberty except according to procedure established by law. Article 19 recognises the right of citizens to various fundamental freedoms including speech and expression, assembly, forming associations, movement, residence, and engaging in any trade, profession or occupation subject to reasonable restrictions imposed on specified grounds.

In India, though a complete separation of powers has not been envisaged in the Constitution, article 50 directs the State to take steps to separate the Judiciary from the executive in the public services of the State. The separation of powers has however, been held to be a part of the 'basic structure' of the Constitution.[97]

The Directive Principles of State Policy which, though not justiciable are stated to be fundamental in the governance of the country and are to be applied by the State in making laws, provided that the State shall strive to promote the welfare of the people by securing and protecting as effectively as it may,

---

97. *His Holiness Kesavananda Bharati Sripadagalvaru* v. *State of Kerala,* (1973) 4 SCC 225: AIR 1973 SC 1461.

a social order in which justice, social, economic and political, shall inform all institutions of national life as well as strive to minimise inequalities in income and eliminate inequalities in status, facilities, and opportunities among individuals as well as among groups residing in different areas or engaged in different vocations (article 38). The other provisions of the Directive Principles also set out welfare objectives to be borne in mind by the State when making laws. Also, the fundamental duties of citizens set out in the Constitution may be compared to the concept of civic virtue.

6. Forms of Government in Other Countries

A large number of states in the world today are republics including many of the states that gained independence from colonial rule such as India. The United States, as mentioned in the previous section, follows the 'Presidential' form of government where the elected head of State exercises both ceremonial functions as well as political functions as head of the executive. Article IV of the Constitution of the United States provides that every state in the union would always enjoy a republican form of government. Although the expression 'republican form of government' was not interpreted by the Supreme Court on the ground that it was a political question, it did observe that the essence of the republican form as understood in the United States is that the government derives its power, directly or indirectly from the bulk of the people.[98]

Other states like India, Ireland, and Germany who have also adopted the republican form of government have an elected head of state who exercises only the ceremonial or non-executive functions while the political functions are exercised by the elected head of government, and is often referred to as the Prime Minister.

Other forms of republican government have also been adopted in some states such as Socialist Republics in countries such as China where the government is 'for and by the

98. See *Chisholm* v. *Georgia*, (1792) 2 Dall 419 quoted in DD Basu, *supra* note 4.

people' but where there are no direct elections and Islamic Republics, which are republics governed in accordance with Islamic Law.[99] Another form of republican government as adopted in countries such as Switzerland is one where there is no full time President but the representational function of the President, who has only limited special powers, is taken over by one or all members in turn such that every member of the government assumes the role once in seven years.[100]

Some states that have hereditary monarchies, such as six member states of the European Union, have monarchs who have been explicitly conferred powers by a democratically adopted Constitution, which position contrasts with the United Kingdom, where power is concentrated in the monarch and is shared with the Parliament.[101]

Britain has and has had a monarchical form of government but is best described as a Constitutional monarchy with a number of republican principles incorporated in its Constitution. Tomkins notes that the Constitutional order that the British Parliament created in 1640-1701 took as their starting-point the republican idea that the government is accountable to Parliament and that continues to form the bedrock of the British Constitution to this day.[102] As mentioned earlier, during the Anglo-Saxon period, the monarch was elected by the supreme council/witan. In the contemporary scenario, the British monarch has tacit approval of the Parliament which turns on assumed continuing acceptability of the continuance of the monarchy to the people.[103] Brazier, taking note of the case against monarchy, examines the issues relating to the possibility of change to a 'republic' in the country pointing out that the very question of which form of government is preferable would depend on many inter-related issues, and would be an intellectually challenging exercise; he suggests

99. See *Supra* note 35.

100. *See* http://swiss-government-politics.all-about-switzerland.info/

101. *Supra* note 7.

102. *Supra* note 15.

103. *Supra* note 7.

that another possibility that can be considered in this regard is of possible return to elective monarchy.[104]

Some former British territories like Canada and Australia continue to have the British monarch as head of the state with a Governor General/Viceroy who carries out the functions of the head of state and is the representative of the Crown in these countries. Canada is described as a 'Democratic Constitutional Monarchy'[105] with the Sovereign as the formal head of State and an elected head of Government, the Prime Minister. The issue of whether a change from a Constitutional Monarchy to a republic can be brought about has been explored in Australia but a referendum on the issue failed.[106] Patmore feels that the trend in public opinion in both Canada and Australia gives reason to anticipate that one day each country will become a republic.[107]

Although a republic is ordinarily understood as the absence of monarchy, as elaborated by many scholars and commentators, the term does not merely imply a government which is not a monarchy but is much wider wherein Sovereignty lies with the people, and the purpose of government that is the common good of the people, conducted through representatives elected periodically by the people and in such a manner that the various interests of different sections of the society are represented in the process of election, becomes important; government is carried on in accordance with the Constitution, and there is an independent judiciary with the rule of law. Its central themes as identified by contemporary theorists include anti-monarchism principle, the idea of freedom/liberty which is defined in terms of non-domination as well as by some as including the more positive component of the notion of self-mastery, and the idea of civic virtue which refers to public participation in the process of

104. *Id.*

105. *See* http://www.canada.gc.ca/aboutgov-ausujetgouv/structure/menu-eng.html.

106. *See* Glenn Patmore, "Choosing the Republic: The Legal and Constitutional Steps in Australia and Canada", 31 Queen's Law Journal 270-295 (2006).

107. *Id.*

government besides a respect for the laws and the country itself.

The concept of republicanism is not one that is new or recently evolved but is one that is often traced back to the ancient roman concept of *res publica* which involved the same elements such as common welfare, as understood in the present time though it cannot be literally translated as republic. Republics are also not new to India which had republics even in ancient times and re-adopted the republican form of government on gaining independence from colonial rule. The republican ideas of ancient Roman writers such as Cicero and Livy as well as the ideas of Machiavelli in Renaissance Italy, Rousseau and Montesquieu influenced many subsequent theorists and writers including the French and American revolutionaries who were influenced by the Principles of Government for the good of the public according to the rule of law. It was at around the time of the French and American revolutions that the term republic acquired the connotation of a free state. Republicanism was again revived by contemporary American historians and theorists who interpreted the classical roman understandings.

Republics in different parts of the world have adopted different forms of government such as the Presidential form or Parliamentary form and even others such as in Switzerland where there is no specific President. There are also many states which are headed by monarchs but still follow a number of Principles associated with republicanism.

The preamble to the Indian Constitution specifically describes the country as a republic, and though there was some debate at the time of drafting of the Constitution on the use of the expression in the light of India's continued membership of the commonwealth, the objections were soon removed with the acceptance by the commonwealth of India's membership after adopting a republican Constitution. The Constitution contains several provisions which incorporate the principles that have been identified as associated with republicanism including elected government with limited tenures, an independent judiciary and equality of all citizens and the separation of powers, though not in a strict sense, has been held as being part of the basic structure of the Constitution. It recognises and protects the basic rights and freedoms of individuals and also sets out under the Directive Principles of State Policy various welfare goals that are to guide the State in the making of laws and policies.

The Constitution of India has thus adopted a republican form of government in both the commonly understood sense of having an elected head of state designated the President as well as in the wider sense wherein sovereignty is ultimately traced to the people and government is to be carried out, by their elected representatives, for the welfare of the people, and protection of the individual rights and freedoms of the people is also guaranteed.

CHAPTER VIII

Justice, Equality, Liberty

Rabindra Kr. Pathak

Framers of the Constitution of India brought to bear on their task their vast experience of life in fields-social, economic and political. Their deliberations, which run into twelve volumes, are a testimony to the time and attention which they gave with care and concern to evolving a generally acceptable instrument for the regulation of the fundamental affairs of the country and the life and liberty of its people.[1] Therefore, it is but logical that they used the words in the constitutional text with a purpose. Every word carries a well-thought meaning. And, preamble being a part of the Constitution is no exception to this. The problem, however, is to ascribe meaning to these words. The Constitution has outlived the framers. One way is to see how these value-laden words have been explored and pondered upon by those who have given content to the meaning of these words. These concepts "though treated as eternal verities, are emptied of the vital occasion which gave them birth and have only that content which each generation must pour into them anew in the light of its experience."[2]

1. Justice: A Conceptual Conundrum

No other question has been discussed so passionately; no other question has caused so much blood and so many bitter

---

1. *A.K. Roy* v. *Union of India*, AIR 1982 SC 710: 1982 Cr LJ 340: (1982) 1 SCC 27.
2. *See*, Upendra Baxi (Edn.), K.K. Mathew on Democracy, Equality and Freedom, 5 (1978).

tears to be shed; no other question has been the subject of so much intensive thinking by the illustrious thinkers from Plato to Kant; and yet this question is today unanswered as it ever was.[3] Ever since men have begun to reflect upon their relations with each other and upon the vicissitudes of the human lot, they have been preoccupied with the meaning of justice, says Allen pointing out that there are aspects of justice which seem essential to its conception, developed over a long period, and which even today continue to be refined and reformulated.

To begin with, one of the important aspects of the conception of justice is the understanding that justice lies in the domain of morality (justice as pure virtue). Secondly, justice is a social virtue. Thirdly, the purpose of justice as "social virtue" is to maintain, or to restore, equilibrium in human affairs. Fourthly, justice as moral principle, postulates *equality of consideration* for all who may come within its scope, which means, in effect, all creatures.[4]

Theorizations about justice have produced a huge corpus of literature which shows that at different times, thinkers and philosophers have tried to devise different approaches to explain and appreciate the idea of justice. However, what St. Augustine said of time equally applies to justice as well. He famously said: "I cannot define it but I know what it is."

At the same time, there have been legal thinkers like Kelsen who believed that justice is an irrational concept, and that there are only interests. Conflict of interests and their solution can be brought about only by sacrifice of one for the sake of other or by compromise between opposing interests.[5] Development of the idea of justice shows that while the ancient approach to justice was religious and sacred, modern approach is a social and secular one. Some of the approaches "have sought eternal and unchanging principles

---

3. Kelsen, What is Justice, 1 (1958).
4. C.K. Allen, Aspect of Justice, 1-33 (1997, Indian reprint).
5. *See;* Hans Kelsen, What is Justice? Justice, Law and Politics in the Mirror of Science, 53-55 (1958) quoted in Upendra Baxi (Ed.), K.K. Mathew on Democracy, Equality and Freedom, 34 (1978).

of justice valid for all times and places, whether in the form of the natural lawyer's search for principles or in the search for principles which makes possible the exercise of free will by all according to Kantian Universal Law" says Stone pin-pointing, at the same time , that recent approaches recognize that criteria of justice cannot be independent of the actual condition of man's social, economic and political life in a particular society at a particular time.[6]

The definitional tangle and the wide conceptual canvass of justice has inspired many a philosophical and jurisprudential endeavor to outline the contours of justice, notwithstanding the Diasian caveat that "quest for justice has been as challenging as the quest for Holy Grail, and as elusive. To some this is because justice is a will-o-the-wisp, to others because it is too vast to be encompassed by one mind."[7] One of the famous and oldest definitions attributed to Ulpian says that justice is the constant and perpetual will to render to everyone that to which he is entitled. Kant, however, defined justice as "the aggregate of those conditions under which the will of one person can be conjoined with the will of another in accordance with a universal law of freedom."[8] His definition is very similar to the one given by Spencer that says: "Every man is free to do that which he wills, provided he infringes not the equal freedom of any other man."[9] Chaim Perelman gives few examples which constitute the most current conception of justice.[10] He believes that it is vain to enumerate all the possible meanings of the idea of justice. However, a succinct summarization of what justice stands for one finds in the following observation of Brian Bix:[11]

---

6. Julius Stone, Human Law and Human Justice, 3 (2008, Indian reprint).
7. Dias, Jurisprudence, 65 (1982).
8. Immanuel Kant, the Metaphysical Element of Justice, 34 (1965).
9. Herbert Spencer, Justice, 46 (1891).
10. 1. To each the same thing; 2. To each according to his works; 3. To each according to his needs; 4. To each according to his rank 5. To each according to his merit 6. To each according to his legal entitlement. *See*, Chaim Perelman, "Concerning Justice" in Edward Allen Kent (Ed), Law and Philosophy (1970) at 474.
11 Brian Bix, Jurisprudence: Theory and Context, 103 (2006).

> "Justice" refers to the family of moral concepts connected particularly with law and politics—politics here being understood broadly in the sense of public decision-making regarding the distribution of goods. Justice is a subset of morality. Thus one can sensibly speak of something as being "right" or "wrong" on occasions where it is inapt to speak of "Justice".

Be that as it may, "Justice has a protean face, capable of change, readily assuming different shapes, and endowed with highly variable features. When we look deeply into this face, trying to unravel the secrets hidden behind its outward appearance, bewilderment is apt to befall us."[12] So, one should tread cautiously in the jurisprudential terrain replete with theories of justice. It is better always to be aware of the different approaches to justice. There are many. In *Book* V of his *Nichomachean Ethics,* Aristotle begins discussion on justice.[13] His conception of justice can be seen in two senses: a broader sense and a narrower sense, which deserves some special attention. Roughly speaking or in the broadest sense, justice is the practice of virtue in one's relation with his neighbour. He says:[14]

> Justice is often thought to be the greatest of virtues, and 'neither evening nor morning star' is so wonderful; proverbially 'in justice is every virtue comprehended'. And, it is complete virtue in its fullest sense, because it is actual exercise of complete virtue. It is complete

12. Edgar Bodenheimer, Jurisprudence, 196 (2001, Indian reprint).
13. To counter the danger of justice becoming over-severe, Aristotle introduced the concept of equity (epieikeia), which he regarded as a quality intimately connected with, but distinct from and more precise than, justice. The equitable approach in law, for Aristotle, is aimed at the prevention of the unfortunate consequences of applying a general rule to a particular case that it does not, at a deep moral level, really cover. The feeling might be that while it is right in general that rule X should be applied, it does not really apply to this particular case Y, despite the formal requirements being fulfilled. For Aristotle, then, the function of the appeal to equity was to allow judges to temper the severity of legal justice, without departing from the constraints of law. Mark Tebbit, Philosophy of Law: An Introduction, 9 (2005). Emphasis added.
14. Edward Allen Kent, Law and Philosophy: Readings in Legal Philosophy, 466 (1970)

> because who possesses it can exercise his virtue not only in himself but towards his neighbors also...

In the narrower sense, justice is concerned with the fair and the unfair in the distribution of honors, wealth, and safety in a political society (particular justice), and it has further sub-divisions in the form of distributive and corrective justice, a distinction that remains one of the best known contributions of Aristotle to the study of jurisprudence. Waldron summarizes:[15]

> Since the time of Aristotle, we have known that justice has a general sense and a particular sense. In its particular sense, it operates in a number of different spheres: distributive justice, corrective justice, cqmmutative justice, retributive justice, political justice, and so on. This is either a retail claim-that criminal law promises retributive justice; tort law, corrective justice; the law of contract, commutative justice; and so on – or it is a general, wholesale claim-that justice in the general sense is what law in general promises.... Aristotle draws a further distinction that cuts across these various spheres of justice: Aristotle distinguishes between *natural justice* and *legal justice* (and thus between natural distributive justice and legal distributive justice, between natural corrective justice and legal corrective justice, and so on).

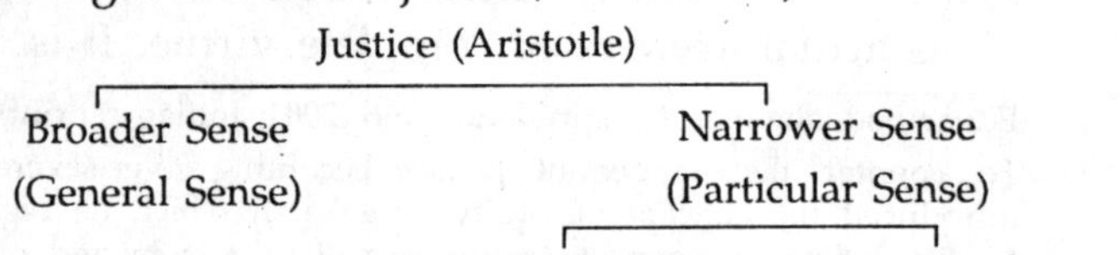

Corrective Justice ('Emendatory' Justice)

Whereas distributive is concerned with equal distribution of goods among members of the community, corrective justice, which relates to the *administration of the law* within a community, is concerned with the "righting of wrongs. If

15. Jeremy Waldron, "Does Law Promise Justice?", 17 Georgia State University Law Review, 759 (2001) at 772-773.

a contract has been broken or a tort has been done, then corrective justice seeks to provide adequate compensation to the wronged party; a crime has been committed, then proper punishment is meted out to the wrongdoer."[16] Aristotle therefore identified corrective justice as "that which plays a rectifying part in transactions between man and man"[17] Malcolm Langford observes:[18]

> Most traditional descriptions of the remedial functions of courts proceed on corrective assumptions, which assume a close connection between the violation of a right and the crafting of a remedy to repair the harm caused by the rights violation. For example, William Blackstone appealed to a theory of corrective justice when he famously wrote that it was 'a settled and invariable principle in the laws of England that every right when withheld must have a remedy and every injury its proper redress'. Blackstone's understanding of remedies informed the decision of *Marbury* v. *Madison*, which asserted powers of judicial review in part on the basis that an individual is entitled 'to claim the protection of the laws, whenever he receives an injury'.

Distributive Justice

What is distinctive about principles of distributive justice is that they refer to that to which people are *entitled*. Aristotle's doctrine of justice of equality is called by him *commutative justice* which requires at least two persons while *distributive justice* requires at least three. Relative equality in treating different persons while granting relief according to need, or reward and punishment according to merit and guilt is the essence of distributive justice. While in commutative justice the two persons confront each other as co-equals, three or more persons are necessary in distributive justice in which

16. Carl J. Friedrich, Constitutional Government and Democracy, 103 (1974).
17. Aristotle, The Nichomachean Ethics, Book 5, Chapters 2–4.
18. Malcolm Langford (Ed.), Social Rights Jurisprudence: Emerging Trends in International and Comparative Law, 48 (2008).

one, who imposes burdens upon or grants advantages to the others, is superior to them. Therefore, it presupposes an act of distributive justice which has granted to those concerned, equality of rights, equal capacity to act, equal status. According to Radbruch, distributive justice is the prototype of justice. In it we have found the idea of justice, towards which the concept of law must be oriented.[19] However, any comprehensive analysis of distributive justice must speak to the following questions:[20]

1. What sorts of entities are included within systems of distributive justice (humans, all sentient creatures, collective entities such as states or nations)?
2. Who are the rightful recipients of goods, and who is obligated to distribute these goods?
3. What should people have fair shares of (income, happiness)?
4. According to what criterion of distributive justice should goods be distributed (equality, according to desert, or the market)?

What should there be fair amounts of? Much has been written on this question. To give some examples: one possibility might be that a theory of justice should ensure that each person has a fair share of 'resources.'[21] Alternatively, one might think that principles of distributive justice should

19. *Gurbax Singh* v. *Financial Commissioner*, AIR 1991 SC 435 (441): JT 1990 (4) SC 114: 1991 (1) SCC (Supp) 167.

20. Simon Caney, Justice Beyond Borders: A Global Political Theory, 103 (2006, Paperback). Caney in his book has made an effort to explore whether there are global principles of distributive justice considering: "One of the striking features of much traditional political philosophy until recently was that it assumed that principles of distributive justice should operate at the state level. That is, the conventional wisdom was, and to some extent still is, that if there are any legitimate principles of distributive justice (and some deny that there are) they should be implemented within states. Duties of distributive justice thus apply within states or nations but do not apply globally. Accordingly, those who affirmed human rights tended to affirm civil and political human rights but deny economic human rights." Id. at 102.

21. Dworkin, Sovereign Virtue: The Theory and Practice of Equality, 65–119 (2000).

be concerned with human happiness and seek to promote welfare. A third position is canvassed by Martha Nussbaum and Amartya Sen, both of whom think that distributive principles should be concerned with peoples' capability to function in certain ways.[22]

2. Equality and Justice

Contemporary theories of justice have two components: formal or legal and economic or legislative. Legal component is presented as equality under the law while the other component is represented as equality through law.[23] Equality is concerned with relative deprivation, and means uniformity. It is comparative in nature deriving its source and limits from the treatments of others. It is simple, and singular but at the same time social as well.[24] For thousands of years, the principle of equality has been dominantly present in western thought, and has made its presence felt through its continuous and sustained articulation in the works of thinkers who have written profusely on issues of justice and its other philosophical aspects. To quote Gregory Vlastos:[25]

> The close connection between justice and equality is manifest in both history and language. The great historic struggle for social justice has centered about some demand for equal rights: the struggle against slaver, political absolutism, economic exploitation, the disenfranchisement of the lower and middle classes

22. Martha Nussbaum, Women and Human Development: The Capabilities Approach, 70–110 (2000); Amartya Sen, "Capability and Well-Being", in Martha Nussbaum and Amartya Sen (eds), The Quality of Life (1993). *Supra* note 18 at 104. Carey.
23. Critical Jurisprudence, 125 (2005).
24. *See*, Peter Westen, "The Empty Idea of Equality", 95 Harvard Law Review (1982) at 537. "The ideal of equality is an inheritance from the inequalities of ancient societies; it is an idea of a peerage – an order or caste of nobles who recognise each other as in some respects and for some purposes equals, while asserting their superiority to the rest of the nation or the rest of the human race... it was in contrast with the subject and the slave that men first felt themselves equal and free." G. Ritchie, Natural Rights, 248 (1903).
25. Gregory Vlastos, " Justice and Equality" in Jeremy Waldron (ed) Theories of Rights, 41 (1984).

and the disenfranchisement women, colonialism, racial oppression.

The not-to-be-ignored relation between equality and justice is, and must be, an integral part of any endeavour to study the nuances of justice as Pennock reminds us that "Equality is not the whole of justice by any means; but to consider questions of justice *without it as starting point* would be like conducting a race without a starting line."[26] Equality is an aspect of justice, with justice being more than simple equality. It is equality *plus*. Equality as an aspect of justice has two phases: *equality as an end to justice* and *equality as means of doing justice*.[27]

Under the Indian Constitution, the concept of equality and equal protection of law guaranteed by Article 14 of the Constitution in its proper spectrum encompasses *social* and *economic justice* in a political democracy as its species to eliminate inequalities in status and to provide facilities and opportunities among the individual and groups of people to secure adequate means of livelihood which is the foundation for stability of political democracy.

Constitution of India (Equality Provisions)

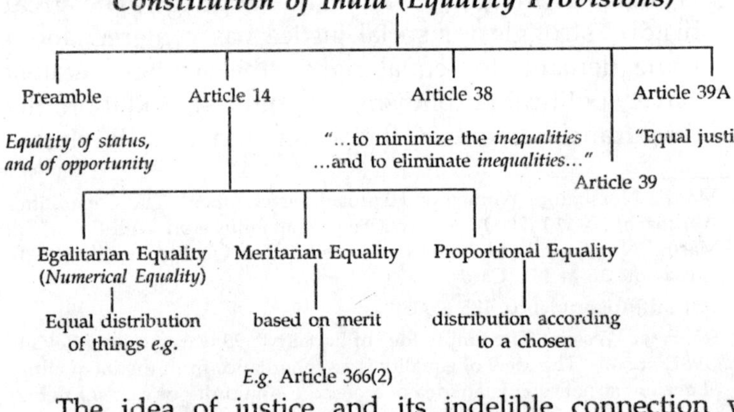

The idea of justice and its indelible connection with equality finds a prominent articulation in the words of Aristotle when he says that injustice arises as much from

26. J.R. Pennock, Democratic Political Theory, 146 (1979) Emphasis added.

27. *See*, Raj Kumar Gupta, "Justice: Unequal But Inseparable", 57 Journal of the Indian Law Institute 29 (1969) at 57.

treating unequals equally as from treating equals unequally. He believed in equality among the equals, *i.e.*, "treat like cases alike" (formal equality). He talks of justice as *proportional equality*.[28] To him, justice is not all about arithmetical equality; it rather involves proportional equality which is maintained by the application of the principle of giving to each according to his *deserts*. Justice consists in giving the morally superior better treatment and granting to the morally inferior a smaller part of the distributed rewards.[29]

The inseparable existence of justice and equality stands well exemplified in the struggle that Ambedkar, *the Aristotle of Indian Dalits*,[30] waged against the prevailing social and political set-up for the emancipation of the *atisudras*. His fight was a fight for equality. He believed that classical Hindu law and jurisprudence not only denied "equality before the law" as a principle to the untouchables, it in doing so erected permanent edifice of *legitimized subalternity* over them down the ages.[31] He felt that equal treatment to unequals would lead to further inequality, in a society where the caste-system has been the anti-thesis of a social order based on the principles of liberty, equality and social justice. Therefore, remedial measures are necessary for the reconstruction of the caste-based system. Oppressed class should be given special facilities and more opportunities to compete with the advanced ones. Reservation for scheduled tribes and scheduled castes is one such facility.[32] In a dispute concerning reservation of seats in Panchayats, the Supreme Court observed:[33]

---

28. To Aristotle, there are two kinds of equality—numerical and proportional.
29. Amal Kumar Mukhoupadhyay , Western Political Thought, 28-29 (1980).
30. *See*, Upendra Baxi, "Does Life Indeed Begin at Sixty? Revisiting the UDHR as a "Single Garment of DESTINY" in a Hyper globalizing World", 23 Emory International Law Review, (2009) at 29.
31. Upendra Baxi, "Emancipation as Justice: Babasaheb Ambedkar's Legacy and Vision" in K.I. Vibhute (ed), Dr. Ambedkar and Empowerment: Constitutional Vicissitudes, 77 (1993). Emphasis added.
32. *See*, J.M. Waghmare, "Dr. Ambedkar's Quest for Social Justice" in K.I. Vibhute (ed), Dr. Ambedkar and Empowerment: Constitutional Vicissitudes, 94 (1993).
33. *Union of India* v. *Rakesh Kumar*, AIR 2010 SC 3244: 2010 AIR SCW 657: (2010) 4 SCC 50 decided on Civil Appeal Nos. 484-491 of 2006.

It is a well-accepted premise in our legal system that ideas such as 'substantive equality' and 'distributive justice' are at the heart of our understanding of the guarantee of 'equal protection before the law'. The State can treat unequals differently with the objective of creating a level-playing field in the social, economic and political spheres. The question is whether 'reasonable classification' has been made on the basis of intelligible differentia and whether the same criterion bears a direct nexus with a legitimate governmental objective. When examining the validity of affirmative action measures, the enquiry should be governed by the standard of proportionality rather than the standard of 'strict scrutiny'. Of course, these affirmative action measures should be periodically reviewed and various measures are modified or adapted from time to time in keeping with the changing social and economic conditions. Reservation of seats in Panchayats is one such affirmative action measure enabled by Part IX of the Constitution.

Fair Equality of Opportunity

Rawls introduced the idea of fair equality of opportunity to correct the defects of formal equality of opportunity. In the scheme of the principles of justice, it has been given priority over the difference principle. It simply means that public offices and social positions are not open only in a formal sense. Rather, all should have a fair chance to attain them. Fair equality to be precise means liberal equality, and to attain its aims, it is necessary that certain requirements must be imposed on the basic structure of the society. The second principle of justice, as propounded by Rawls, recognizes the fact that there would be inequalities. However, such an inequality has to be of the greatest benefit of the least advantaged of the society. The second part of the second principle, known as difference principle, is concerned with making the worst-off members of the society as well off as possible. It is concerned with distributive equity as well as overall efficiency. This principle indicates the importance of equity in social arrangements so that attention is drawn particularly to the predicament of the worst-off people.[34] The point is that inequality in distribution of resources is justified only when it is in the interests of such people.

The (Basic) Liberties

Norman Barry writes that the concept of liberty is perhaps one of the 'most' difficult concepts to elucidate. It is suffused with emotive appeal. He however believes that 'a person is free to the extent that her actions and choices are not impeded by actions of others'.[35] Liberty, however, can be positive liberty or negative liberty, as Sir Isaiah Berlin has written in the classic work, *The Two Concepts of Liberty*.[36] Answer to the question, "what is the area within which the subject—a person or a group of persons—is or should be left to do or be what he is able to be, without interference by other persons?"[37] Reflects the negative sense of the term "liberty". And, the positive sense of "liberty" may be said to be clear in the answer to the question: "what, or who, is the source of control or interference that can determine someone to do, or be, this rather than that?"[38]

The equal basic liberties in the first principle of justice, as propounded by Rawls, are specified by a list as follows: freedom of thought and liberty of conscience;[39] the political liberties (*e.g.* the right to vote and to participate in politics) and freedom of association, as well as the freedoms specified by the liberty and integrity of the person; and finally, the rights and liberties covered by the rule of law.[40] That is, Rawls identifies four categories of liberties. The second and fourth categories are familiar and widely used, and might respectively be called *rights of political participation* and

34. *See*, Amartya Sen, The Idea of Justice, (2009).
35. Norman Barry, Modern Political Theory, 188-200 (2000). He uses the word "liberty" and "freedom" "interchangeably".
36. Sir Isaiah Berlin, The Two Concepts of Liberty, (1969).
37. Id. at 121.
38. Id. at 122.
39. It includes rights protecting thought, belief, inquiry, expression, and association.
40. John Rawls, Tanner Lectures, (1981).

due process rights. However, the third category is the most vague, and Rawls never offers a comprehensive listing of its contents.[41] Nickel points out that if we compare the four categories of basic liberties enlisted by Rawls with the historic and contemporary bill of rights, there are notable omissions, of which the important ones are:[42]

(1) Rights to security (protections against wrongful killing, torture, rape, harm, and deprivation of property); and

(2) Liberties in the area of family, lifestyle, and reproduction, including rights of privacy and (limited) control by parents of the rearing and education of children.

However, the noticeable point is that Rawls's first principle protects only certain *basic liberties* which cannot be interfered with and not liberty in general. And it is in this sense that the first principle of justice differs from classical liberal principle.

When a Constitutional text embodies provisions recognizing right to liberty, along with life, many questions are bound to crop. One such question is: what is the extent of "liberty" recognized by a Constitution? Can a state through a "process" of law deprive people of their cherished personal liberty? And if yes, what is the nature and extent of such deprivation? What about the implications that arise from the debate that talk about "due process of law" and "procedure established by law" as regard the protection and violation of personal liberty? These questions and answers to these form part of a long history of great Constitutional consequence.

3. The Preambular Promise: The Constitutional Perspective

The Preamble to the Constitution of India promises socio-economic justice, the fundamental rights confer certain justiciable socio-economic rights and the Directive Principles

41. *See*, James W. Nickel, "Rethinking Rawls's Theory of Justice and Liberty", 69 Chicago-Kent Law Review 763 (1994) at 766.

42. *Ibid*.

fix the socio-economic goals which the State must strive to attain.[43] These three together constitute the core and conscience of the Constitution.[44] It begins with a preambular

---

43. "To establish an egalitarian social order, the trinity, the Preamble, the Fundamental Rights in Part III and Directive Principles of State Policy in Chapter IV of the Constitution delineated the socio-economic justice. The word 'justice' envision in the Preamble is used in broad spectrum to harmonise individual right with the general welfare of the society. The Constitution is the supreme law. The purpose of law is realisation of justice whose content and scope vary depending upon the prevailing social environment. Every social and economic change causes change in the law. In a democracy governed by rule of law, it is not possible to change the legal basis of socio-economic life of the community without bringing about any corresponding change in the law. In interpretation of the Constitution and the law, endeavour needs to be made to harmonise the individual interest with the paramount interest of the community keeping pace with the realities of ever changing social and economic life of the community envisaged in the Constitution. Justice in the Preamble implies equality consistent with the competing demands between distributive justice with those of cumulative justice. Justice aims to promote the general well-being of the community as well as individual's excellence. The principal end of society is to protect the enjoyment of the rights of the individuals subject to social order, well-being and morality. Establishment of priorities of liberties is a political judgment". See, *Dalmia Cement (Bharat) Ltd.* v. *Union of India,* (1996) 10 SCC 104: 1996 AIR SCW 3652.
44. *Jacob M. Puthuparambil* v. *Kerala Water Authority,* (1991) 1 SCC 28: AIR 1990 SC 2228: 1990 Lab IC 1918, para 5. "The Constitution guarantees 'equality', abhors discrimination, prohibits and penalises forced labour in any form whatsoever and extends protection against exploitation of labour including child labour. After extending these guarantees, amongst others, the Constitution makers proceeded to chart out the course for the Governance of the country in Part IV of the Constitution entitled 'Directive Principles of State Policy'. These Principles reflect the hopes and aspirations of the people. Although the provisions of this part are not enforceable by any court, the Principles laid down therein are nevertheless fundamental in the Governance of the country and the State is under an obligation to apply them in making laws. The Principles laid down therein, therefore, define the objectives and goals which the State must endeavour to achieve over a period of time. Therefore, whenever the State is required to make laws it must do so consistently with these principles with a view to securing social and economic freedom so essential for the establishment of an egalitarian society. This part, therefore, mandates that the State shall strive to promote the welfare of the people by minimizing the inequalities in income and eliminating inequalities in status, facilities and opportunities; by directing its policy towards securing, amongst others, the distribution of the material resources of the community to subserve the common good; by so operating the economic system as not to result in concentration of wealth; and by making effective provision

Contd. on next page

proclamation of securing justice, social, economic and political. Interestingly, constitutional articulation of securing liberty and equality in the preamble, echoing Rawls's twin principles, predates his famed *Theory of Justice* (1971). Justice as a primary objective of government is concerned with two things: first, to ensure that all person are put in a position to get what they are entitled to under the law; and second, to ensure that no one injured, that is, suffers injury to life or limb unless he has infringed the law, law here meaning not merely the positive enactments of Legislative Authority, rather encompassing standards of fairness, reasonableness, and the like.[45]

Accordingly, when the Constitution of India was being framed, in the Constituent Assembly, detailed provisions were made to ensure that people were not deprived of their cherished rights and entitlements as can be seen under Part III and Part IV of the Constitution. However, working of the Indian Constitution in the last six decades archives both the instances of right-protection and right-deprivation.

Whereas *economic justice* is enshrined in article 39 of the Constitution, *social justice* is enshrined in article 38.[46]

Contd. from previous page

for securing the right to work as also to public assistance in cases of unemployment, albeit within the limits of its economic capacities. There are certain other provisions which enjoin on the State certain duties, *e.g.* securing to all workers work, a living wage, just and humane conditions of work, a decent standard of life, participation in management, etc. which are aimed at improving the lot of the working classes." *Ibid.*

45. Friederich op. cit, at 103.

46. "Justice is the generic sense and social justice is its facet, a dynamic device to mitigate the sufferings of the disadvantaged and to eliminate handicaps so as to elevate them to the level of equality to live life with dignity of person, social justice is not a simple or single idea of a society but is an essential part of complex social change to relieve the poor etc. from handicaps, penury, to ward them off from distress and to make their lives livable for greater good of the society at large. Social justice, therefore, gives substantial degree of social, economic and political equality, which is the constitutional right of every citizen."

"The constitutional concern of social justice, as an elastic continuous process, is to transform and accord justice to all sections of the society by providing facilities and opportunities to remove handicaps and disabilities

Contd. on next page

Political justice relates to the Principle of Rights of the people, *i.e.* right to universal suffrage, right to democratic form of Government and right to participation in political affairs.[47] In fact, Constitution incorporates a particular socio-economic and political philosophy, so well reflected by, and interwoven in the Constitution, "a document of social revolution which casts an obligation on every instrumentality including the Judiciary, which is a separate but equal branch of the State, to transform the status *quo ante* into a new human order in which justice, social, economic and political will inform all institutions of national life and there will be equality of status and opportunity for all."[48] We would do well to remember that justice – social, economic and political – is preamble to our Constitution. Administration of justice can no longer be merely protector of *legal rights* but must whenever possible be dispenser of social justice.[49] The Constitution of India, in its historical background provided Directive Principles *vis-a-vis* the fundamental rights to realize social and economic democracy for successful working of political democracy in which the state is bound to provide to every person in the society equality of opportunity in economic arrangements. Material resources and operation of the economic system shall be so organized as to establish the egalitarian social order.[50]

Contd. from previous page

with which the poor etc. are languishing. It aims to secure dignity of their person. It is the duty of the state to accord justice to all members of the society in all facets of human activity. The concept of social justice embeds equality to flavor and enlivens practical content of life. Social justice and equality are complementary to each other so that both should maintain their vitality. Rule of Law, therefore, is a potent instrument of social justice to bring about equality in result." See, *Suresh Kumar Dalmia Cement (Bharat) Ltd.* v. *Union of India*, decided by the Supreme Court of India on 25 April, 1996.

47. See, *Raghunathrao Ganpatrao* v. *Union of India*, AIR 1993 SC 1267 (1289).
48. *S.P. Gupta* v. *President of India*, AIR 1982 SC 149 (197): 1982 Rajdhani LR 389: (1981) Supp SCC 87 (210).
49. *Sadhuram Bansal* v. *Pulin Behari Sarkar*, AIR 1984 SC 1471 (1479): (1984) 3 SCC 410. Emphasis added.
50. *Jilubhai Nanbhai Khachar* v. *State of Gujarat*, 1994 AIR SCW 4181: AIR 1995 SC 142 (164): 1995 Supp (1) SCC 596. Within the system of economic

Contd. on next page

One of the essential aspects of justice under the Indian Constitution has been the concept of economic justice. Economic justice means the abolition of those economic conditions which ultimately result in the inequality of economic value between men *viz.* concentration of wealth and means of production in the hands of a few. It also means equality of reward for equal work. Every man should get his just dues for his labour.[51] It means that there shall be no distinction between man and man from the standpoint of economic value. In short, it aims at establishing economic democracy and a welfare state. The ideal of economic justice is to make equality of status meaningful and the life worth living at its best removing inequality of opportunity and of status – social, economic and political.[52]

Our Constitution permits and even directs the State to administer what may be termed "distributive justice". The concept of distributive justice in the sphere of law-making connotes, *inter alia,* the removal of economic inequalities and rectifying the injustice resulting from dealings or transactions between unequals in society. *Law should be used as an instrument of distributive justice to achieve a fair division of wealth among the members of society based upon the Principle: "From each according to his capacity, to each according to his needs"*. Distributive justice comprehends more than achieving lessening of inequalities by differential taxation, giving debt relief of distribution of property owned by one too many who have none by imposing ceiling on holdings, both agricultural

Contd. from previous page

justice as defined by Louis Kelso and Mortimer Adler, there are three essential and interdependent Principles: The Principle of Participation, The Principle of Distribution, and The Principle of Harmony. Like the legs of a three-legged stool, if any of these Principles is weakened or missing, the system of economic justice will collapse. http://www.cesj.org/thirdway/economicjustice-defined.htm, (last accessed on 23.02.11). The ideal of economic justice is to make equality of status meaningful and the life worth living at its best removing inequality of opportunity and of status- social, economic and political.

51. *See,* DC Jain, "Economic Justice and the Indian Constitution", (1971) 2 SCJ 26.

52 *Suresh Kumar Dalmia Cement (Bharat) Ltd.* v. *Union of India,* decided on 25 April, 1996

and urban, or by direct regulation of contractual transaction by forbidding certain transactions and, perhaps, by requiring others. It also means that those who have been deprived of their properties by unconscionable bargaining should be restored their property. All such laws may take the form of forced redistribution of wealth as a means of achieving a fair division of material resources among the members of society or there may be Legislative control of unfair agreements.[53] In *Central Inland Water Transport Corporation Ltd.* v. *Brijonath Ganguly,* the Supreme Court observed:[54]

> When our Constitution states that it is being enacted in order to give to all the Citizens of India "JUSTICE social, economic and political", when clause (1) of Art 38 of the Constitution directs the State to strive to promote the welfare of the people by securing and protecting as effectively as it may the social order in which social, economic and political justice shall inform all the institutions of the national life, when clause (2) of Art. 38 directs the State, in particular, to minimize the inequalities in income, not only amongst individuals but also amongst groups of people residing in different areas or engaged in different vocations, and when Art. 39 directs the State that it shall, in particular, direct its policy towards securing that the citizens, men and women equally, have the right to an adequate means of livelihood and that the operation of the economic system does not result in the concentration of wealth and means of production to the common detriment and that there should be equal pay for equal work for both men and women, it is the doctrine of distributive justice which is speaking through these words of the Constitution.

The "noble and grand vision" vision of the Constitution of India was "was put in words in the preamble and carried out

53. *Lingappa Pochanna Appealwar* v. *State of Maharashtra,* AIR 1985 SC 389: (1985) 1 SCC 479: (1985) 2 SCR 224.

54. AIR 1986 SC 1571 (1606-7): (1986) 3 SCC 156: 1986 (2) Supreme 479 (para 83).

in part by conferring fundamental rights on the people. The vision was directed to be further carried out by the application of Directive Principles.[55] And two such fundamental rights of great constitutional importance are right to personal liberty and equality. In *Kharak Singh* v. *State of Uttar Pradesh*,[56] it was observed that "the term "personal liberty" is used in article 21 as a compendious term to include within itself all the varieties of rights which go to make up the "personal liberties" of man other than those dealt with in the several clauses of article 19(I). While article 19(1) deals with particular species or attributes of that freedom, "personal liberty"' in article 21 takes in and comprises the residue."

In *Bolling* v. *Sharpe*,[57] the Supreme Court of America observed that the expression "liberty" was not confined to mere freedom from bodily restraint and that liberty under law extended to the full range of conduct which the individual was free to pursue. But this absolute right to liberty was regulated to protect other social interests by the State exercising its powers. In *Kharak Singh*, it was aptly observed that "In India the word "liberty" has been qualified by the word "personal", indicating thereby that it is confined only to the liberty of the person. The other aspects of the liberty have been provided for in other Articles of the Constitution. Even in the most advanced and orderly democratic societies in the world in which political equality is to a large extent achieved, the content of liberty is more and more recognized to be the product of social and economic justice without which all freedoms become meaningless.[58]

As regards the conceptual interplay of the preambular values, it can be said;[59]

55. *Kesavananda Bharati* v. *State of Kerala*, (1973) 4 SCC 225: AIR 1973 SC 1461, para. 15.
56. AIR 1963 SC 1295: (1963) 2 Cr LJ 329: (1964) 1 SCR 332. The court explained that "The right of personal liberty in article 21 implies a right of an individual to be free from restrictions or encroachments on his person, whether those restrictions or encroachments are directly imposed or indirectly brought about by calculated measures."
57. (1954) 347 US 407 (499).
58. *Kesavananda*, para 1329.
59. *Id.* at 1353.

The pre-eminent place in the Preamble is given to JUSTICE-social, economic and political, and it is obvious that without JUSTICE the other concepts of LIBERTY, EQUALITY and FRATERNITY would be illusory. In a democratic country whose institutions are informed by JUSTICE-social, economic and political, the other three concepts of LIBERTY, EQUALITY and FRATERNITY will be automatically fostered. Social and political Justice takes care of Liberty; and Justice, social and economic, takes care of Equality of status and of opportunity.

CHAPTER IX

Fraternity

Deepa Kansra

The making (and remaking) of Constitutions, designated as the constituent power, manifests the power, strength, and movement of the multitudes. Constitutions as grammars of the constituted power often tend towards the reduction of the constituent power, thus diminishing the range of the political. If we were to regard constituent power as 'the origin of the political,' then the negation of the political by the constituted power invites continual 'struggles to emerge in order to emerge as strength'[1]

The Preamble of the Constitution of India affirms the determination to secure amongst the people a feeling of fraternity, ensuring the dignity of the individual and the unity of the nation.[2]

The historic ideal of fraternity integrated with liberty and equality (the trinity) has been an omnipresent feature of Indian

---

1. Upendra Baxi, *"Preliminary Notes of Transformative Constitutionalism"*, BISA Conference: Courting Justice (Delhi 2008). Available at http://www.conectas.org/IBSA/UBNotesonTransformativeConstitutionalism.pdf.
2. The Preamble of the Constitution of India.

   Text also embodied by the National Commission to Review the Working of the Constitution: A Consultation Paper on Literacy in the Context of Constitution of India, Vigyan Bhawan (2001). Available at http://lawmin.nic.in/ncrwc/finalreport/v2b1-5.htm (Last visited 10-1-2013).

   In *Pradip Jain* v. *Union of India*, AIR 1984 SC 1420 the court stated; Preamble of the Constitution is framed with great care and deliberation so that it reflects the high purpose and the noble objective of the Constitution makers.

democratic politics. The significance of the constitutional trinity has been highlighted in *Kartar Singh* v. *State of Punjab*,[3] wherein the court makes a reference to the closing speech of Dr. Ambedkar in the Constituent Assembly;

> "The Principle of Liberty, equality and fraternity are not to be treated as separate entities but in a trinity. They form the union or trinity in the sense that to divorce one from the other is to defeat the very purpose of democracy. Liberty cannot be divorced from equality. Nor can equality and liberty be divorced from fraternity".

Even so, fraternity has more than often been absent from the miniscule exploration of the constitutional ideals present under the Preamble.[4] Observably, it is the "forgotten element of democracy."[5]

Historically, 'liberty, equality, fraternity became a major influence on political thought after the French Revolution. The Revolution marked the triumph of the people and pronounced the Declaration on Rights of Man and of the Citizen in 1789. According to Johnston, even then fraternity was rather less central to the preconceptions of the enlightenment predecessors of the revolutionary era, their emphasis being

3. (1994) 3 SCC 569: (1994) 2 SCR 375: 1994 Cr LJ 3139 (SC).
4. In 2011, scholar and historian K.N. Panikkar while interacting with the students in Chennai levelled a critical narrative of the Constitutional promises. He expressed; that "while Indian Democracy had evolved an institutional structure on the basis of the principles and prescriptions laid down in the Constitution, there existed a wide gulf between precept and practice", "while cultural plurality was the strength of the Indian civilization, the absence of cultural equality had led to the exclusion of many from the mainstream life", "the widening gulf between religious communities, coinciding with the influence of religion from the private to the public sphere, has led to a religionisation of society and commodification of religion." *See* Special Correspondent, "Several Basic Guarantees of Statute Remain Inaccessible to Vast Sections of Population", The Hindu (Chennai, July 2011). Available at http://www.thehindu.com/news/national/article 2219573.ece (Last visited 10.1 2013).
5. Justice Charles Gonthier, "Liberty, Equality, Fraternity: The Forgotten Leg of the Trilogy, or Fraternity The Unspoken Third Pillar of Democracy" 45 McGill Law Journal 569 (2000).

   Justice Gonthier refers to "fraternity" as an essential value as that of liberty and equality. However, fraternity has not been discussed more often in comparison to the other two values.

given rather to the 'rights of man' and to the equality of entitlement to those rights.[6]

In the present, although there are many differences in interpretation...the idea of fraternity is less directly accepted.[7] Till date, the pre-occupation with liberty and equality has left vacant a conceptual upbringing of *fraternity* in the postcolonial context.

1. Popularizing *Fraternity*

From the literature available it can be gathered that *fraternity* has been subjected to several interpretations and linked with several virtues. For a few, it stands close to the actualities of solidarity, humanity, compassion, companionship, brotherhood.[8] For others, it is the "glue that binds equality and liberty to the civil society" and "presents a sense of continuity with the past and the future".[9]

Omvedt replaces the word fraternity with "community", an important component of a human vision for the new millennium along with equality and justice.[10] According to Wilson McWilliams (*The Idea of Fraternity in America*, 1973) fraternity – a relation of affection founded on shared values and goals, is a permanent social and psychological need of human development, yet one that is discouraged and inhibited by the institutions and processes of modern industrial societies.[11]

---

6. Gerald Johnston, "Liberty, Equality, Fraternity: Democratic Ideals and Educational Effects", Vol. 12 No. 4 British Journal of Sociology of Education 492 (1991).
7. Paul Spicker, Liberty, Equality, Fraternity, The Policy Press, UK 1 (2006).
8. The Universal Declaration of Human Rights states that all human beings are born free and equal in dignity and rights. They are endowed with reason and conscience and should act towards one another in a spirit of brotherhood. *See* Universal Declaration of Human Rights, GA Res. (1948).
9. *Supra* note 5.
10. Gail Omvedt, "Liberty, Equality, Community: Dr. Ambedkar's Vision of a New Social Order" Available at http://www.ambedkar.org/research/LibertyEquality.htm.
11. Wilson Carey McWilliams, The Idea of Fraternity in America, University of California Press, London 7 (1973).
    McWilliam also argues that fraternity is a bond based on intense interpersonal affection; involves shared values or goals considered more important than mere life; implies a necessary tension with loyalty to society at large.

In addition to the Indian Constitution, Constitutions across the globe have committed themselves to the vision of brotherhood and harmony in society. The Preamble of the Constitution of Brazil (New Constitution in 1988) states;

> We, the representatives of the Brazilian People, assembled in the National Constituent Assembly to institute a Democratic State for the purpose of ensuring the exercise of social and individual rights, liberty, security, well-being, development, equality and justice as supreme values of a fraternal, pluralist and unprejudiced society...[12]

In the more recent times, fraternity has aroused the enthusiasm of scholars and states amidst global disintegration and unrest. In *S.* v. *Makwanyane,*[13] the South African court referred to *ubuntu* or shared solidarity as a constitutional value;

> "The concept of *ubuntu* is of some relevance to the values we need to uphold. It is a culture which places some emphasis on communality and on the interdependence of the members of a community. It recognizes a person's status as a human being, entitled to unconditional respect, dignity, value and acceptance from the members of the community such person happens to be part of. It also entails the converse, however. The person has a corresponding duty to give the same respect, dignity, value and acceptance to each member of that community. More importantly, it regulates the exercise of rights by the emphasis it lays on sharing and co-responsibility and the mutual enjoyment of rights by all".

In 1993, the Parliament of the World's Religions with the support of two hundred leaders from diverse backgrounds

12. R.C. Lahoti, Preamble: The Spirit and Backbone of the Constitution of India, Eastern Book Company 126 (2004).

    Also, the Italian Constitution under article 2 provides; "the Republic expects that the fundamental duties of political, economic and social solidarity be fulfilled." *See* Xenophon Contiades and Alkmene Fotiadou, "Social Rights in the Age of Proportionality: Global Economic Crisis and Constitutional Litigation" Vol. 10 No. 3, 660-686 International Journal of Constitutional Law 664 (2012).
13. (1995) 3 SA 391 (CC).

adopted the declaration *Towards a Global Ethic*. The Declaration personifies the values of fraternity;

> "We must treat others as we wish others to treat us. We make a commitment to respect life and dignity, individuality and diversity, so that every person is treated humanely, without exception. We must have patience and acceptance. We must be able to forgive, learning from the past but never allowing ourselves to be enslaved by memories of hate. Opening our hearts to one another, we must sink our narrow differences for the cause of the world community, practicing a culture of solidarity and relatedness."[14]

In 2011, the Canadian Institute for the Administration of Justice in collaboration with the McGill University organized a symposium on *Responsibility, Fraternity and the Sustainability in Law* to highlight fraternity as an intrinsic value and a mode of conduct aiming for the realization of human and social needs.[15] In Latin America (since 2006) there has been a collaborative effort between scholars and state officials to conceptualize *fraternity*. More specifically, *The Forgotten Principle: Fraternity in Law and Politics* (First published in 2006) by Antonio Baggio has taken the lead in bringing the study of fraternity back to the mainstream of political and historic discussions.[16] According to Baggio there are many forms

14. The Parliament of the World's Religions, The Declaration *Towards a Global Ethic*. Chicago, USA (September 1993). Available at http://www.parliamentofreligions.org/_includes/FCKcontent/File/TowardsAGlobalEthic.pdf.
15. *See* Jola Gjuzi, "Substantiating the Principle of Sustainable Development with the Principle of Fraternity: The case of Corporate Social Responsibility" Available at http://cisdl.org/gonthier/public/pdfs/papers/Conférence%20Charles%20D%20Gonthier%20-%20Jola%20Gjuzi.pdf.
16. Rodrigo Mardones, "Fraternity in Politics: New Scholarship and Publications from Latin America" Vol. 1 No. 2 Journal of Dialogue and Culture 72 (October 2012).

    Mardones deals in brief with the contemporary works on fraternity; Antonio M. Baggio, Fraternity in Political Perspective (2009), Osvaldo Barreneche, ed., Recent Studies about Fraternity (2010), Pablo Ramírez, ed., Fraternity and Conflict (2011), Domingo Ighina, The Ember under the Ashes (2012).

by which fraternity among human beings may be fulfilled, but in the end the concept needs to be translated into the political sphere in order for it to have a positive impact on the community at large.[17] Baggio identifies the two conditions that he considers key for fraternity to become a political category. First, it must properly be a criterion for political decisions; and second, it must affect the way the other two political categories (liberty and equality) are conceived. "Baggio has underlined how fraternity is a dynamic reality, signifying a co-belonging to the other, and constitutes the beginning of a reality to be reckoned with, in which liberty and equality represent the other poles of confrontational differences".[18]

There is visibly an attempt to define fraternity as a political or legal value, more simply than a historic/rhetoric one. Fraternity is seen to be reflected in the everyday lives of the community, wherein there is sharing of common experiences, threats, and values. The inability to re-construct fraternity as a reality would obstruct us from rationalizing the process of mass/social mobility, integration or cohesion in general and situationally. Fraternity as solidarity or brotherhood may very well be read with the conditions of mass conflict or social disintegration. It is certainly a dynamic and propelling ideal within law and society, worthy of the same respect as the values of equality and liberty.

2. The Global Fraternity

Global fraternity or universal brotherhood is a theme worth entertaining for several scholars. Universal fraternity basically reflects "diverse fraternities"[19] or situationally expressing the "solidarity of global resistance."[20] The experience of globalization and interdependence underlies the existence of common problems and the need for coordinated solutions to these problems.

---

17. *Ibid* at 74.
18. Marco Luppi, "Myth and Fraternity" (2012). Available at http://www.iu-sophia.org/_News_1399 (Last visited 10-1-2013).
19. Sophia University Institute, "Fraternity as a Relational Principle, in Law and Politics" Available at http://www.iu-sophia.org/_News_1377.
20. *Supra* note 1 at 19.

In addition to the increasing literature on *fraternity*, brotherhood and social cohesion, the ideal has also paved the way for global reforms to instill the value of *brotherhood* in the younger generations. Globalization of political values like that of fraternity has affected the paths of several "multicultural nation-states".[21] For instance, in *Grutter* v. *Bollinger*,[22] the US court has highlighted the role of education as the foundation of good citizenship.

3. *Fraternity* and the Indian Society

India has rich diversity which the Constitution has preserved and respected. The Constitution itself incorporates the zeal of the nation and "it is the creation of the people of India who, being dissatisfied with the then existing constitutional arrangements, wanted to make a fresh start".[23] The Constitution does embody the essence of fraternity through its text and interpretations.

> Fraternity means a sense of common brotherhood of all Indians...In a country like ours with so many disruptive forces of regionalism, communalism and linguism, it is necessary to emphasize and re-emphasise that the unity and integrity of India can be preserved only by a spirit of brotherhood.[24]

In *Rajasthan State Electricity Board* v. *Sultan Mohd.*[25] the High Court of Rajasthan stated that;

> The expression "fraternity" has not been defined in the Constitution but it appears that this expression is

21. Paul Enriquez, "Deconstructing Transnationalism: Conceptualizing Metanationalism as a Putative Model of Evolving Jurisprudence" Vol. 43: 1265 Vanderbilt Journal of Transnational Law 1295 (2010).
22. 539 US 306 (331) (2003).
23. Mahendra P. Singh and Surya Deva, "The Constitution of India: Symbol of Unity in Diversity"53 Yearbook of Public Law Germany 649-686 (2005). Also *see* Nicholas Robinson, "India's Constitutional Anxiety: Has the Constitution Transformed Indian Society?" (Book Review) The Caravan: A Journal of Politics and Culture (November 2012). Available at http://www.caravanmagazine.in/books/indias-constitutional-anxiety.
24. Words of Dr. Ambedkar quoted in Justice R.C. Lahoti, Preamble: The Spirit and Backbone of the Constitution of India, Eastern Book Company 106 (2004).
25. (2000) III LLJ 691 Raj.

wide enough to include every bond of unity between two or more human beings, whether the bond, is temporary or it is permanent, whether it is contractual or sacramental; whether it is voluntary or commanded by law. Suffice it to say that fraternity referred to in the preamble to the Constitution of India, refers to human bonds among the people as well as the bonds between the sovereign and the subjects. The bond of fraternity, not only binds the parties to it, it creates mutuality of interaction and shifting of certain responsibilities according to the nature and form of the bond. Whatever may or may not be the obligation of the parties on account of the bond of fraternity between them, one thing is very obvious that unless the parties to the bond of fraternity would not honour, protect and enforce the rights of other parties to the bond, the bond of fraternity cannot survive... Fraternity, in our opinion, imposes a duty on every party, to honour, protect and enforce the rights of the other parties to the bond and this appears to be at the root of the maxim that wherever there is a right there must be a corresponding duty on some other fellow and there must be a remedy available for enforcing the right. The bond of fraternity which exists between the sovereign and subjects, makes it obligatory on the part of sovereign to enforce the rule of law and to administer justice to all citizens by honouring their rights and by taking appropriate steps to protect and enforce the same even if the citizen does not ask for it...

Under Part IVA of the Constitution of India, fundamental duties (article 51A) have been prescribed. The provision states under clause (e); it shall be the duty of every citizen of India- to promote harmony and the spirit of common brotherhood amongst all people of India transcending religious, linguistic, and regional or sectional diversities...[26] Fundamental duties have been interpreted so that citizens must exercise their fundamental rights keeping in mind the duties provided

26. Fundamental Duties were incorporated by the 42nd Amendment Act.

under the Constitution.[27] Part IVA "re-endorses fraternity as cited in the Preamble...the framers of the Constitution gave a new dimension to the concept of fraternity. It was not only to raise the status of many who were looked down upon by the privileged castes but also to bring about harmony and understanding between the various segments of the Indian society so that the country appeared to be one, for all intents and purposes".[28]

Part III of the Constitution dealing with fundamental rights gives freedom to minorities and "accommodation is the key concept that characterizes this constitutional approach to diversity..."[29] To many, fraternity is often referred to specifically in the context of backward classes and religious minorities.[30] In *Indira Sawhney* v. *Union of India*,[31] "fraternity was used by in two distinct, yet related fashions: to defend the practice of reservations under the Constitution on the basis of fraternity, and also to warn of its effects on fraternal relations when undertaken in an unguided manner."[32]

In *Ashok Kumar Thakur* v. *Union of India*,[33] the apex court stated; the Preamble to the Constitution of India secures, as one of its objects, fraternity assuring the dignity of the individual and the unity and integrity of the nation to 'we

27. *See* J.C. Johari, The Constitution of India: A Political-Legal Study, 4th Ed. Sterling Publishers Pvt. Ltd. 95-96 (2007).
28. Aparajita Baruah, Preamble of the Constitution of India: An Insight and Comparison with other Constitutions, Deep and Deep Publications 63-64 (2007).
29. Balveer Arora, "Diversity and Unity in the Republic of India" in Luis Moreno, Cesar Coleno (Eds.), Diversity and Unity in Federal Countries, McGill-Queens University Press 200-226 (2010). Also available http://www.academia.edu/450290/Diversity_and_Unity_in_the_Republic_of_India (Last visited 10-1-2013).
30. Muchkund Dubey, S.N. Jha, and Rajiv Balakrishnan, Social Development in India – The Policy Canvas: An Overview of the Last Fifty Years & Emerging Issues for the Twenty-First Century, Council for Social Development, New Delhi.
31. (1992) Supp (3) SCC 217: AIR 1993 SC 477: 1902 AIR SCW 3682.
32. Smaran Shetty and Tanaya Sanyal, "Fraternity and the Constitution: A Promising Beginning in *Nandini Sundar* v. *State of Chhattisgarh*, 4 NUJS Law Review 455 (July-September, 2011).
33. (2008) 5 SCALE 1: AIR 2008 SC (Supp) 1: 2008 AIR SCW 2899.

the people of India'. Reservation unless protected by the Constitution itself, as given to us by the founding fathers and as adopted by the people of India, is sub-version of fraternity, unity and integrity and dignity of the individual.

In *Krishna Swami* v. *Union of India,*[34] the apex court emphasized upon the role of the courts *vis-à-vis* the ideal of fraternity. The court stated; the independence of the judiciary in the scheme is essential to establish real parliamentary democracy and maintenance of rule of law to usher in an egalitarian social order, removing the existing imbalances, social and economic inequalities, assuring liberty, equality, fraternity and to further justice-social, economic and political with dignity of the persons and fraternity to integrate Bharat. Independence of judiciary thus constitutes the cornerstone and the foundation on which our democratic polity itself is to rest and work on sound principles.

Evidently, the "ideal of fraternity imposes specific duties on the state in order to promote social cohesion and solidarity. In particular, it requires the state to ensure a certain minimum degree of well-being for 'socially excluded people."[35] Several endeavors keep the spirit of fraternity alive amongst the Indian community. In 2002 the Bhopal Conference: Charting a New Course for Dalits for the 21st Century was held to deliberate upon the welfare of the Scheduled Caste and Scheduled Tribes. The Bhopal Conference endorsed the ideals of civil society enshrined in the Constitution of India; reaffirmed that concerted action by the community as a whole is necessary for upbringing of the oppressed sections; conscious that the hurdles that caste Hindu society- and its tentacles in government, media, voluntary sector, etc. is likely to hurt any serious movement that challenges the entrenched system of discrimination and exclusion; hoping that this country will no longer remain an exception to the global norm of progress,

34. (1992) 1 SCALE 484: (1992) 4 SCC 605: AIR 1993 SC 1407. Also see *Consumer Education and Research Centre* v. *Union of India,* (1995) 1 SCALE 354: (1995) 3 SCC 42: AIR 1995 SC 922.

35. Tarunabh Khaitan, "Fraternity", Outlook India (15th May, 2009). Available http://www.outlookindia.com/article.aspx?240443.

equality, justice, peace and social harmony. The Conference was a citizen-government initiative to pave the way for social inclusion and respect.[36]

In 2005 the Prime Minister set up a High Level Committee to prepare a report on the social, economic and educational status of the Muslim community of India. The Committee known as the Sachar Committee in 2006 made recommendations for the formulation of policies that "sharply focus on inclusive development and 'mainstreaming' of the Community while respecting diversity."[37] Over the years, the Constitution has offered "affirmative programmes for the disadvantaged sections", "and make special provisions for the protection of different languages and linguistic groups in the country".[38]

The Indian civil society has also played a significant role in generating and preserving the feelings of togetherness and solidarity.[39] More recently, the Indian state witnessed the strength of "community" while addressing the concerns over good governance/corruption, or the deplorable conditions of safety and wellbeing of women. In a contemporary perspective, the disregard for fundamental rights of the citizens has espoused a sense for recreating a better sense of belonging and compassion amongst the members of the community. The quality of brotherhood/integrity/respect is evidently an inherent feature of the Indian Society.

---

36. Text available at http://www.ambedkar.org/News/TASKFORCE RECOMMENDATIONS1312003.PDF.
37. Priya Parker, "Summary of Sachar Committee Report" (2006) Available at http://www.prsindia.org/administrator/uploads/general/1242304423~~Summary%20of%20Sachar%20Committee%20 Report.pdf.
38. *Supra* note 23 at 686.
39. *See* Prabhakar Singh, "Constitutionalism in International Law during the Times of Globalization: A Sociological Appraisal", Indian Yearbook of International Law and Policy (2009); Neera Chandokhe, "The 'Civil' and the 'Political' in the Society: The Case of India" in Peter Burnell and Peter Calvert, "Civil Society in Democratization", Frank Cass. London (2004); Pranab Bardhan, "Our Self Righteous Civil Society", XLVI Vol. No. 29 Economic and Political Weekly (July 2011).

So can this energy and desire for collective harmony be constructively utilized? Can community lead the way for a duty shaped society? Must law dampen the enthusiasm with the use of violence? Must not the young citizens be educated about the historic and modern values of solidarity/inclusion? To what extent may we utilize the freedom conferred by the state to achieve fraternity; inclusion, respect and love? Is it true that the "Indian unity and fraternity today suffers a syndrome of divisiveness, disparity and despair.[40]

On a conclusive note the global and local developments certainly emphasise upon the articulation, recognition and promotion of fraternity. The promotion and recognition of *'fraternity'* will pave the way for the Indian democracy; specifically the way for better realization of liberty and social justice. "The importance of fraternity, in both a historical and legal sense, would then be in the recognition of the importance of the group's identity, as well as the fundamental rights of the persons constituting such groups."[41] Fraternity may have been forgotten in the debates and explorations of politics, but it continues to live and reflect in the aspirations and strength of the community.

---

40. Justice V.R. Krishna Iyer, "The Indian Constitution in 2050", Halsbury's Law Monthly (October 2008), available at http://www.halsburys.in/the-indian-constitution-in2050.html.

41. 41 Smaran Shetty and Tanaya Sanyal, "Fraternity and the Constitution: A Promising Beginning in *Nandini Sundar* v. *State of Chhattisgarh,* 4 NUJS Law Review, 461 (July-Sept. 2011)

SUBJECT INDEX

N

P

Q

R

S

•••